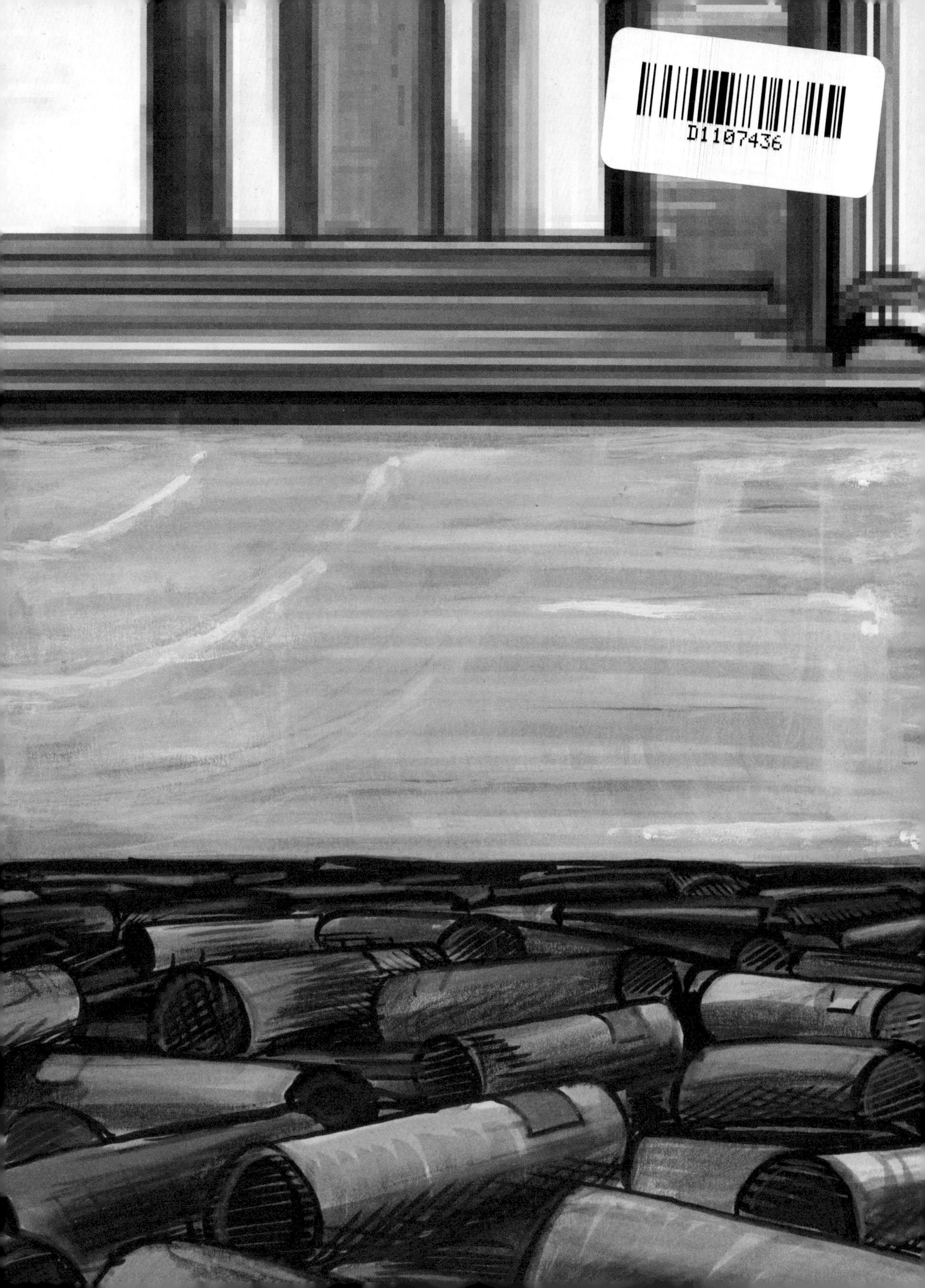

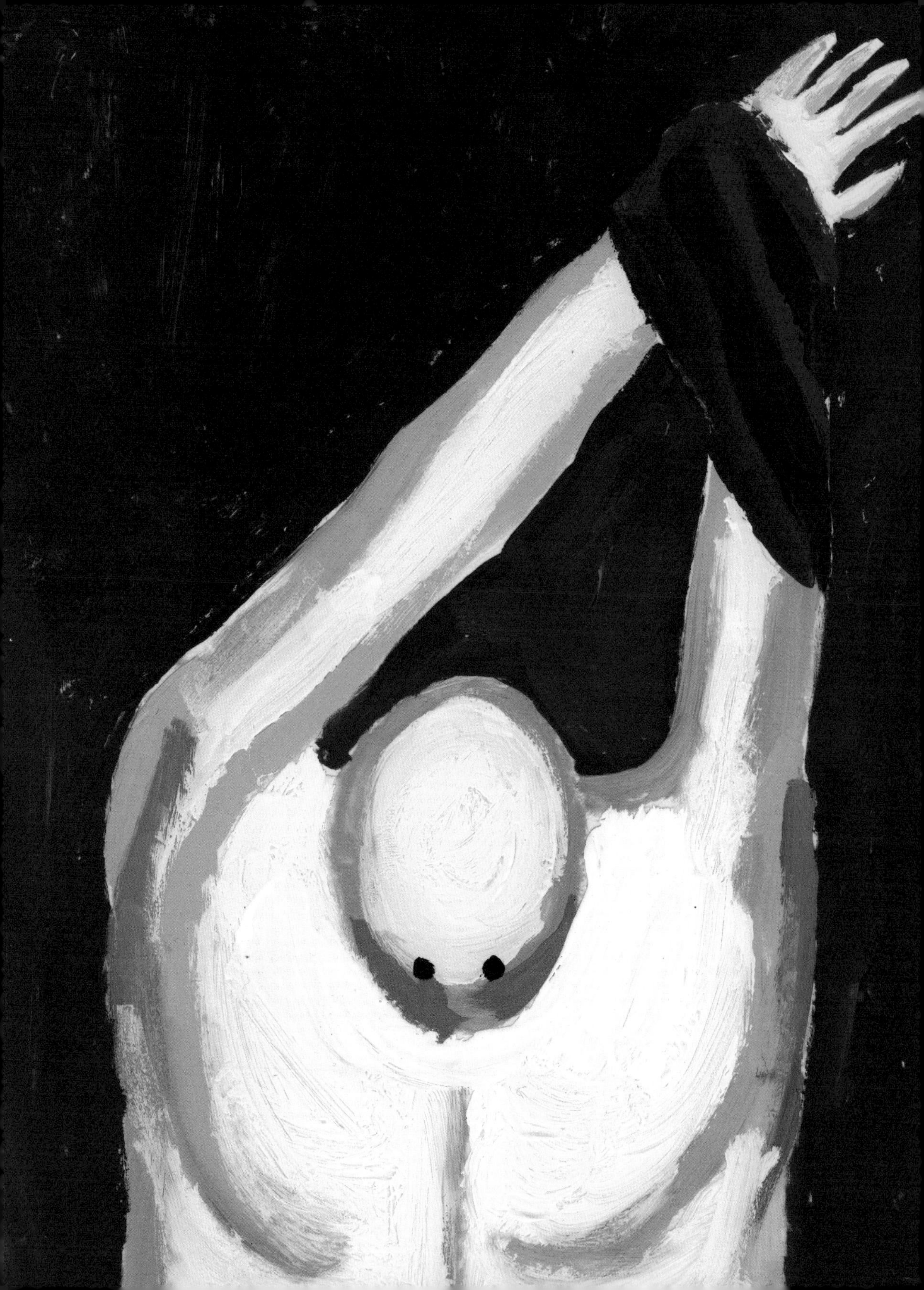

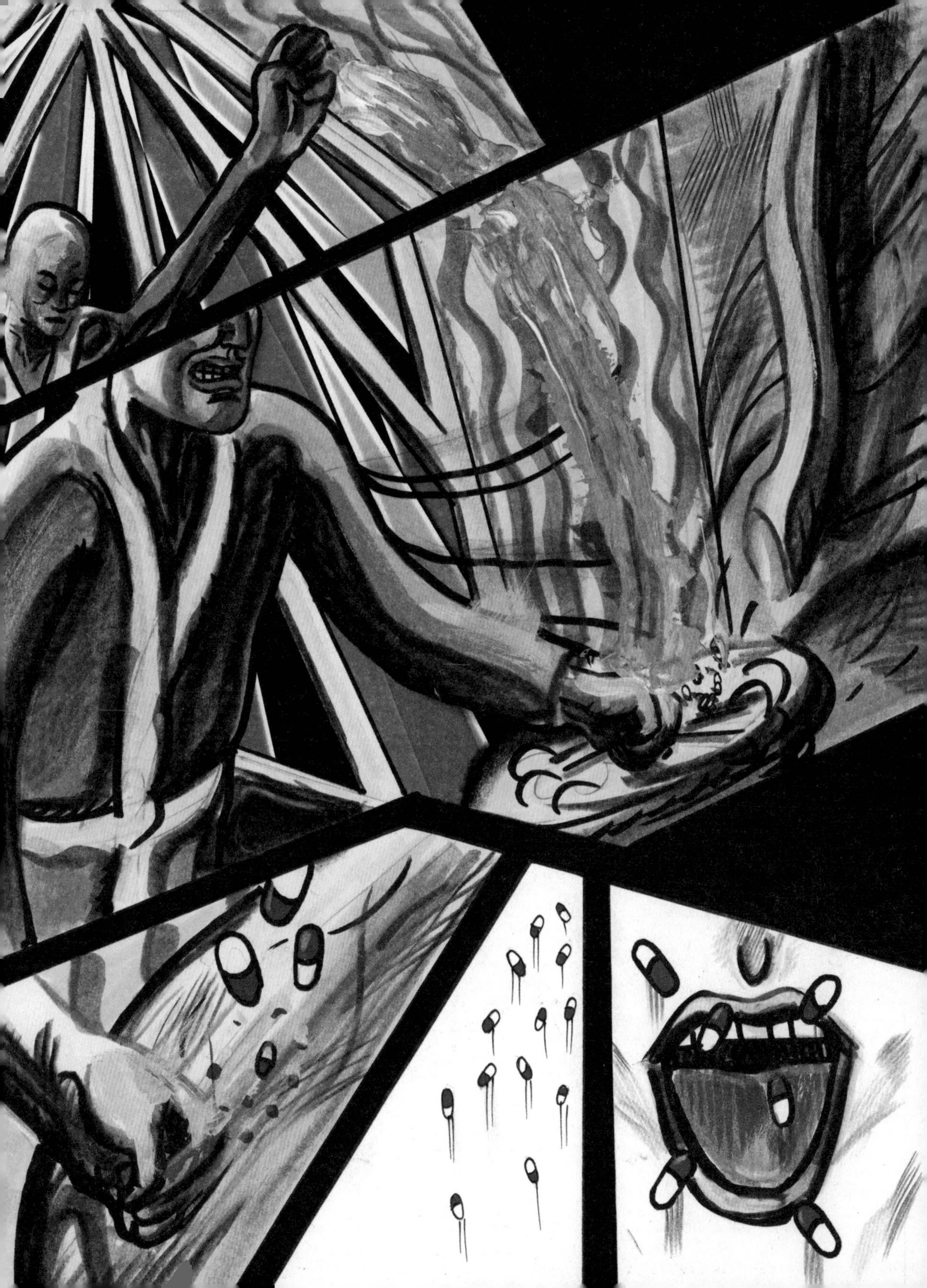

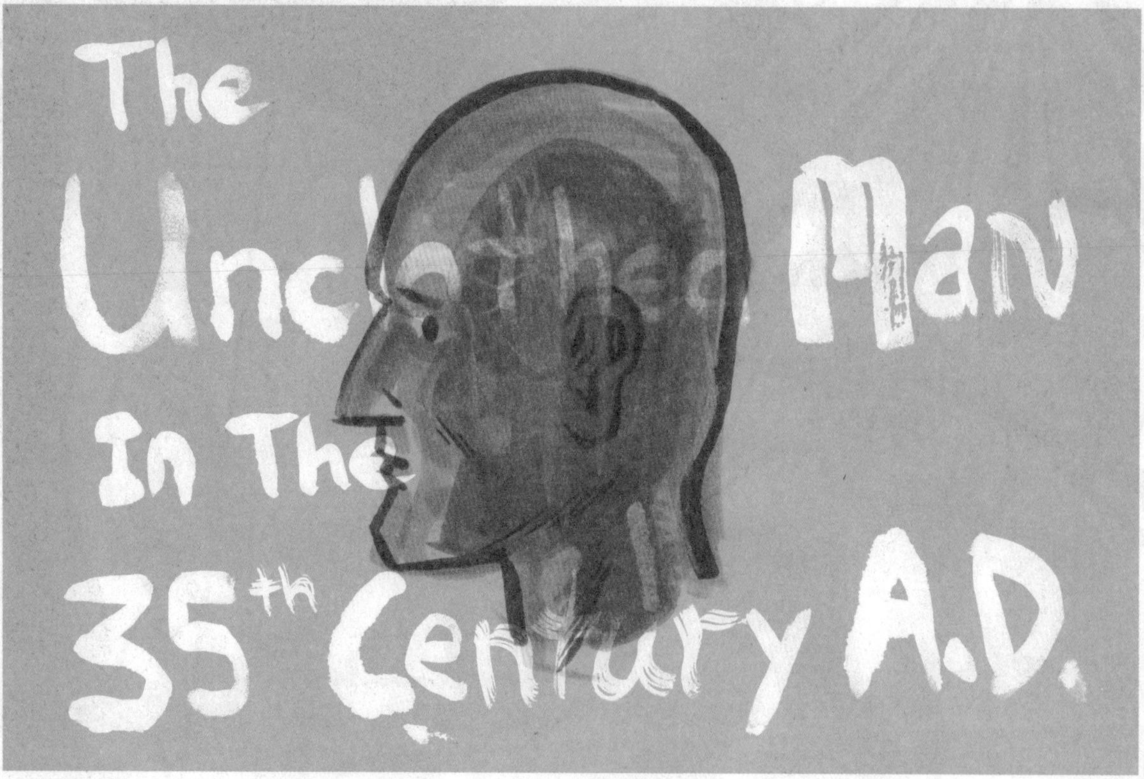
The
Unclothed Man
In The
35th Century A.D.

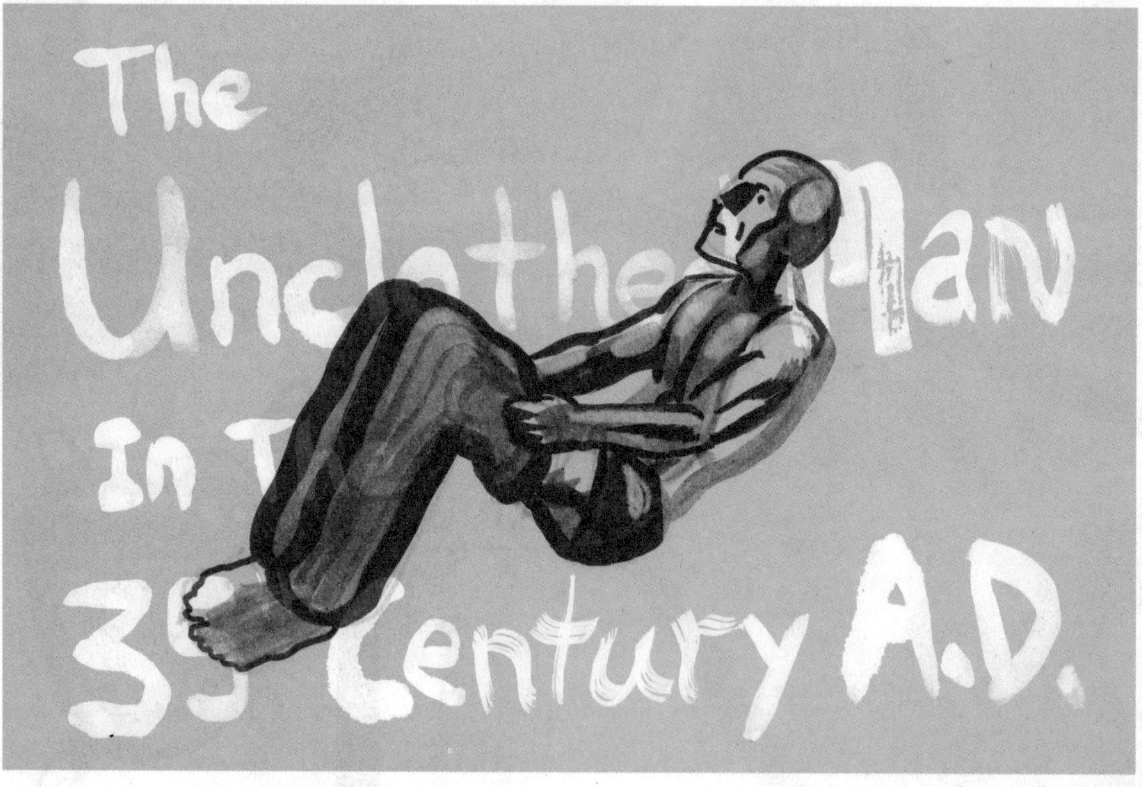
The
Uncl the Man
In T
3 Century A.D.

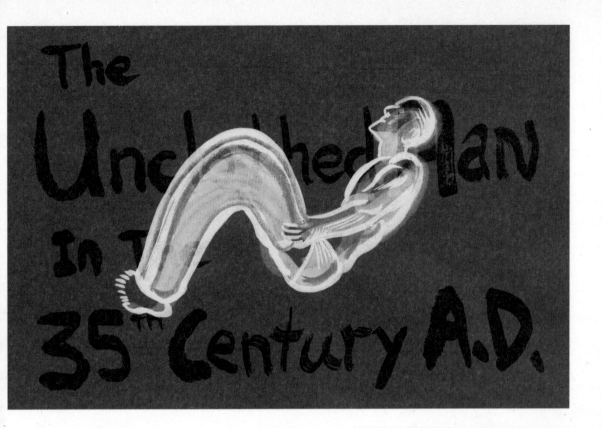

The Unclothed Man In The 35th Century A.D.

The Unclothed Man In The 35th Century A.D.

■ THIS BOOK IS DIVIDED INTO TWO PARTS:

1 The first 24 pages are a collection of storyboards, comics, and animation work from the ifc. com series, "The Unclothed Man in the 35th Century A.D." While I directed and drew a lot of the IFC series, great credit goes to Jane Samborski for collaborating on the imagery, as well as James Lucido, for sound/music, and executive producers Colin Moore and Craig Parks. I've included some of Jane Samborski's artwork in this book: she did the backgrounds on pages 17 and 18, the rotating satellite animation seen on page 5 and 9, as well as penciled figure on the bottom of page 13. Her other contributions included are more integrated: she'd pencil a figure I'd later ink, or she'd create a background where I provided a foreground figure. A black dot in the upper right hand corner marks a page or image where she made a contribution.

2 The last 80 pages are a collection of my comic short stories, most of which originally appeared in "Mome," the Fantagraphics quarterly anthology.

■ I HOPE THAT THIS BOOK INVITES COMPARISONS between animation/storyboards and comics. A debt is owed to the Japanese animation industry's practice of publishing complete storyboards for animated series. It is unlikely that any of these books will be translated into English but I recommend seeking out these archives from stores, such as Kinokuniya in the States, or online.

—DS

■ THIS BOOK IS DEDICATED TO JANE SAMBORSKI.
  Special thanks go to Colin Moore and Eric Reynolds.

Editor: Gary Groth
Design: Dash Shaw and Jacob Covey
Associate Publisher: Eric Reynolds
Gary Groth and Kim Thompson, publishers

Visit Dash Shaw's website at www.dashshaw.com
Visit Jane Samborski's website at www.jane.Iamsam.com
Visit IFC's website at www.IFC.com
Visit Fantagraphics Books' website at www.fantagraphics.com

Distributed in the U.S. by W.W. Norton and Company, Inc. (212-354-5500)
Distributed in Canada by Canadian Manda Group (416-516-0911)
Distributed in the United Kingdom by Turnaround Distribution (208-829-3009)

First edition: September, 2009. Printed in China. ISBN: 978-1-60699-307-1

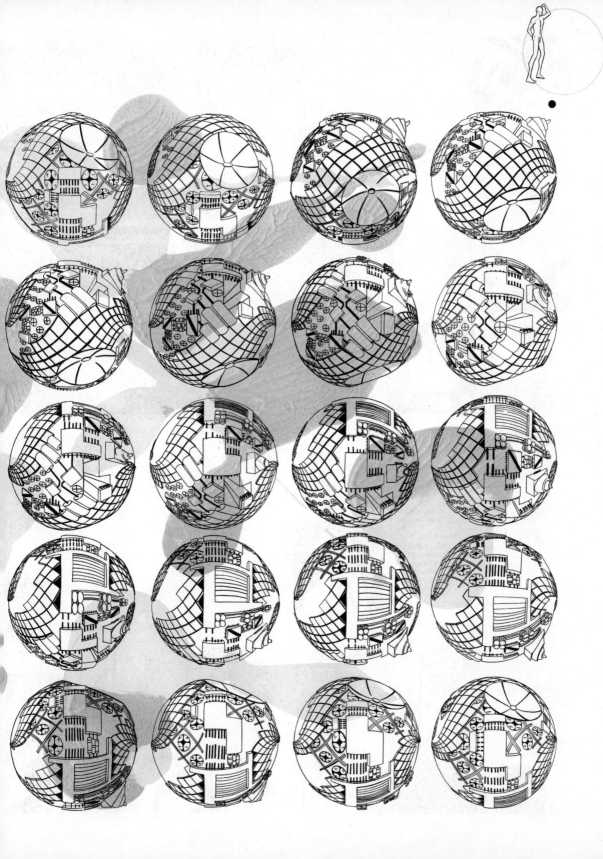

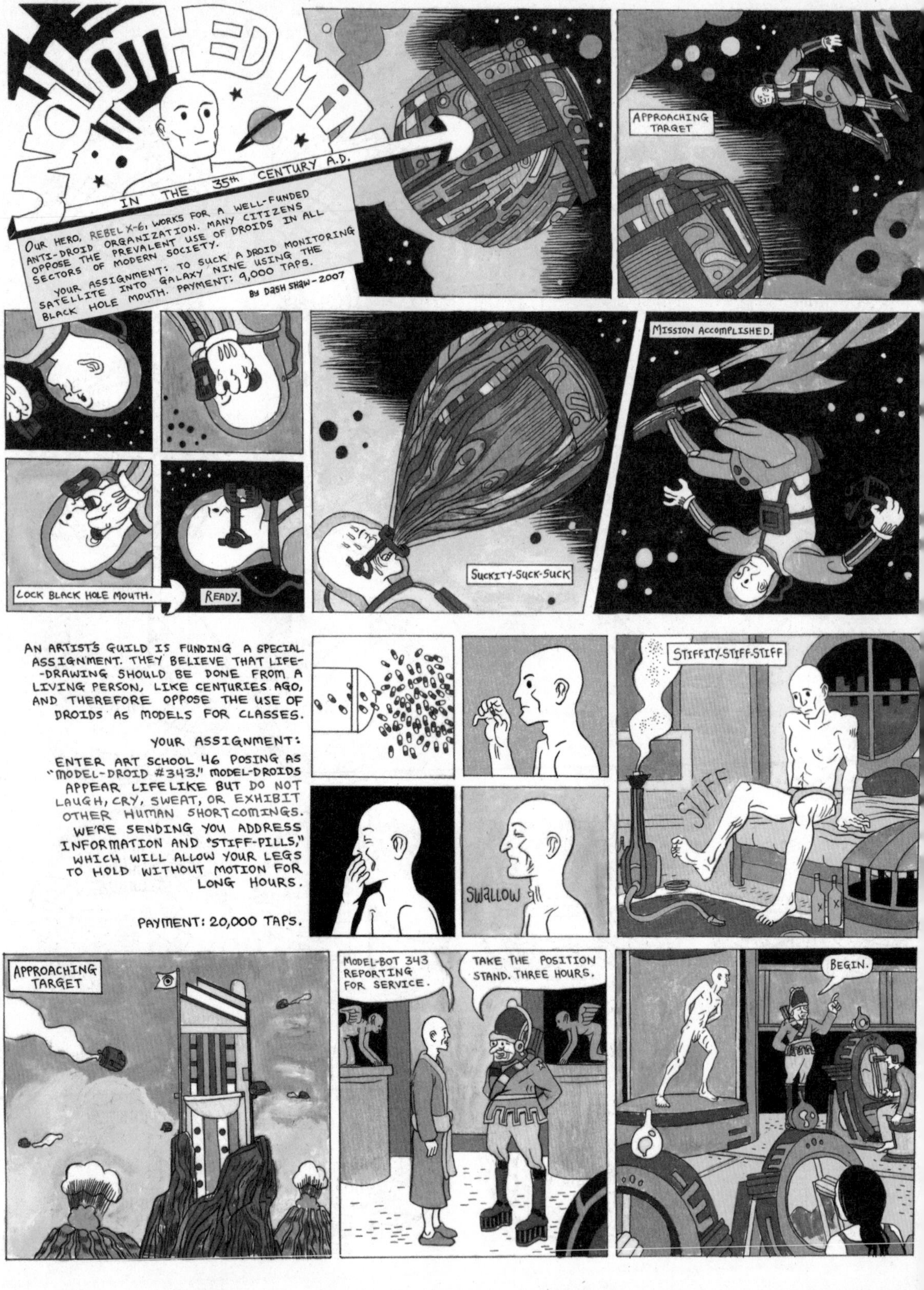
UNCLOTHED MAN
IN THE 35th CENTURY A.D.
OUR HERO, REBEL X-6, WORKS FOR A WELL-FUNDED ANTI-DROID ORGANIZATION. MANY CITIZENS OPPOSE THE PREVALENT USE OF DROIDS IN ALL SECTORS OF MODERN SOCIETY.
YOUR ASSIGNMENT: TO SUCK A DROID MONITORING SATELLITE INTO GALAXY NINE USING THE BLACK HOLE MOUTH. PAYMENT: 9,000 TAPS.
BY DASH SHAW-2007
APPROACHING TARGET
LOCK BLACK HOLE MOUTH.
READY.
SUCKITY-SUCK-SUCK
MISSION ACCOMPLISHED.
AN ARTIST'S GUILD IS FUNDING A SPECIAL ASSIGNMENT. THEY BELIEVE THAT LIFE-DRAWING SHOULD BE DONE FROM A LIVING PERSON, LIKE CENTURIES AGO, AND THEREFORE OPPOSE THE USE OF DROIDS AS MODELS FOR CLASSES.
YOUR ASSIGNMENT:
ENTER ART SCHOOL 46 POSING AS "MODEL-DROID #343." MODEL-DROIDS APPEAR LIFELIKE BUT DO NOT LAUGH, CRY, SWEAT, OR EXHIBIT OTHER HUMAN SHORTCOMINGS. WE'RE SENDING YOU ADDRESS INFORMATION AND "STIFF-PILLS," WHICH WILL ALLOW YOUR LEGS TO HOLD WITHOUT MOTION FOR LONG HOURS.
PAYMENT: 20,000 TAPS.
SWALLOW
STIFFITY-STIFF-STIFF
STIFF
APPROACHING TARGET
MODEL-BOT 343 REPORTING FOR SERVICE.
TAKE THE POSITION STAND. THREE HOURS.
BEGIN.

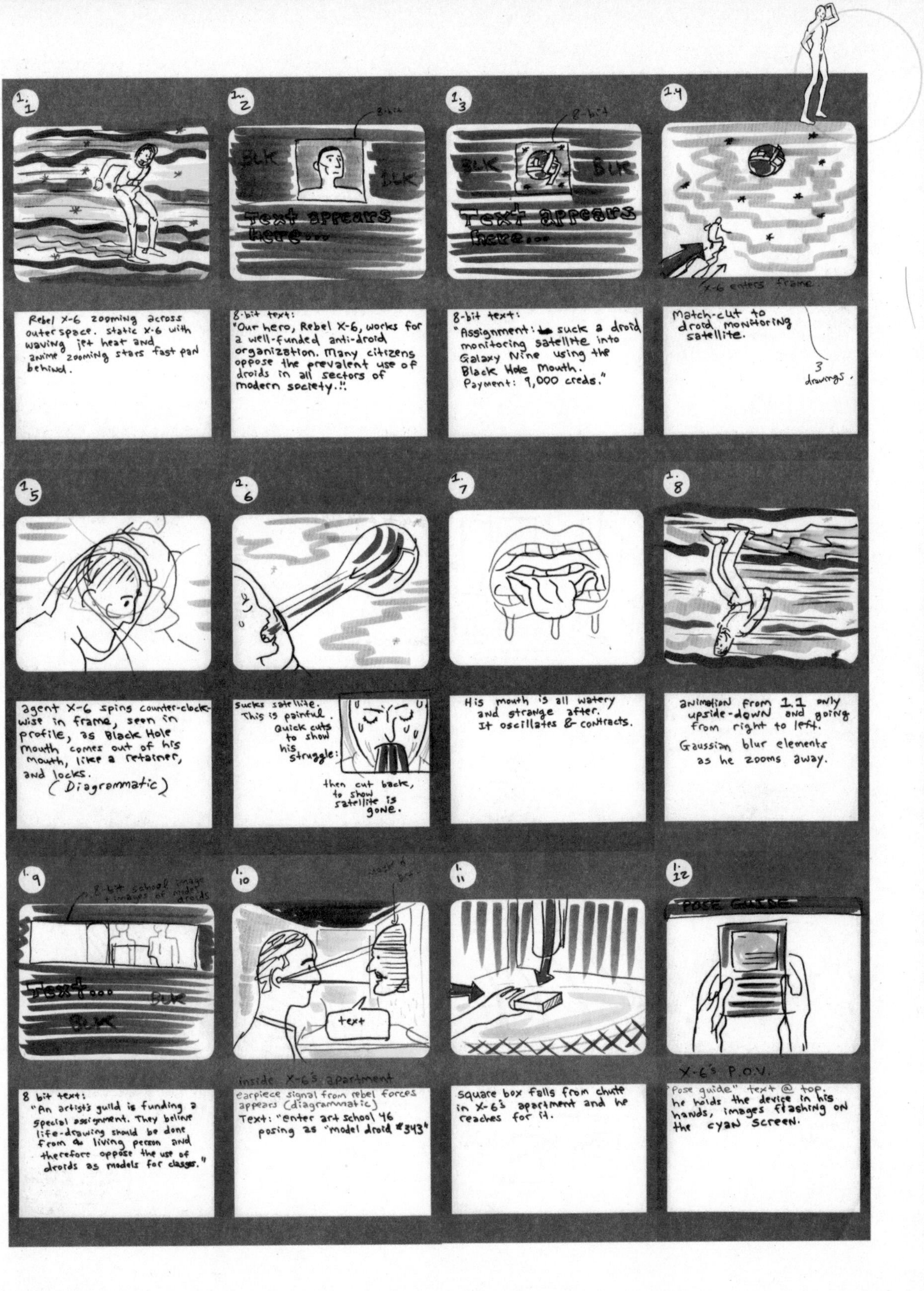

1.1

Rebel X-6 zooming across outer space. Static X-6 with waving jet heat and anime zooming stars fast pan behind.

1.2

BLK   8-bit   BLK
Text appears here...

8-bit text:
"Our hero, Rebel X-6, works for a well-funded anti-droid organization. Many citizens oppose the prevalent use of droids in all sectors of modern society."

1.3

8-bit
BLK   BLK
Text appears here...

8-bit text:
"Assignment: to suck a droid monitoring satellite into Galaxy Nine using the Black Hole mouth. Payment: 9,000 creds."

1.4

X-6 enters frame.

Match-cut to droid monitoring satellite.

3 drawings.

1.5

agent X-6 spins counter-clockwise in frame, seen in profile, as Black Hole mouth comes out of his mouth, like a retainer, and locks.
(Diagrammatic)

1.6

Sucks satellite. This is painful. Quick cuts to show his struggle.

then cut back to show satellite is gone.

1.7

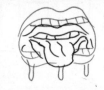

His mouth is all watery and strange after. It oscillates & contracts.

1.8

animation from 1.1 only upside-down and going from right to left.

Gaussian blur elements as he zooms away.

1.9

8-bit school image + images of model droids

Text... BLK
BLK

8 bit text:
"An artist's guild is funding a special assignment. They believe life-drawing should be done from a living person and therefore oppose the use of droids as models for classes."

1.10

text

inside X-6's apartment
earpiece signal from rebel forces appears (diagrammatic)
Text: "enter art school 46 posing as 'model droid #343'"

1.11

Square box falls from chute in X-6's apartment and he reaches for it.

1.12

POSE GUIDE

X-6's P.O.V.

"Pose guide" text @ top. he holds the device in his hands, images flashing on the cyan screen.

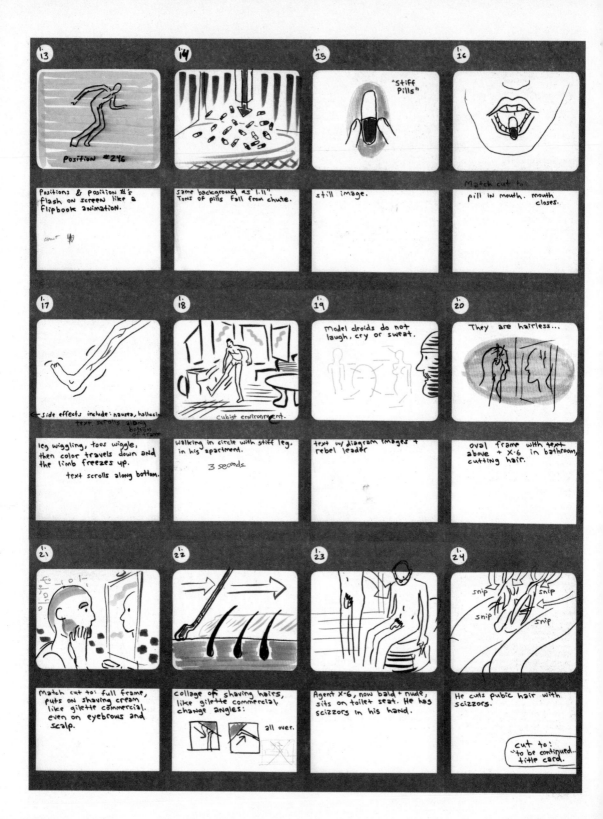

1.13 — Positions & Position #'s flash on screen like a flipbook animation. about 40 (Position #246)

1.14 — same background as "1.11". Tons of pills fall from chute.

1.15 — still image. ("Stiff Pills")

1.16 — Match cut to: pill in mouth. mouth closes.

1.17 — side effects include: nausea, hallucin... text scrolls along bottom of frame. leg wiggling, toes wiggle, then color travels down and the limb freezes up. text scrolls along bottom.

1.18 — Cubist environment. walking in circle with stiff leg, in his apartment. 3 seconds.

1.19 — Model droids do not laugh, cry or sweat. text w/ diagram images + rebel leader

1.20 — They are hairless... oval frame with text above + X-6 in bathroom, cutting hair.

1.21 — Match cut to: full frame, puts on shaving cream like gilette commercial. even on eyebrows and scalp.

1.22 — collage of shaving hairs, like gilette commercial. change angles: all over.

1.23 — Agent X-6, now bald + nude, sits on toilet seat. He has scizzors in his hand.

1.24 — He cuts pubic hair with scizzors. snip snip snip snip. cut to: "to be continued... title card.

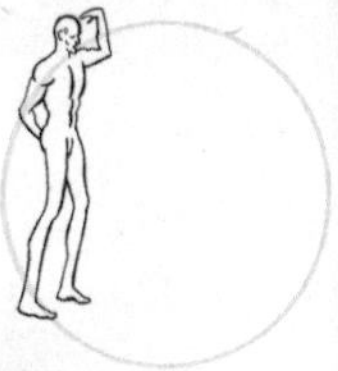

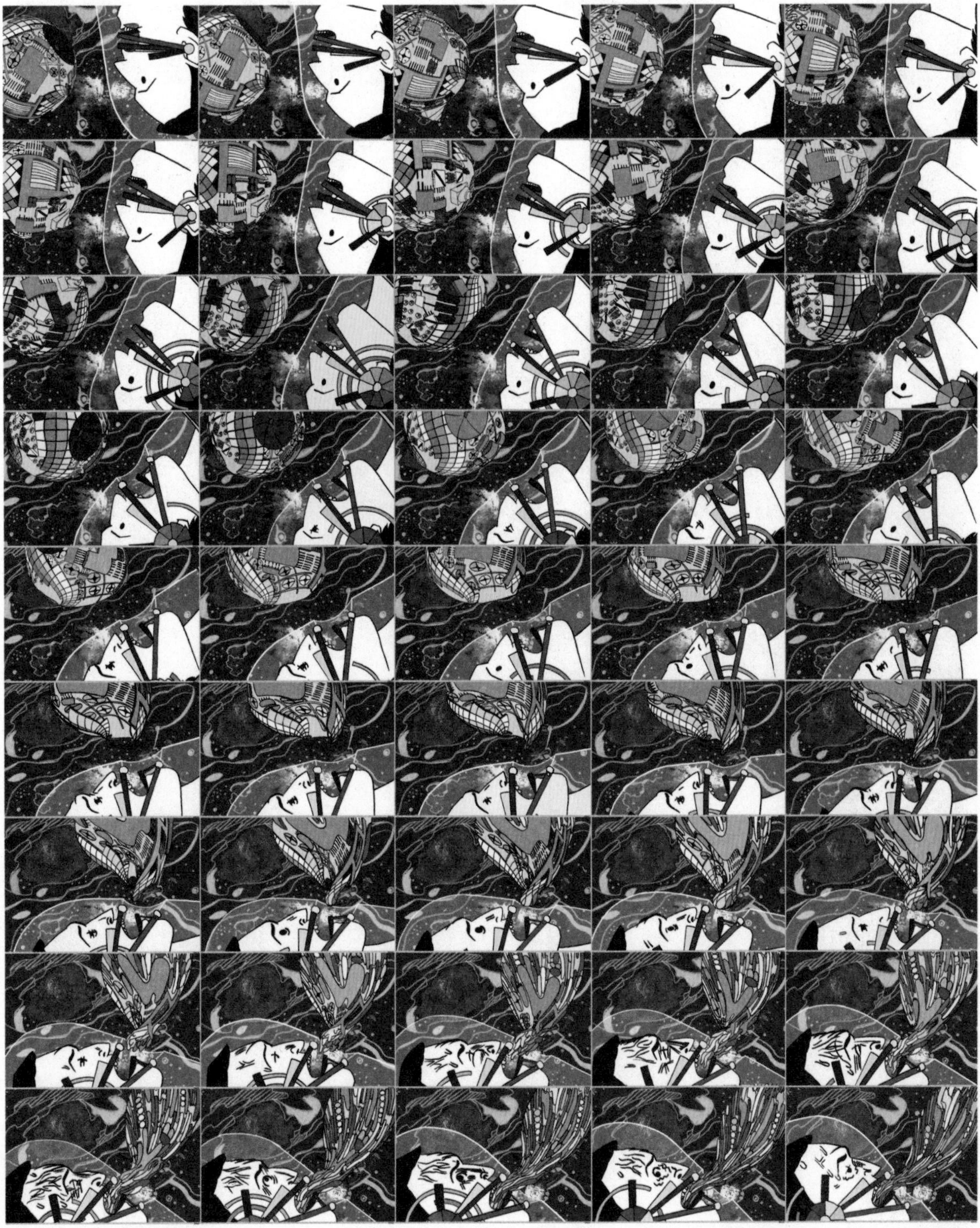

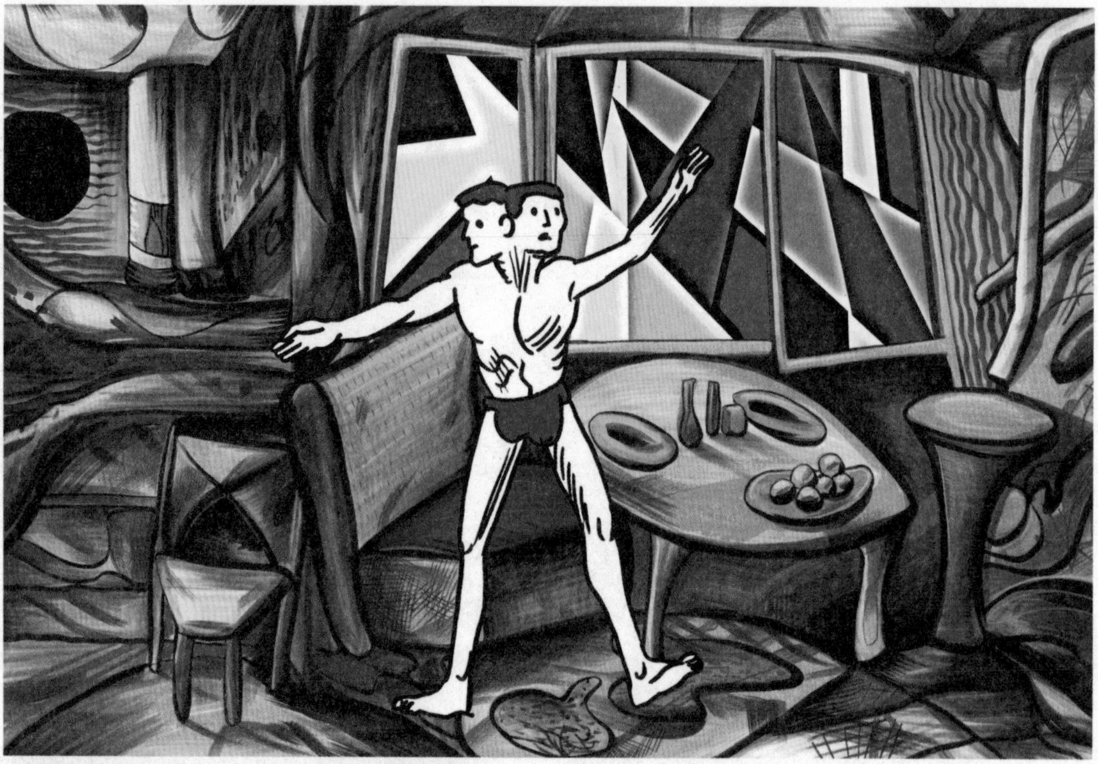
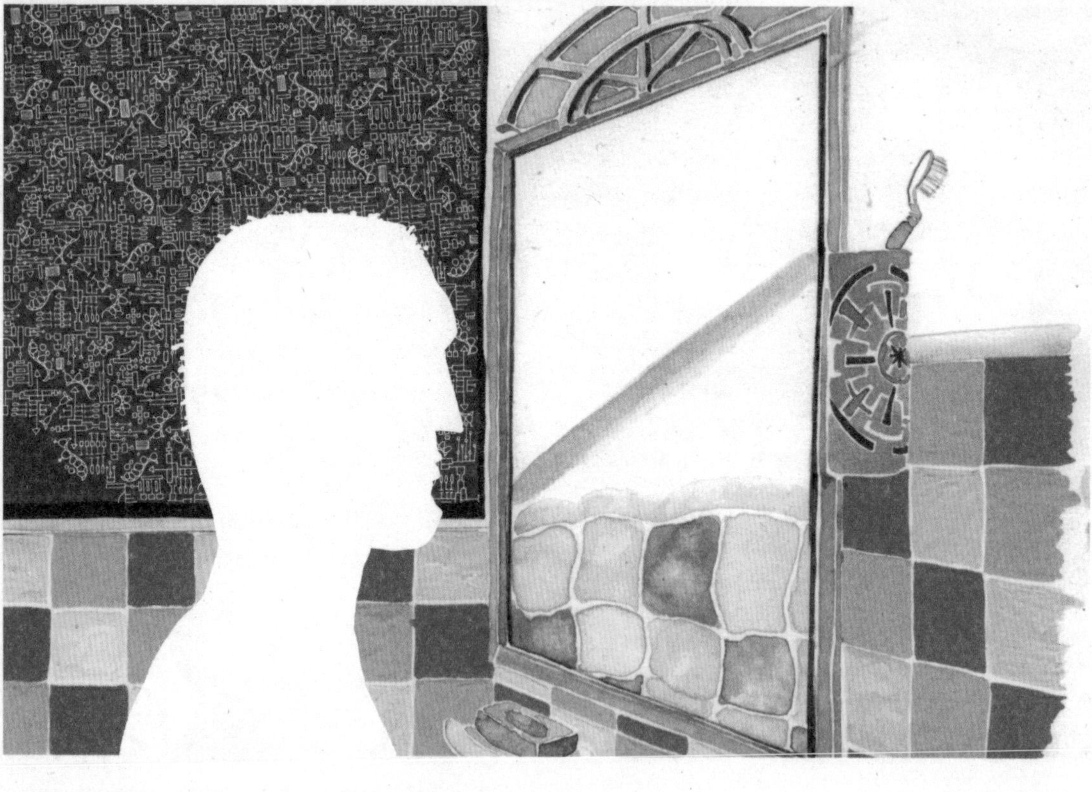

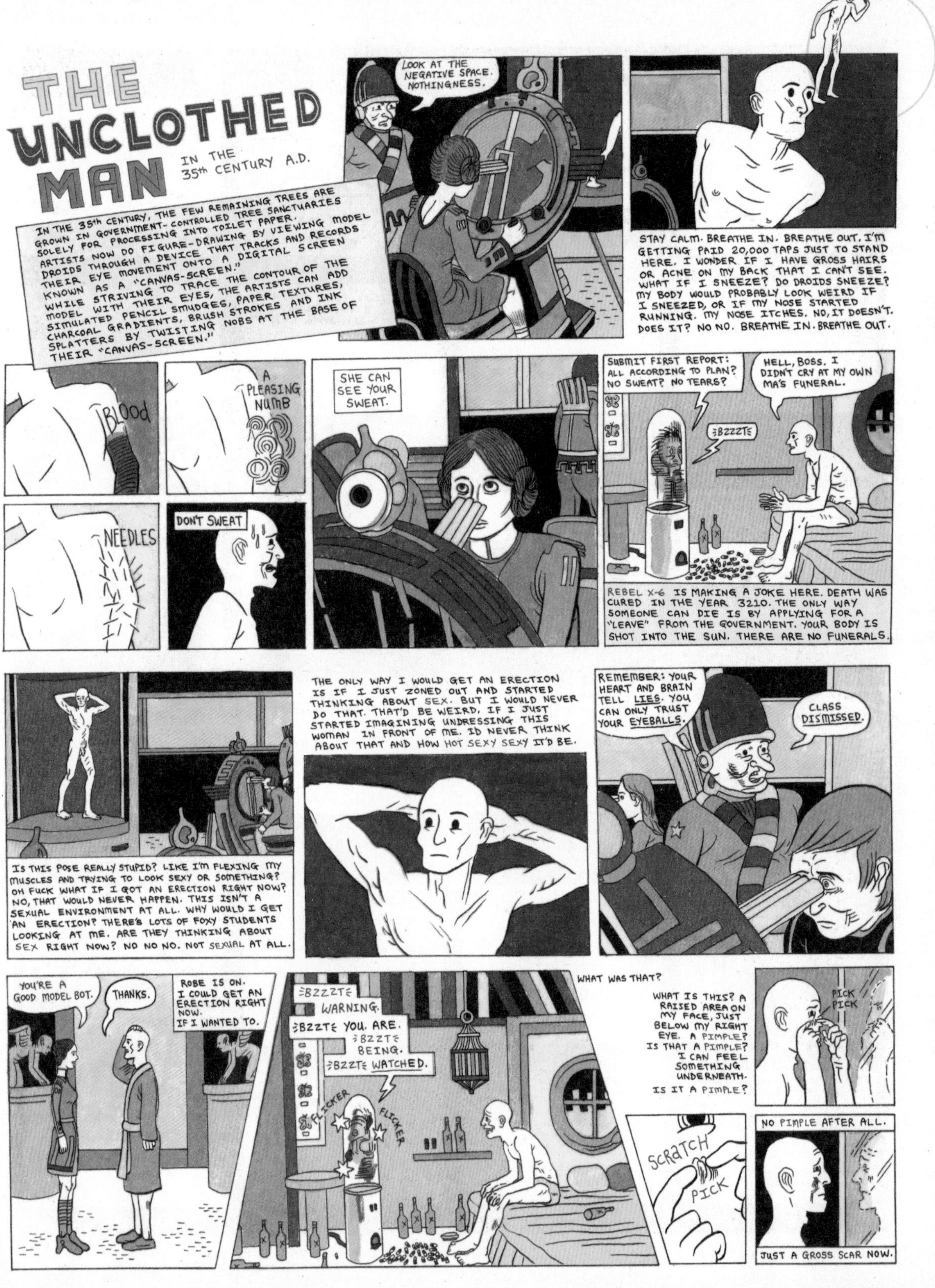
THE UNCLOTHED MAN
IN THE 35th CENTURY A.D.
IN THE 35th CENTURY, THE FEW REMAINING TREES ARE GROWN IN GOVERNMENT-CONTROLLED TREE SANCTUARIES SOLELY FOR PROCESSING INTO TOILET PAPER. ARTISTS NOW DO FIGURE-DRAWING BY VIEWING MODEL DROIDS THROUGH A DEVICE THAT TRACKS AND RECORDS THEIR EYE MOVEMENT ONTO A DIGITAL SCREEN KNOWN AS A "CANVAS-SCREEN." WHILE STRIVING TO TRACE THE CONTOUR OF THE MODEL WITH THEIR EYES, THE ARTISTS CAN ADD SIMULATED PENCIL SMUDGES, PAPER TEXTURES, CHARCOAL GRADIENTS, BRUSH STROKES AND INK SPLATTERS BY TWISTING NOBS AT THE BASE OF THEIR "CANVAS-SCREEN."
LOOK AT THE NEGATIVE SPACE. NOTHINGNESS.
STAY CALM. BREATHE IN. BREATHE OUT. I'M GETTING PAID 20,000 TAPS JUST TO STAND HERE. I WONDER IF I HAVE GROSS HAIRS OR ACNE ON MY BACK THAT I CAN'T SEE. WHAT IF I SNEEZE? DO DROIDS SNEEZE? MY BODY WOULD PROBABLY LOOK WEIRD IF I SNEEZED, OR IF MY NOSE STARTED RUNNING. MY NOSE ITCHES. NO, IT DOESN'T. DOES IT? NO NO. BREATHE IN. BREATHE OUT.
BLOOD
A PLEASING NUMB
NEEDLES
DON'T SWEAT
SHE CAN SEE YOUR SWEAT.
SUBMIT FIRST REPORT: ALL ACCORDING TO PLAN? NO SWEAT? NO TEARS?
BZZZT
HELL, BOSS. I DIDN'T CRY AT MY OWN MA'S FUNERAL.
REBEL X-6 IS MAKING A JOKE HERE. DEATH WAS CURED IN THE YEAR 3210. THE ONLY WAY SOMEONE CAN DIE IS BY APPLYING FOR A "LEAVE" FROM THE GOVERNMENT. YOUR BODY IS SHOT INTO THE SUN. THERE ARE NO FUNERALS.
IS THIS POSE REALLY STUPID? LIKE I'M FLEXING MY MUSCLES AND TRYING TO LOOK SEXY OR SOMETHING? OH FUCK WHAT IF I GOT AN ERECTION RIGHT NOW? NO, THAT WOULD NEVER HAPPEN. THIS ISN'T A SEXUAL ENVIRONMENT AT ALL. WHY WOULD I GET AN ERECTION? THERE'S LOTS OF FOXY STUDENTS LOOKING AT ME. ARE THEY THINKING ABOUT SEX RIGHT NOW? NO NO NO. NOT SEXUAL AT ALL.
THE ONLY WAY I WOULD GET AN ERECTION IS IF I JUST ZONED OUT AND STARTED THINKING ABOUT SEX. BUT I WOULD NEVER DO THAT. THAT'D BE WEIRD. IF I JUST STARTED IMAGINING UNDRESSING THIS WOMAN IN FRONT OF ME. I'D NEVER THINK ABOUT THAT AND HOW HOT SEXY SEXY IT'D BE.
REMEMBER: YOUR HEART AND BRAIN TELL LIES. YOU CAN ONLY TRUST YOUR EYEBALLS.
CLASS DISMISSED.
YOU'RE A GOOD MODEL BOT.
THANKS.
ROBE IS ON. I COULD GET AN ERECTION RIGHT NOW. IF I WANTED TO.
BZZZT
WARNING.
BZZT YOU. ARE.
BZZT BEING.
BZZT WATCHED.
FLICKER
FLICKER
WHAT WAS THAT?
WHAT IS THIS? A RAISED AREA ON MY FACE, JUST BELOW MY RIGHT EYE. A PIMPLE? IS THAT A PIMPLE? I CAN FEEL SOMETHING UNDERNEATH. IS IT A PIMPLE?
PICK PICK
SCRATCH
PICK
NO PIMPLE AFTER ALL.
JUST A GROSS SCAR NOW.

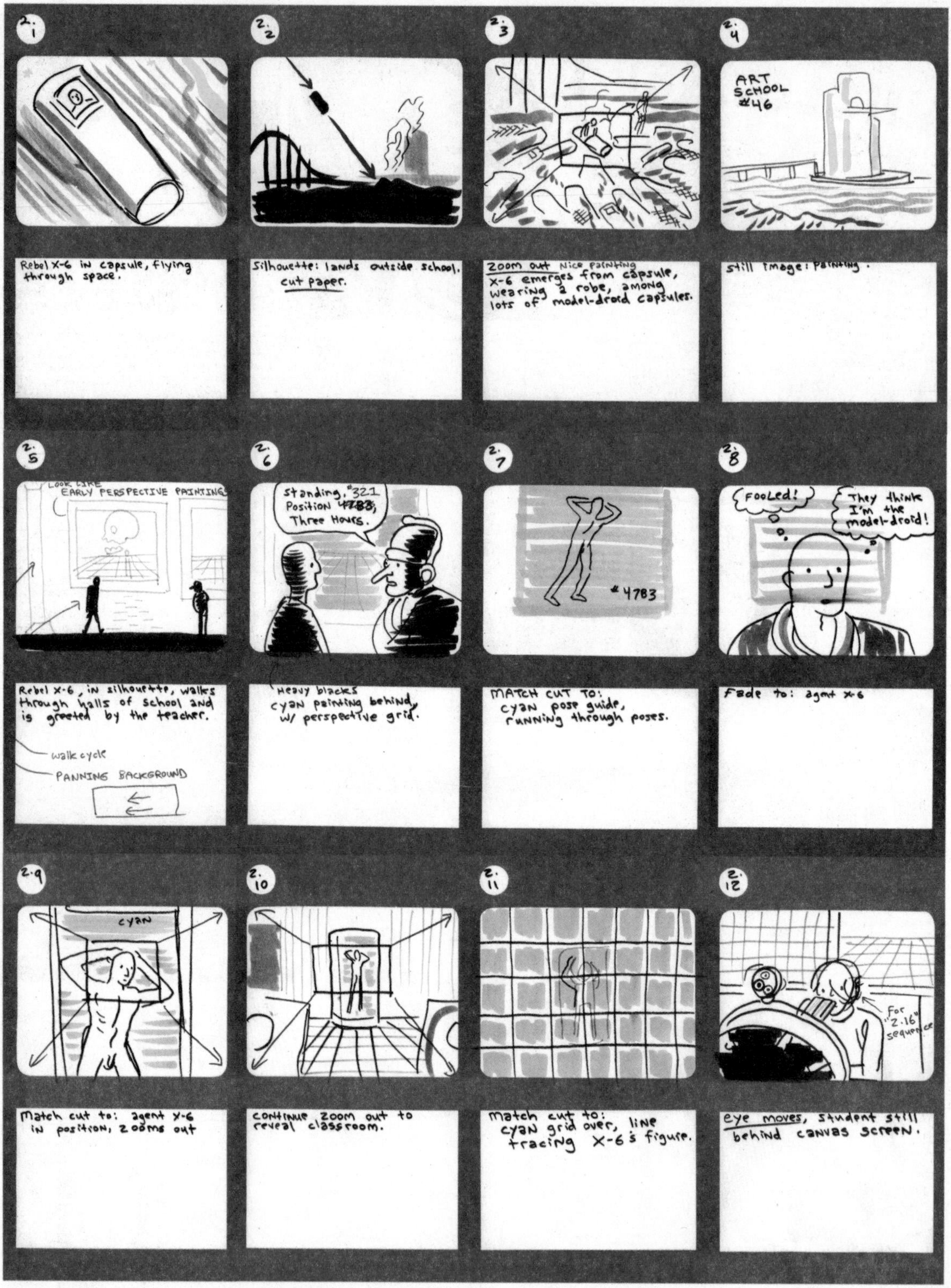
2.1
Rebel X-6 in capsule, flying through space.
2.2
Silhouette: lands outside school.
cut paper.
2.3
Zoom out Nice painting
X-6 emerges from capsule, wearing a robe, among lots of model-droid capsules.
2.4
ART SCHOOL #46
still image: painting.
2.5
LOOK LIKE EARLY PERSPECTIVE PAINTINGS
Rebel X-6, in silhouette, walks through halls of school and is greeted by the teacher.
walk cycle
PANNING BACKGROUND
2.6
Standing, #321 Position 4783, Three Hours.
Heavy blacks
cyan painting behind, w/ perspective grid.
2.7
#4783
MATCH CUT TO: cyan pose guide, running through poses.
2.8
Fooled!
They think I'm the model-droid!
Fade to: agent X-6
2.9
cyan
Match cut to: agent X-6 in position, zooms out
2.10
continue zoom out to reveal classroom.
2.11
match cut to: cyan grid over, line tracing X-6's figure.
2.12
For "2.16" sequence
eye moves, student still behind canvas screen.

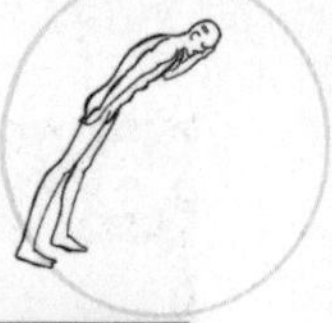
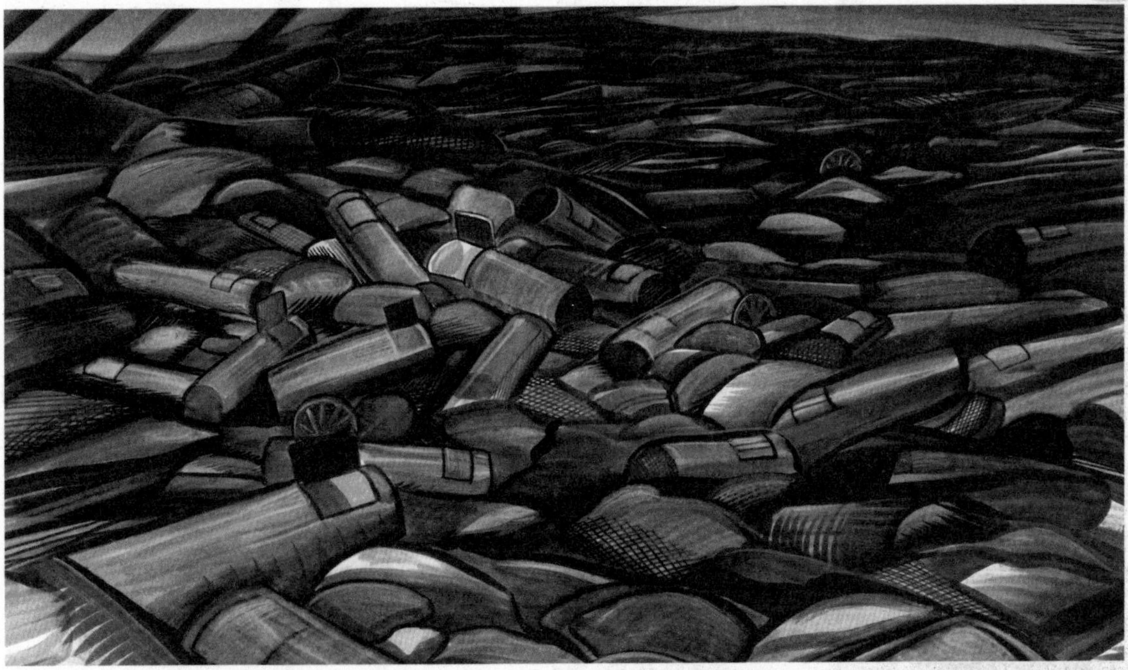
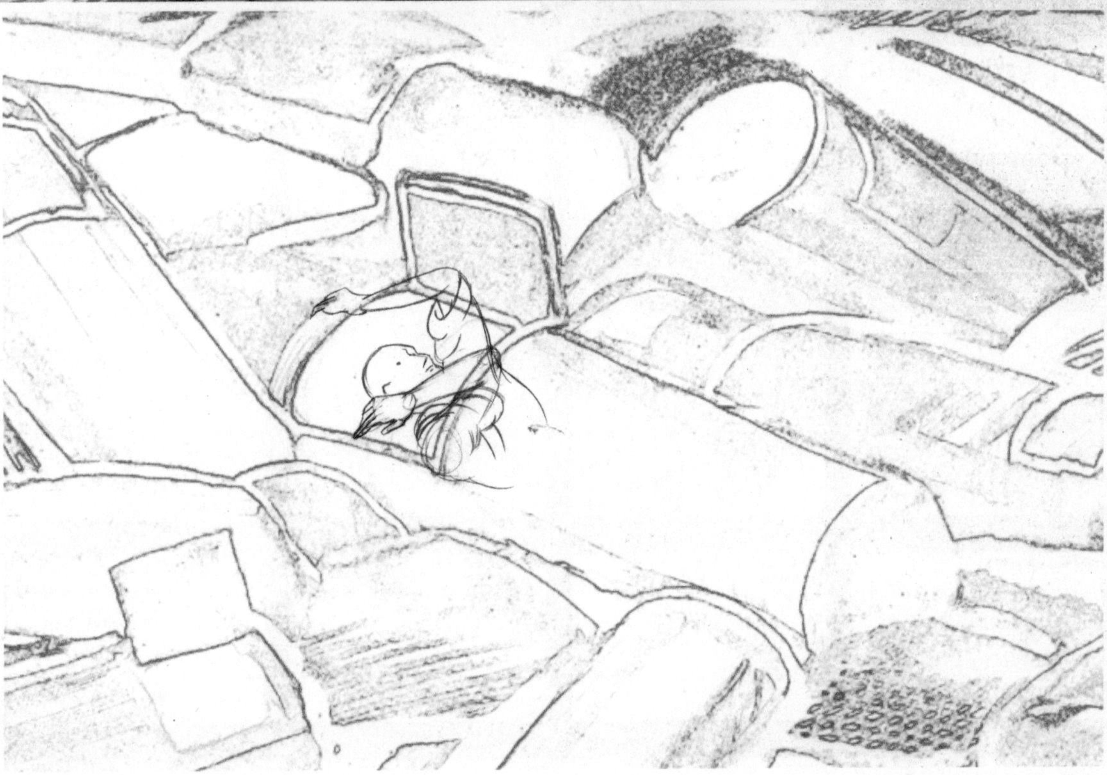

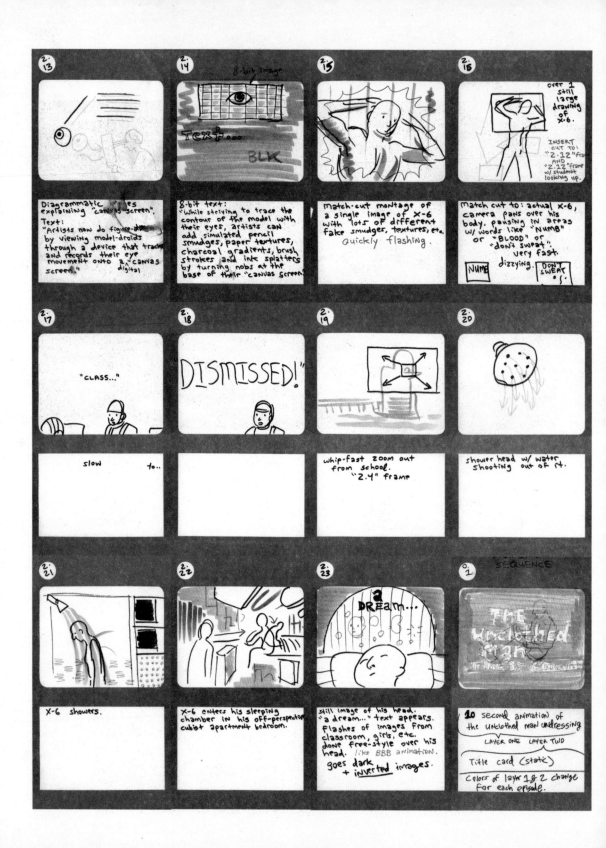

2.13 — Diagrammatic [images] explaining "canvas-screen".
Text:
"Artists now do figure-[drawing] by viewing model-droids through a device that tracks and records their eye movement onto a 'canvas screen.'"   digital

2.14 — 8-bit image
8-bit text:
"While striving to trace the contour of the model with their eyes, artists can add simulated pencil smudges, paper textures, charcoal gradients, brush strokes and ink splatters by turning nobs at the base of their 'canvas screen.'"
Text...
BLK

2.15 — Match-cut montage of a single image of X-6 with lots of different fake smudges, textures, etc. Quickly flashing.

2.16 — over 1 still large drawing of X-6.
INSERT CUT TO: "2.12" frame AND "2.12" frame w/ student looking up.
Match cut to: actual X-6, camera pans over his body. pausing in areas w/ words like "NUMB" or "BLOOD" or "don't sweat". very fast. dizzying.
NUMB
DON'T SWEAT.

2.17 — "CLASS..."
slow   to..

2.18 — DISMISSED!"

2.19 — whip-fast zoom out from school. "2.4" frame

2.20 — shower head w/ water shooting out of it.

2.21 — X-6 showers.

2.22 — X-6 enters his sleeping chamber in his off-perspective cubist apartment bedroom.

2.23 — a DREAM...
still image of his head. "a dream..." text appears. Flashes of images from classroom, girls, etc. done free-style over his head. like BBB animation. goes dark + INVERTED images.

0.1 — SEQUENCE
THE unclothed man
10 second animation of the unclothed man undressing
LAYER ONE   LAYER TWO
Title card (static)
Colors of layer 1 & 2 change for each episode.

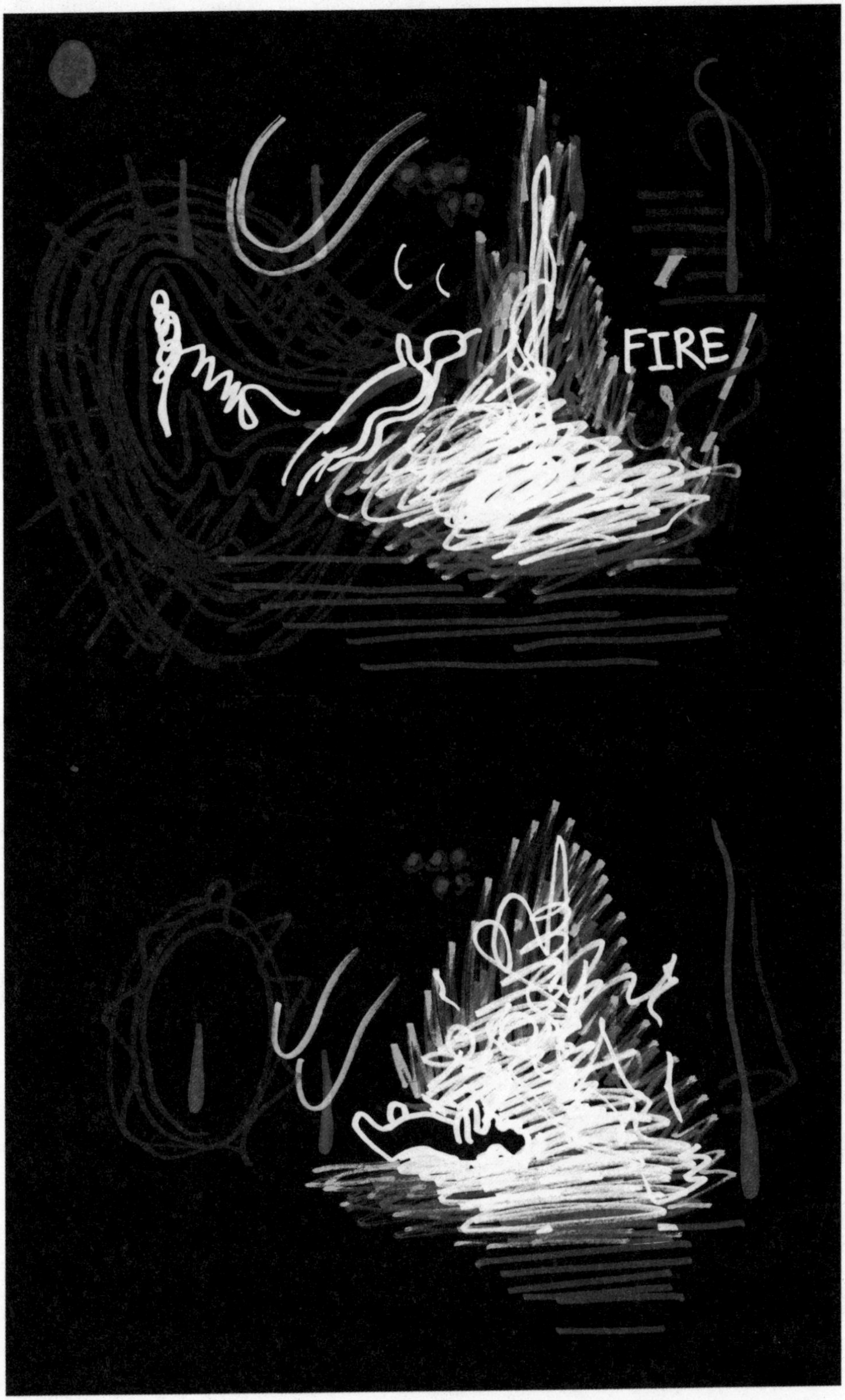
FIRE

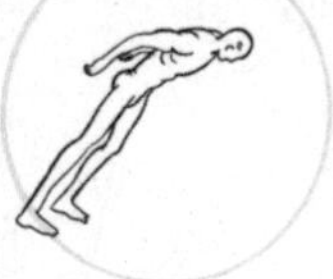

THE UNCLOTHED MAN IN THE 35TH CENTURY A.D.

DON'T MOVE. DON'T SWEAT. DON'T LAUGH. STAY CALM.

FOCUS. BREATHE IN. BREATHE OUT.

THUMP

A TERRIFYING DREAM:
I'M STARVING AND STRAPPED INTO SOME KIND OF TORTURE CHAIR AND MOUTH PIECE. A HOT DOG IS INFRONT OF ME. IF I REACH FOR IT OR OPEN MY MOUTH OR SALIVATE A MILLION NEEDLES PIERCE INTO MY HEAD AND CHEST.

GAAAAA!

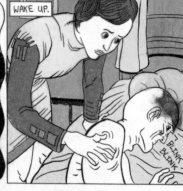

WAKE UP.

BLINK BLINK

WE THOUGHT YOU WERE DEAD. ER, "NOT OPERATING."... I GUESS DROIDS ARE ALWAYS DEAD.

UM. IS THIS YOUR PLACE?

YEAH. I COLLECT OLD THINGS.

YOU'RE NOT LIKE OTHER DROIDS. YOU SWEAT AND SHAKE. ARE YOU A NEW MODEL?

YES. THE, UH, LATEST MODEL.

YOU KNOW WHAT I HEARD? I HEARD THE OLD PAINTERS—MATISSE, REMBRANDT—THEY PAINTED LIVING PEOPLE.

NOT SCULPTURES LIKE WHAT PROFESSORS SAY.

I WANT TO DRAW A LIVING PERSON. TO GET THAT RUSH OF SEEING ANOTHER HUMAN BEING, YOU KNOW? A REAL PERSON WITH REAL FEELINGS AND MOVEMENT.

I DON'T GET THAT LOOKING AT YOU. YOU'RE ALL MECH UNDER THERE. WIRES. PROGRAMMING. NOTHING REAL AT ALL.

UM. ...

SHRUG

MY PROGRAMMING IS REAL. WIRES ARE REAL.

MISSION ACCOMPLISHED

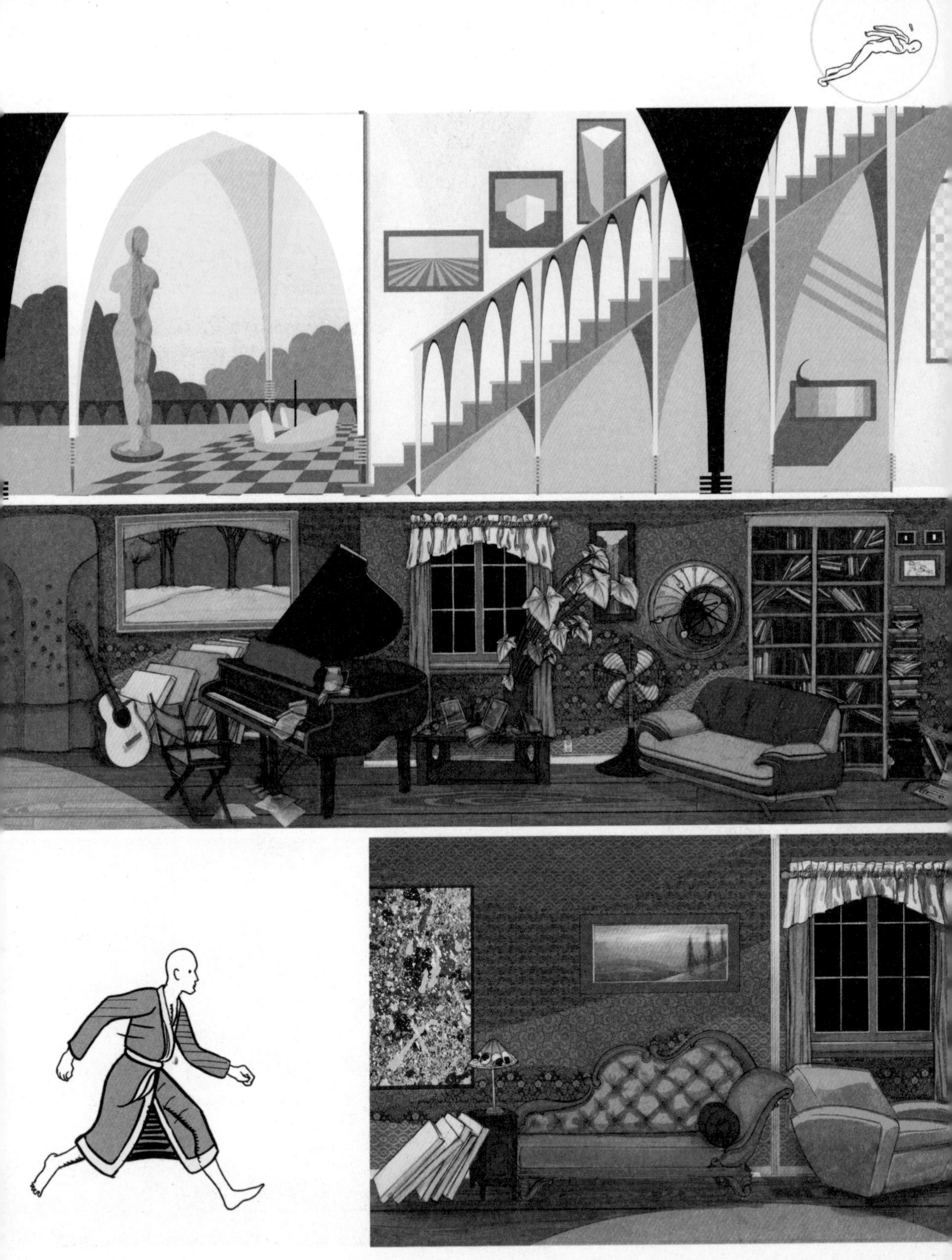

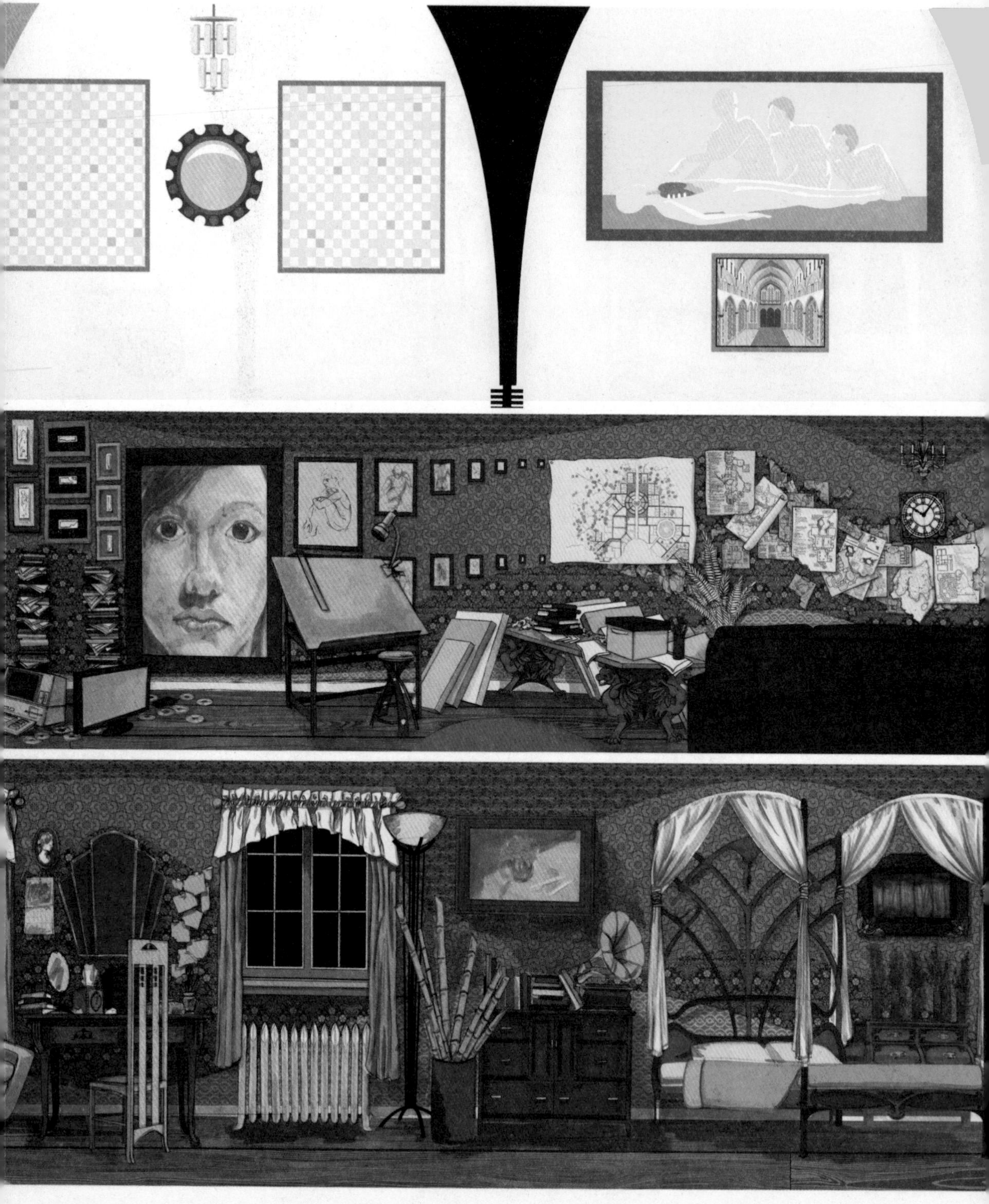

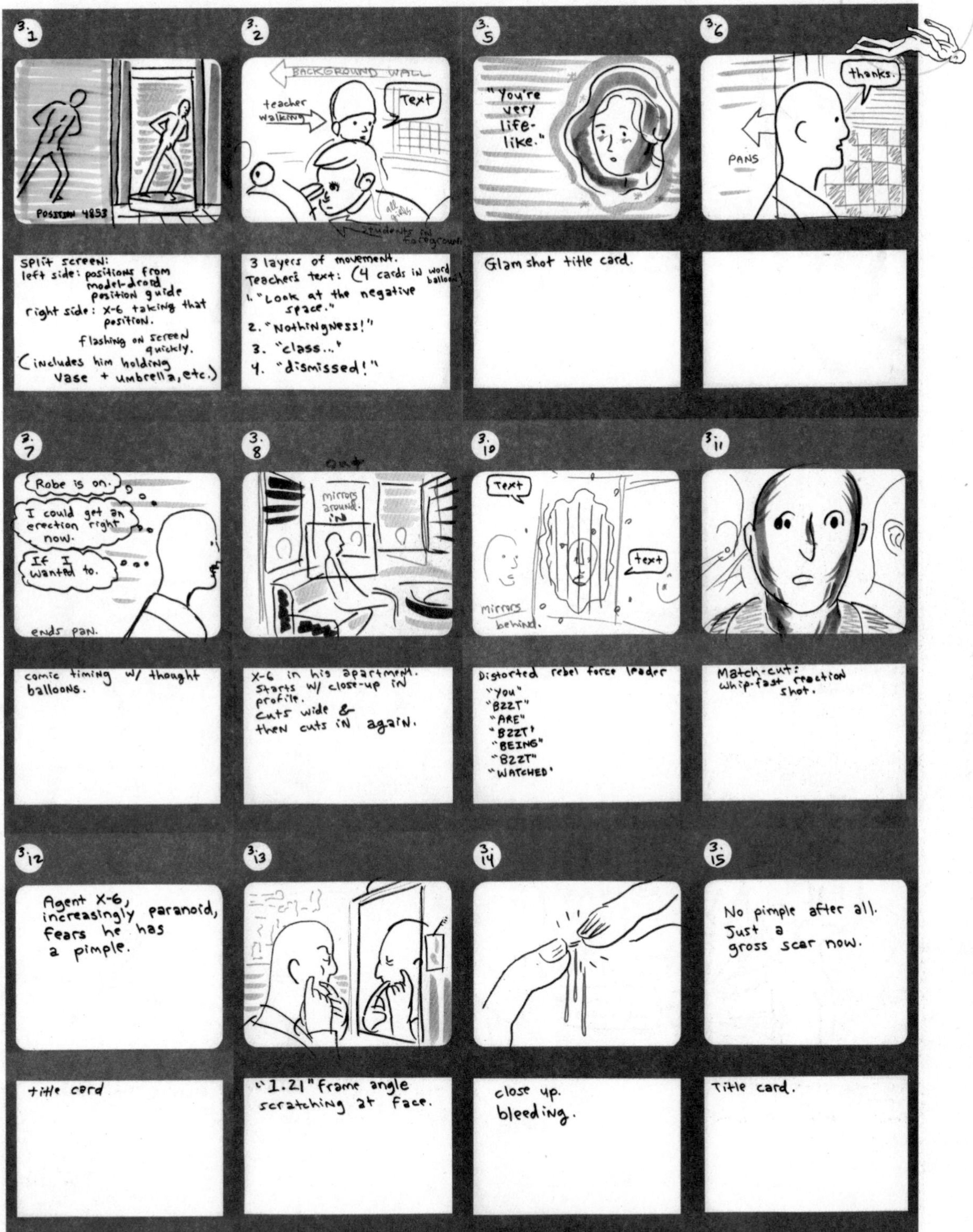
3.1
POSITION 4853
Split screen:
left side: positions from model-droid position guide
right side: X-6 taking that position.
flashing on screen quickly.
(includes him holding vase + umbrella, etc.)
3.2
BACKGROUND WALL
teacher walking
Text
students in foreground
3 layers of movement.
Teacher's text: (4 cards in word balloon)
1. "Look at the negative space."
2. "Nothingness!"
3. "class..."
4. "dismissed!"
3.5
"You're very life-like."
Glam shot title card.
3.6
thanks.
PANS
3.7
Robe is on.
I could get an erection right now.
If I wanted to.
ends pan.
comic timing w/ thought balloons.
3.8
mirrors around.
X-6 in his apartment. Starts w/ close-up in profile.
cuts wide & then cuts in again.
3.10
Text
text
mirrors behind.
Distorted rebel force leader
"YOU"
"BZZT"
"ARE"
"BZZT"
"BEING"
"BZZT"
"WATCHED"
3.11
Match-cut: whip-fast reaction shot.
3.12
Agent X-6, increasingly paranoid, fears he has a pimple.
title card
3.13
"1.21" frame angle scratching at face.
3.14
close up. bleeding.
3.15
No pimple after all. Just a gross scar now.
Title card.

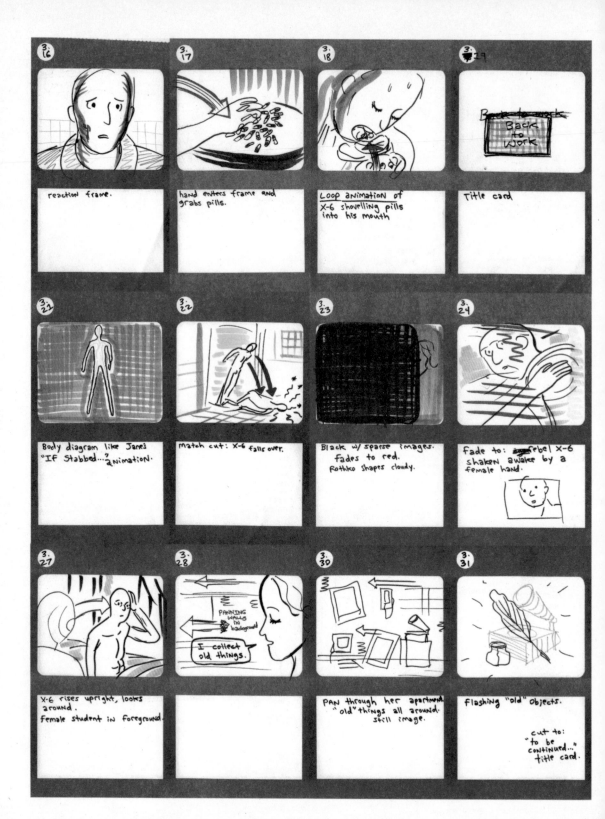

3.16

reaction frame.

3.17

hand enters frame and grabs pills.

3.18

Loop animation of X-6 shovelling pills into his mouth

3.19

Back to work
Back to Work

Title card

3.21

Body diagram like Jane's "If Stabbed..." animation.

3.22

match cut: X-6 falls over.

3.23

Black w/ sparse images. fades to red. Rothko shapes cloudy.

3.24

fade to: rebel X-6 shaken awake by a female hand.

3.27

X-6 rises upright, looks around.
Female student in foreground.

3.28

PANNING WALLS IN background
I collect old things.

3.30

PAN through her apartment. "old" things all around. still image.

3.31

Flashing "old" objects.

cut to: "to be continued..." title card.

4.2

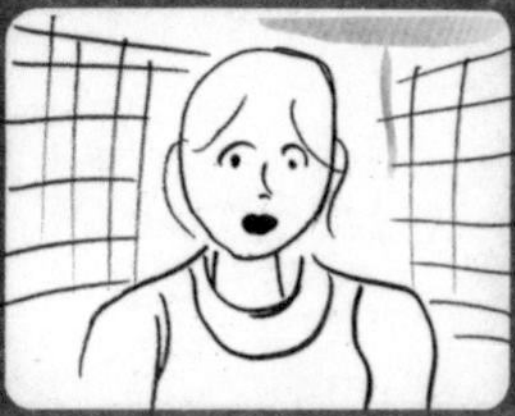

"3.25" image with strangely moving mouth on separate layer.

4.3

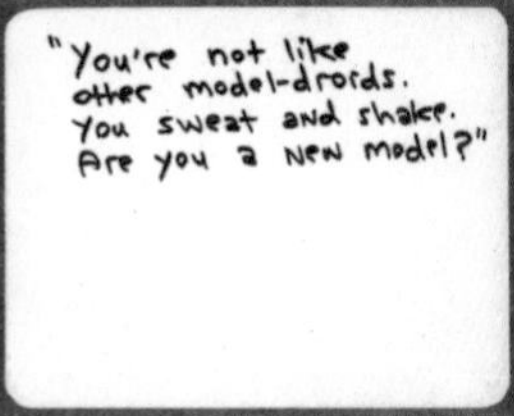
"You're not like other model-drords. You sweat and shake. Are you a new model?"

Title card

4.4

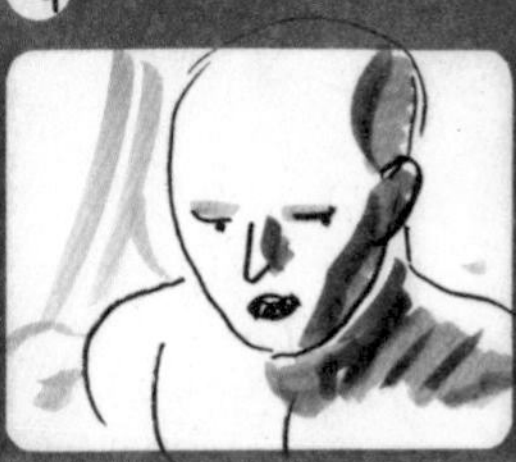

still image w/ strangely moving mouth on separate layer.

4.5

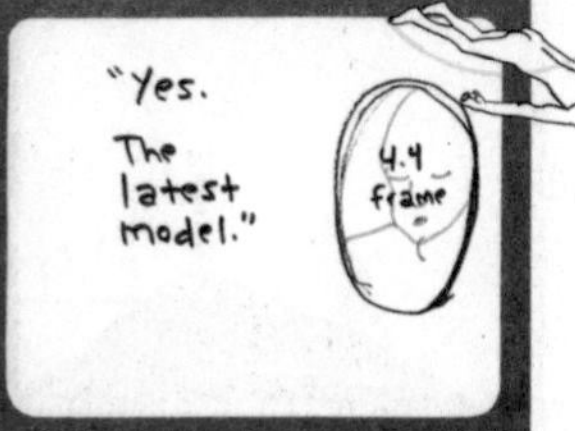
"Yes.
The latest model."
4.4 frame

title card w/ image insert.

4.8

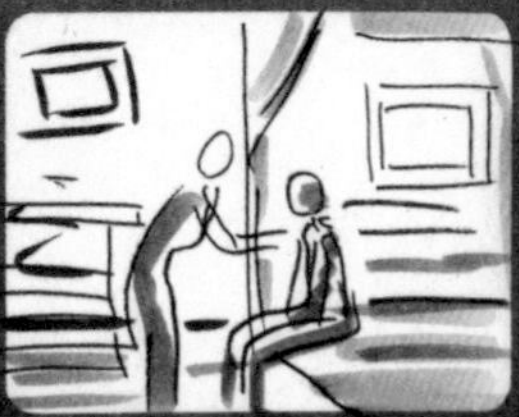

wide shot: she pokes @ him.

4.10

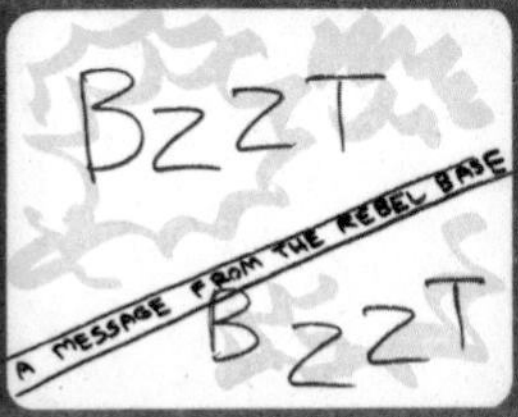
BZZT
A MESSAGE FROM THE REBEL BASE
BZZT

Flashing text. w/ scrolling text.

4.12

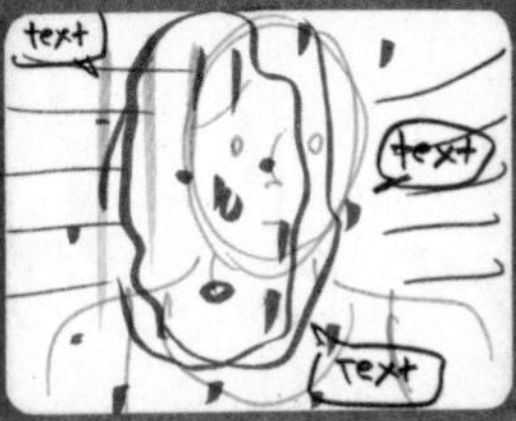
text
text
text

Rebel leaders staticy, distorted image over "3.25" image. X-6's P.O.V.
Text:
"They've caught on to us!"
"mission ABORTED!"
"Destroy the [redacted] craft school!"

4.13

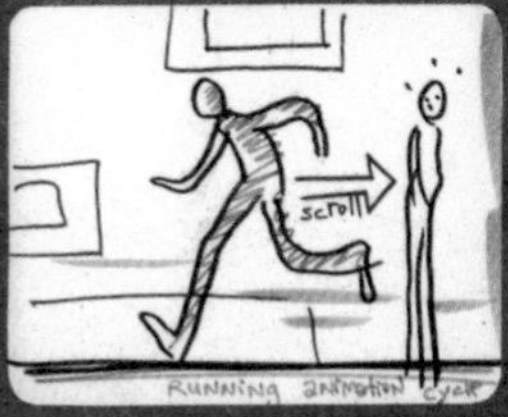
scroll
RUNNING ANIMATION CYCLE

X-6 runs ← past her.
running animation loop. background scrolling by.

4.14

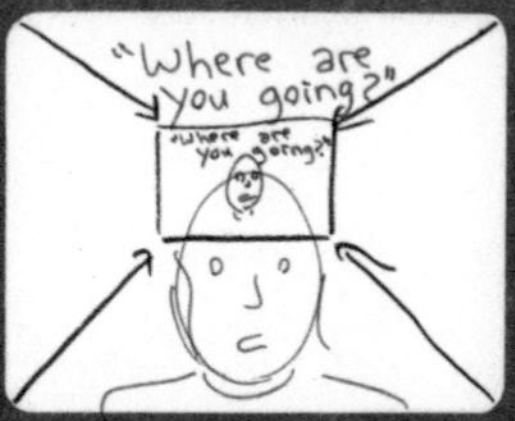
"Where are you going?"
"where are you going?"

whip-fast title card, getting farther away

4.15

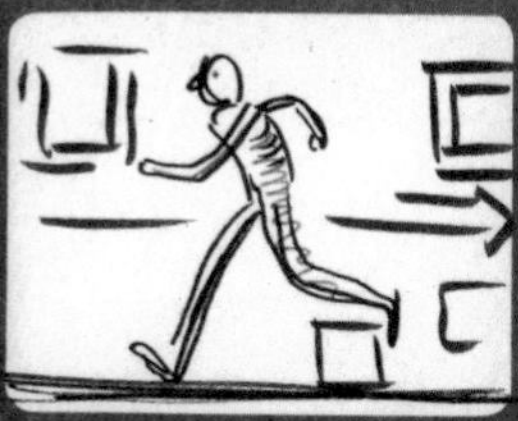

hold animation loop (Scooby-Doo style) of running past the same objects, too long.

4.19

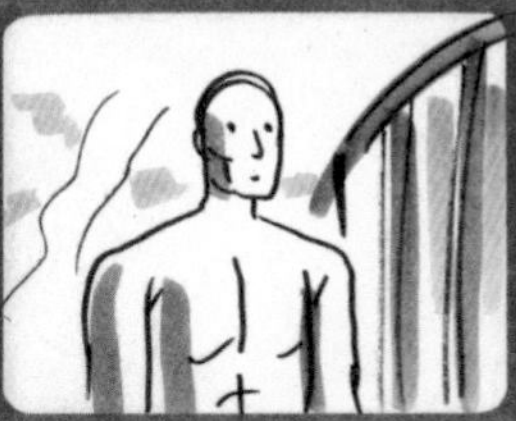

X-6 looks @ the school.

4.20

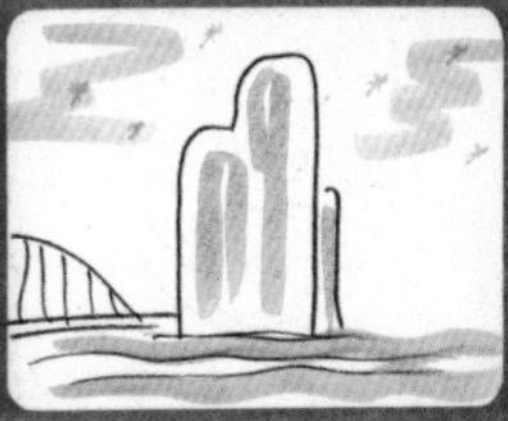

shot of the school. cuts to different areas inside the school.

classroom long hallway.

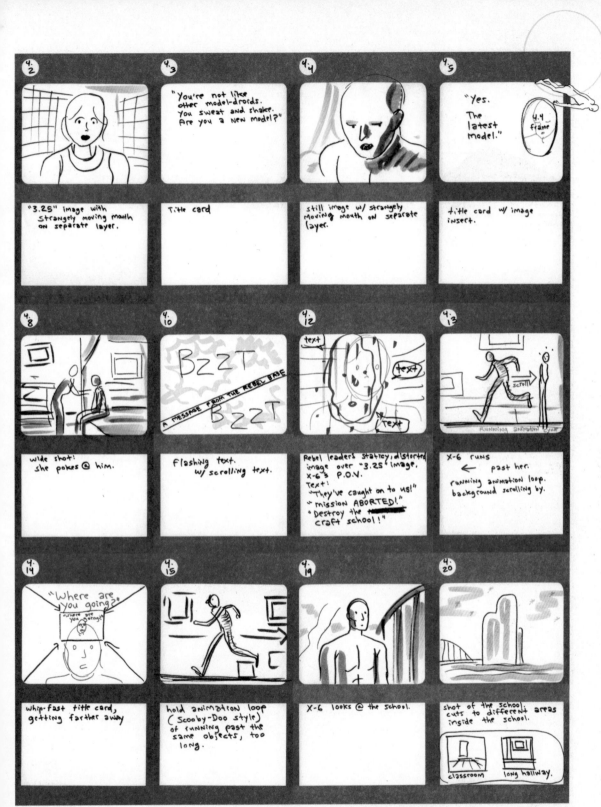

4.21

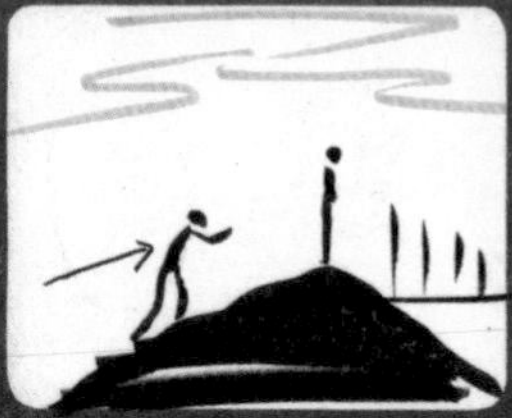

silhouette w/ X-6 standing. Female student approaches from behind.

Cut paper?

4.22

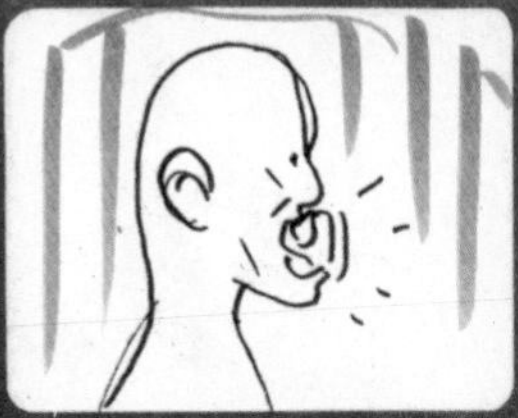

BLACK HOLE MOUTH COMES OUT.

4.23

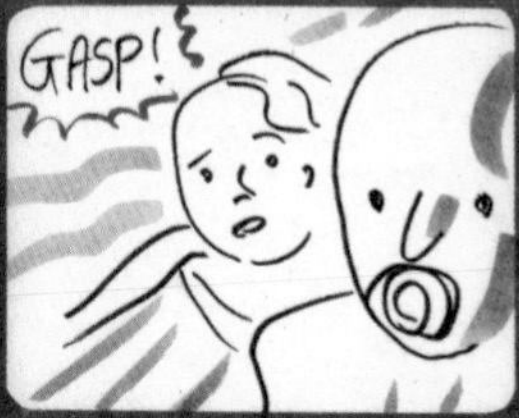
GASP!

whip-fast cut

4.24

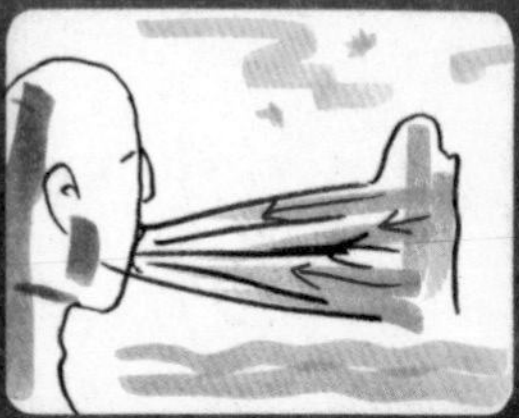

X-6 sucks up the school using black hole mouth.

4.25

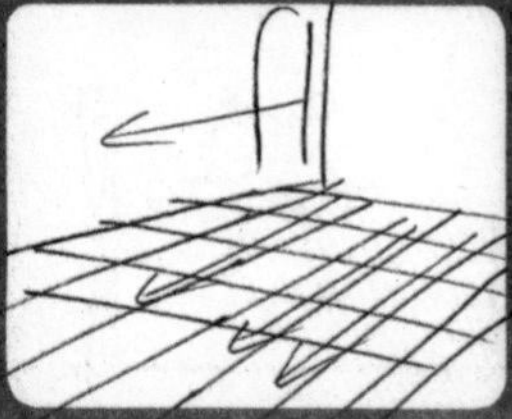

MONTAGE

shots of classrooms, parts of school being sucked iN.

4.26

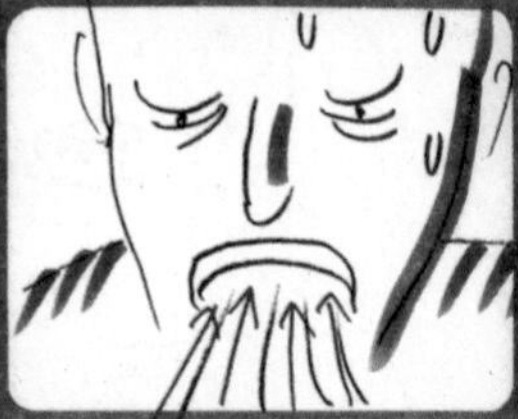

This is painful for X-6

4.27

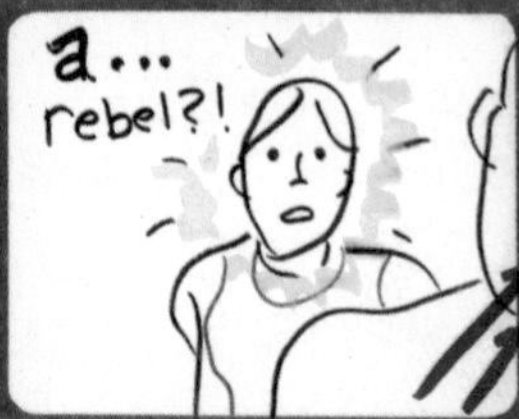
a...
rebel?!

whip-fast reaction shot of female student.

4.28

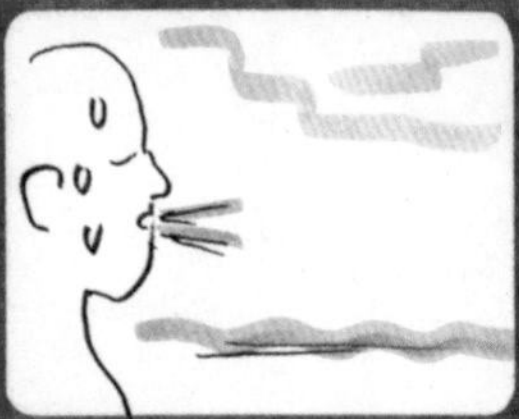

school is all gone.

4.29

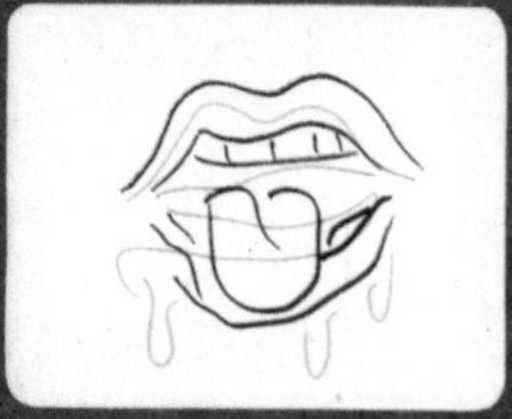

like "1.7" animation of weird post-black hole mouth.

4.30

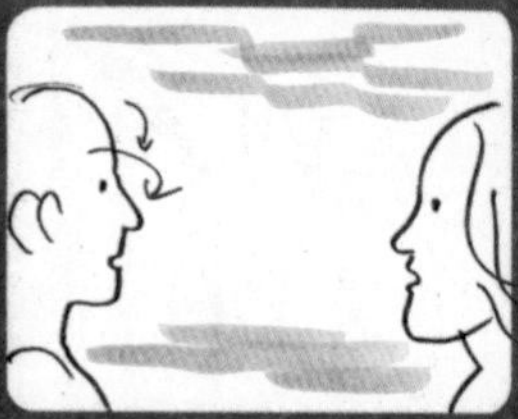

X-6 turns to see student.

4.31

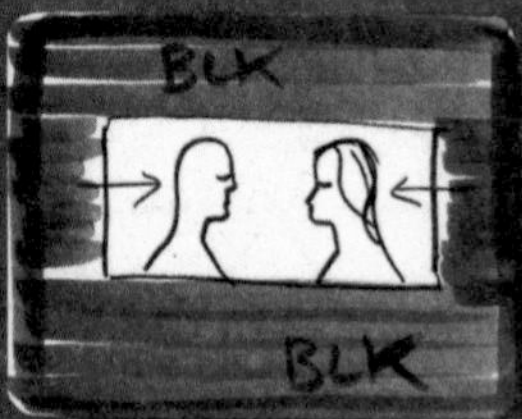
BLK
BLK

8-bit slide towards each other like ending to Ninja Gaiden.

4.32

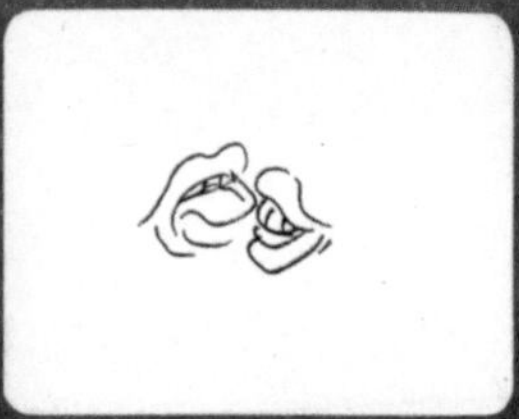

animation of just mouths (no people) kissing. his mouth is still weird from using the Black Hole mouth.

cut to: "The End" title card.

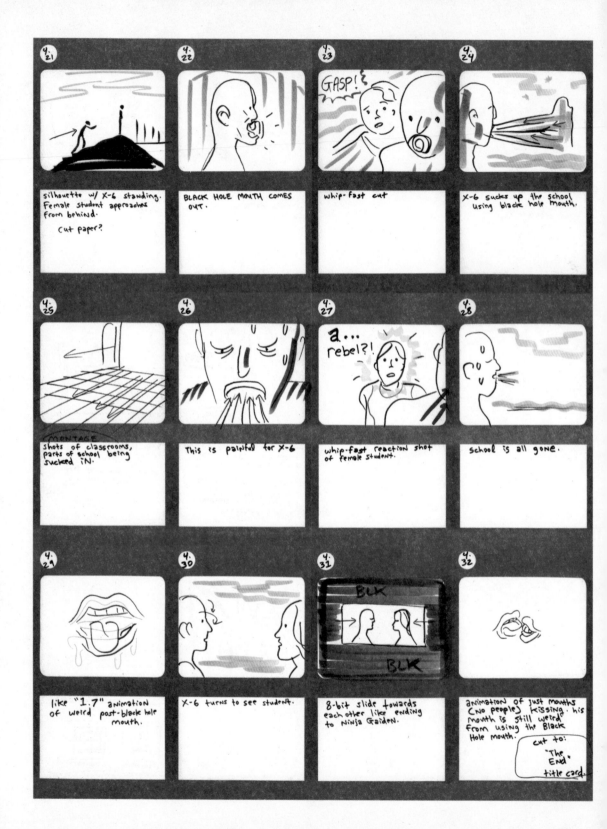

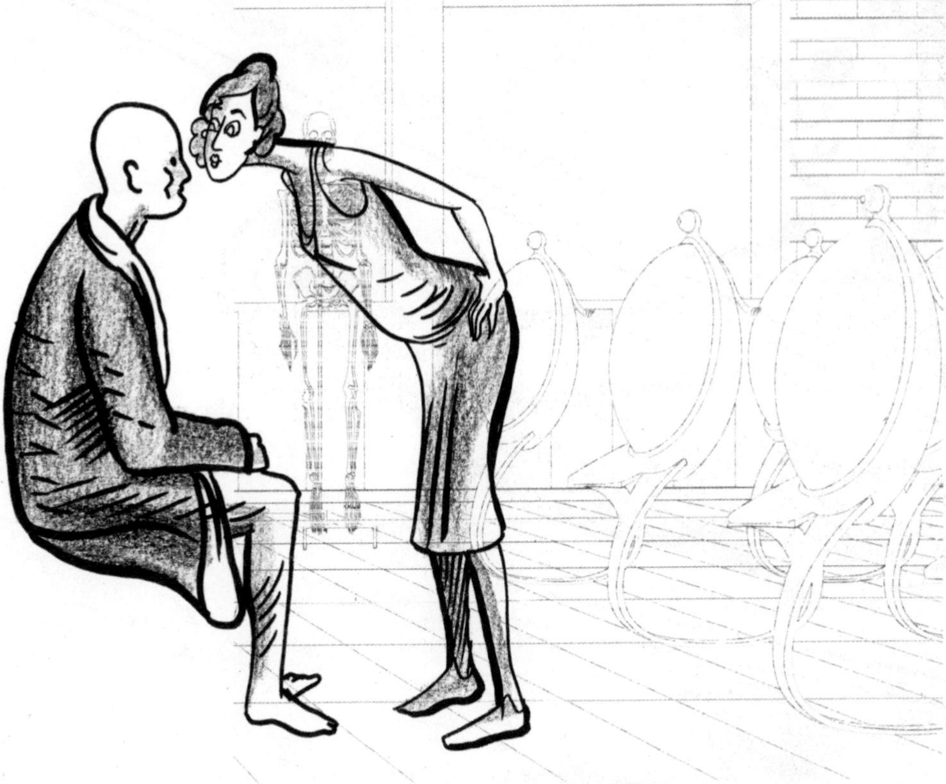

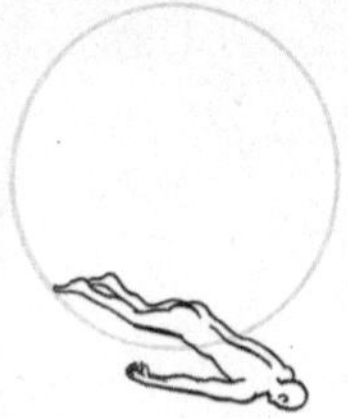

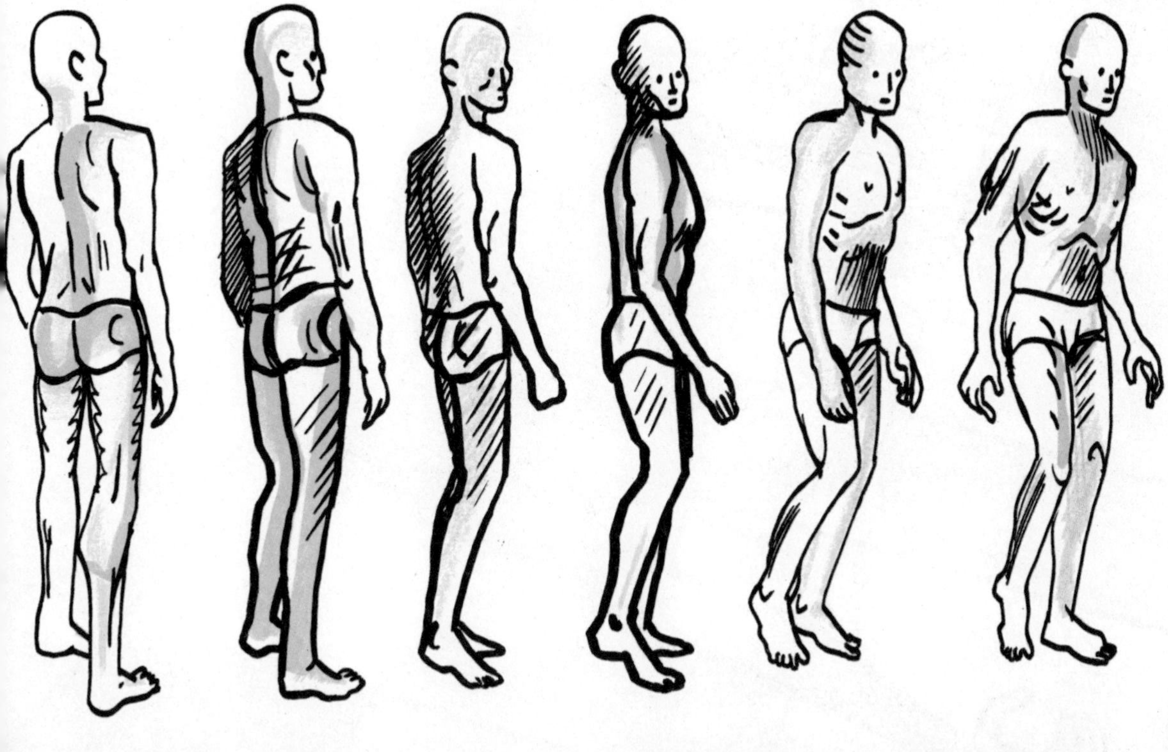

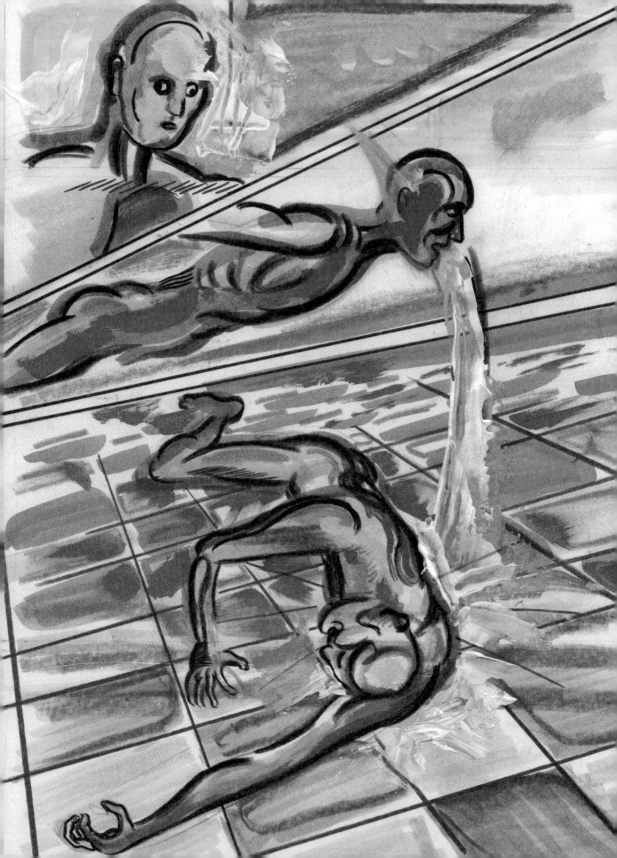

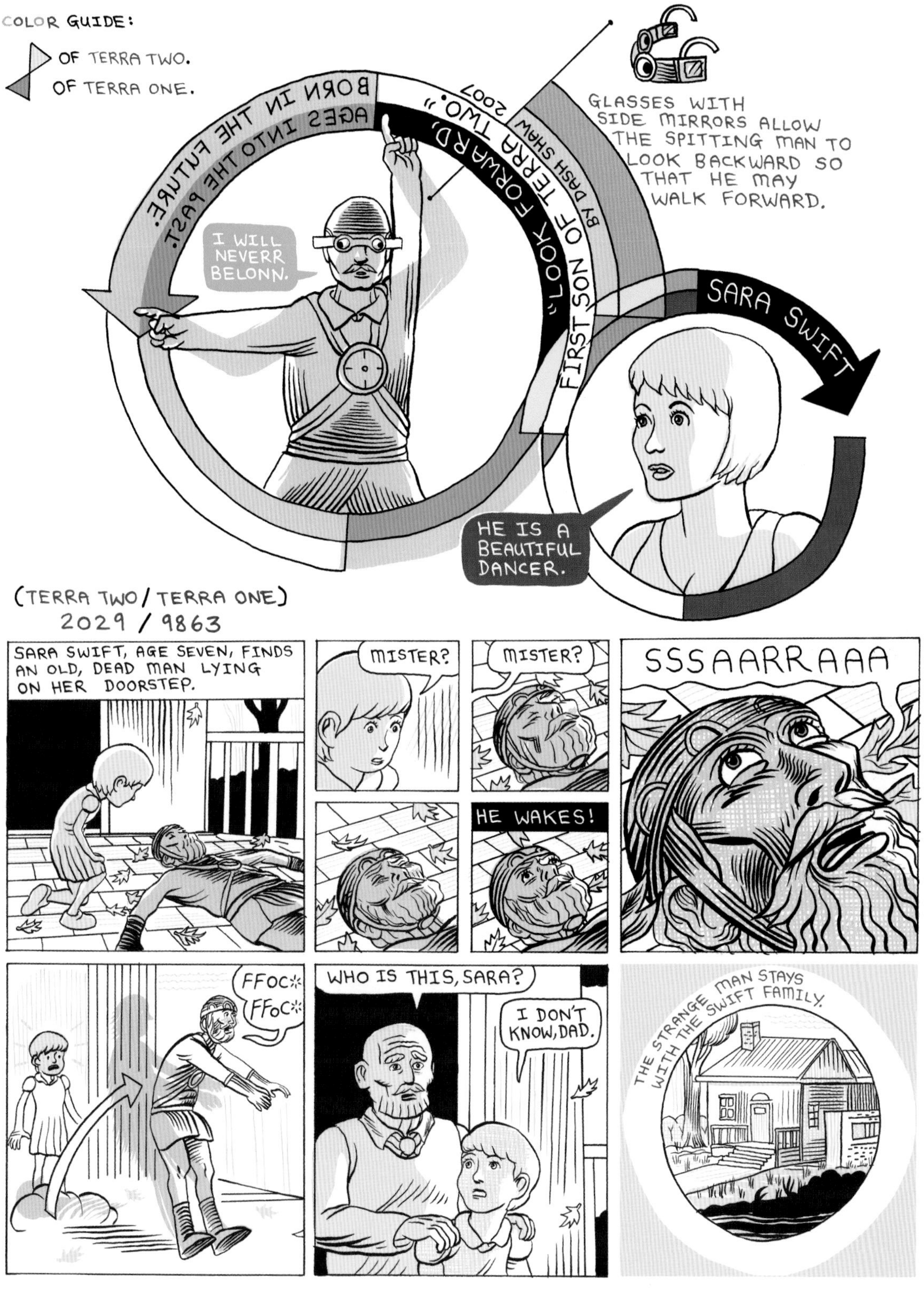

COLOR GUIDE:
OF TERRA TWO.
OF TERRA ONE.
BORN IN THE FUTURE.
AGES INTO THE PAST.
"LOOK FORWARD," FIRST SON OF TERRA TWO.
BY DASH SHAW 2007
GLASSES WITH SIDE MIRRORS ALLOW THE SPITTING MAN TO LOOK BACKWARD SO THAT HE MAY WALK FORWARD.
I WILL NEVERR BELONN.
SARA SWIFT
HE IS A BEAUTIFUL DANCER.
(TERRA TWO / TERRA ONE)
2029 / 9863
SARA SWIFT, AGE SEVEN, FINDS AN OLD, DEAD MAN LYING ON HER DOORSTEP.
MISTER?
MISTER?
HE WAKES!
SSSAARRAAA
FFOC
FFOC
WHO IS THIS, SARA?
I DON'T KNOW, DAD.
THE STRANGE MAN STAYS WITH THE SWIFT FAMILY.

SPIT SPIT

THE STRANGER PULLS FOOD OUT OF HIS MOUTH AND PLACES IT ON THE EMPTY PLATE INFRONT OF HIM.

FINALLY, HIS SPIT (CLEARLY ORANGE JUICE) RISES FROM THE GLASS INTO AN EMPTY PITCHER.

I WASS BOREN AT THE MADISON SQARR GARDEN STADIUM.

THAT'S STRANGE. I WAS JUST ABOUT TO ASK WHERE HE WAS FROM.

THIS CONVERSATION NEVER TAKES PLACE IN OUR WORLD LINE, SINCE THE SPITTING MAN WOULD NOT RESPOND TO A QUESTION THAT WAS NEVER ASKED.

YOU TEACHED ME YOUR NAMM ANED HOW TO TALK TO YOU.

HOW DID YOU KNOW MY NAME?

(SARA, YEARS LATER, IS THE FIRST TO CONVERSE WITH THE SPITTING MAN IN OUR WORLD LINE.)

YOUNGER.

OLDER.

...

MOST CONVERSATIONS WITH PEOPLE (DOCTORS, SCIENTISTS, REPORTERS) SIMPLY DO NOT OCCUR IN OUR WORLD LINE. ALL SUCH PARADOXICAL PROBLEMS ARE DUMPED INTO THE "GARBAGE WORLD LINE." AN INSANE, SCARY PLACE.

INSANE TO US, BUT SANE, EVEN MUNDANE, TO THOSE WHO INHABIT IT.

2046-2060 / 9846-9832

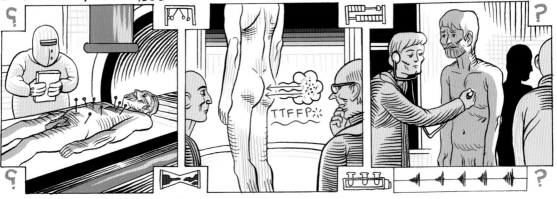

TTFFP

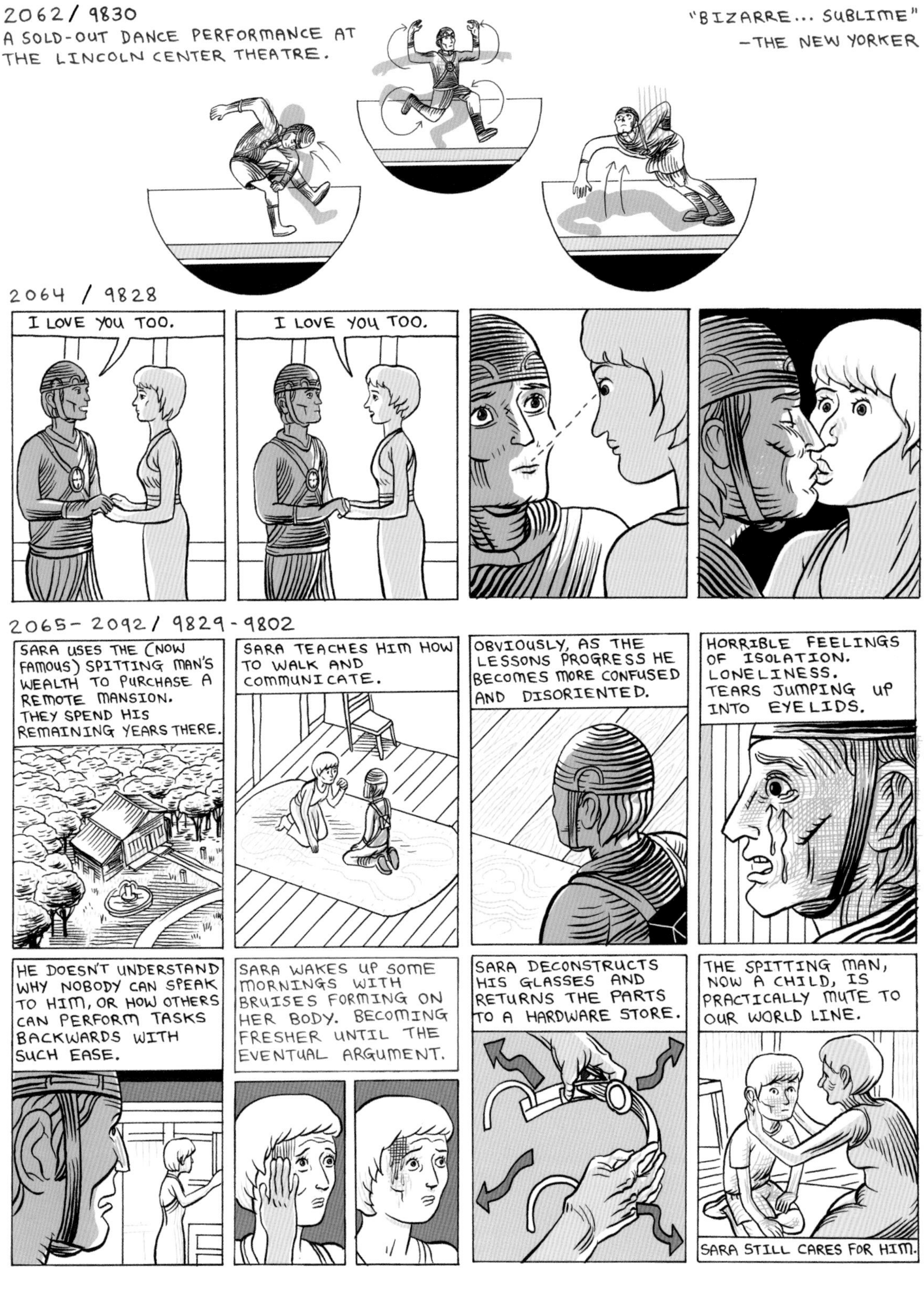

2062/ 9830
A SOLD-OUT DANCE PERFORMANCE AT THE LINCOLN CENTER THEATRE.
"BIZARRE... SUBLIME"
—THE NEW YORKER
2064 / 9828
I LOVE YOU TOO.
I LOVE YOU TOO.
2065-2092/ 9829-9802
SARA USES THE (NOW FAMOUS) SPITTING MAN'S WEALTH TO PURCHASE A REMOTE MANSION. THEY SPEND HIS REMAINING YEARS THERE.
SARA TEACHES HIM HOW TO WALK AND COMMUNICATE.
OBVIOUSLY, AS THE LESSONS PROGRESS HE BECOMES MORE CONFUSED AND DISORIENTED.
HORRIBLE FEELINGS OF ISOLATION. LONELINESS. TEARS JUMPING UP INTO EYELIDS.
HE DOESN'T UNDERSTAND WHY NOBODY CAN SPEAK TO HIM, OR HOW OTHERS CAN PERFORM TASKS BACKWARDS WITH SUCH EASE.
SARA WAKES UP SOME MORNINGS WITH BRUISES FORMING ON HER BODY. BECOMING FRESHER UNTIL THE EVENTUAL ARGUMENT.
SARA DECONSTRUCTS HIS GLASSES AND RETURNS THE PARTS TO A HARDWARE STORE.
THE SPITTING MAN, NOW A CHILD, IS PRACTICALLY MUTE TO OUR WORLD LINE.
SARA STILL CARES FOR HIM.

WHAT WILL HAPPEN TO THE SPITTING MAN? WHERE WILL HE GO? IT IS A MASSIVE MEDIA EVENT, HELD AT THE MADISON SQUARE GARDEN STADIUM.
SARA SWIFT, NOW IN HER SEVENTIES, HOLDS THE BABY.

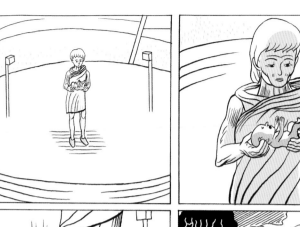

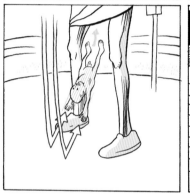

AH!

HUK!

I WILL NEVER LOVE ANOTHER.

DIZZY DIZZY

DIZZY CAP

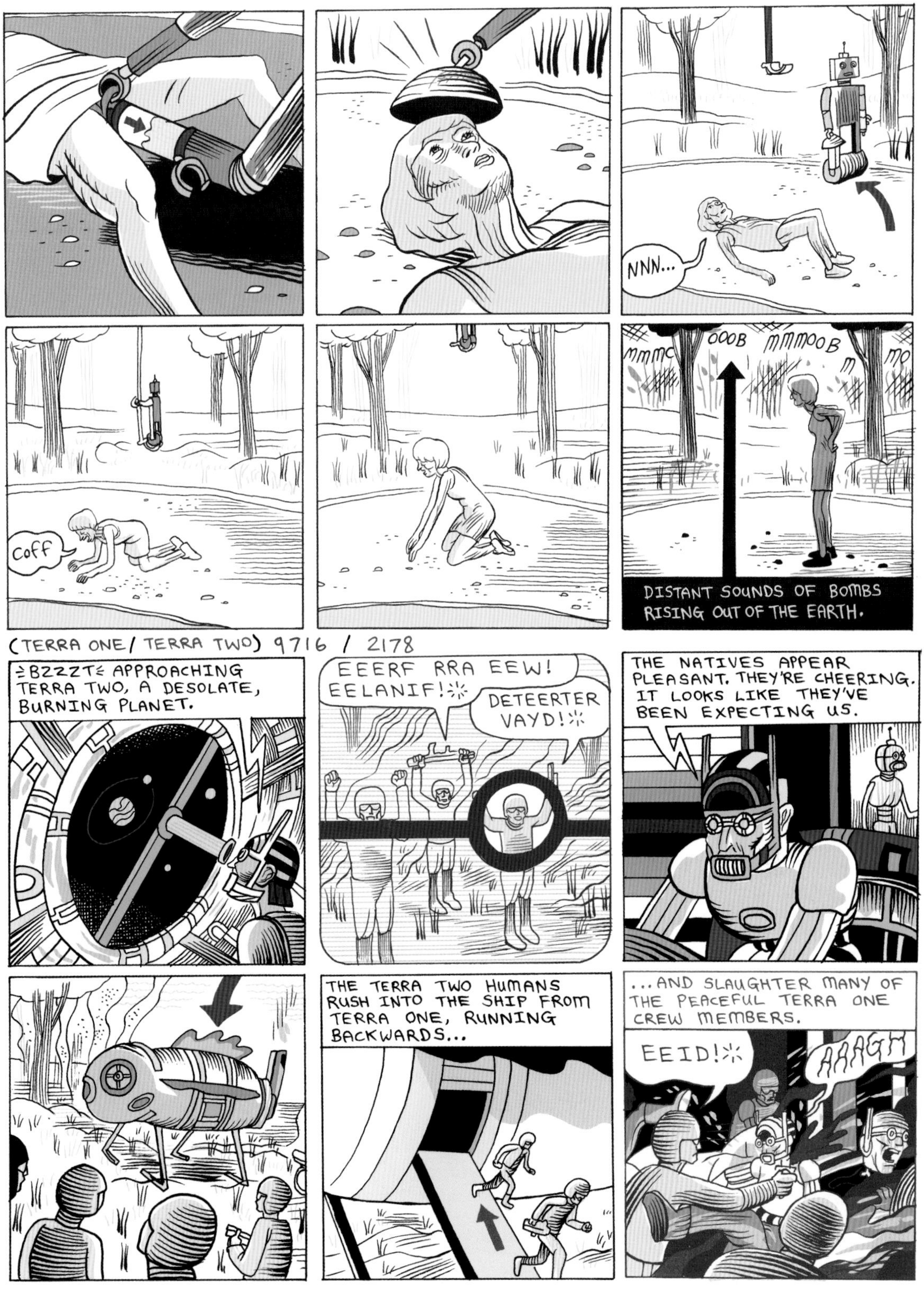
NNN...
COFF
MMMC
OOOB
MMMOOB
M
MO
DISTANT SOUNDS OF BOMBS RISING OUT OF THE EARTH.
(TERRA ONE/ TERRA TWO) 9716 / 2178
BZZZT APPROACHING TERRA TWO, A DESOLATE, BURNING PLANET.
EEERF RRA EEW! EELANIF!
DETEERTER VAYD!
THE NATIVES APPEAR PLEASANT. THEY'RE CHEERING. IT LOOKS LIKE THEY'VE BEEN EXPECTING US.
THE TERRA TWO HUMANS RUSH INTO THE SHIP FROM TERRA ONE, RUNNING BACKWARDS...
...AND SLAUGHTER MANY OF THE PEACEFUL TERRA ONE CREW MEMBERS.
EEID!
AAAGH

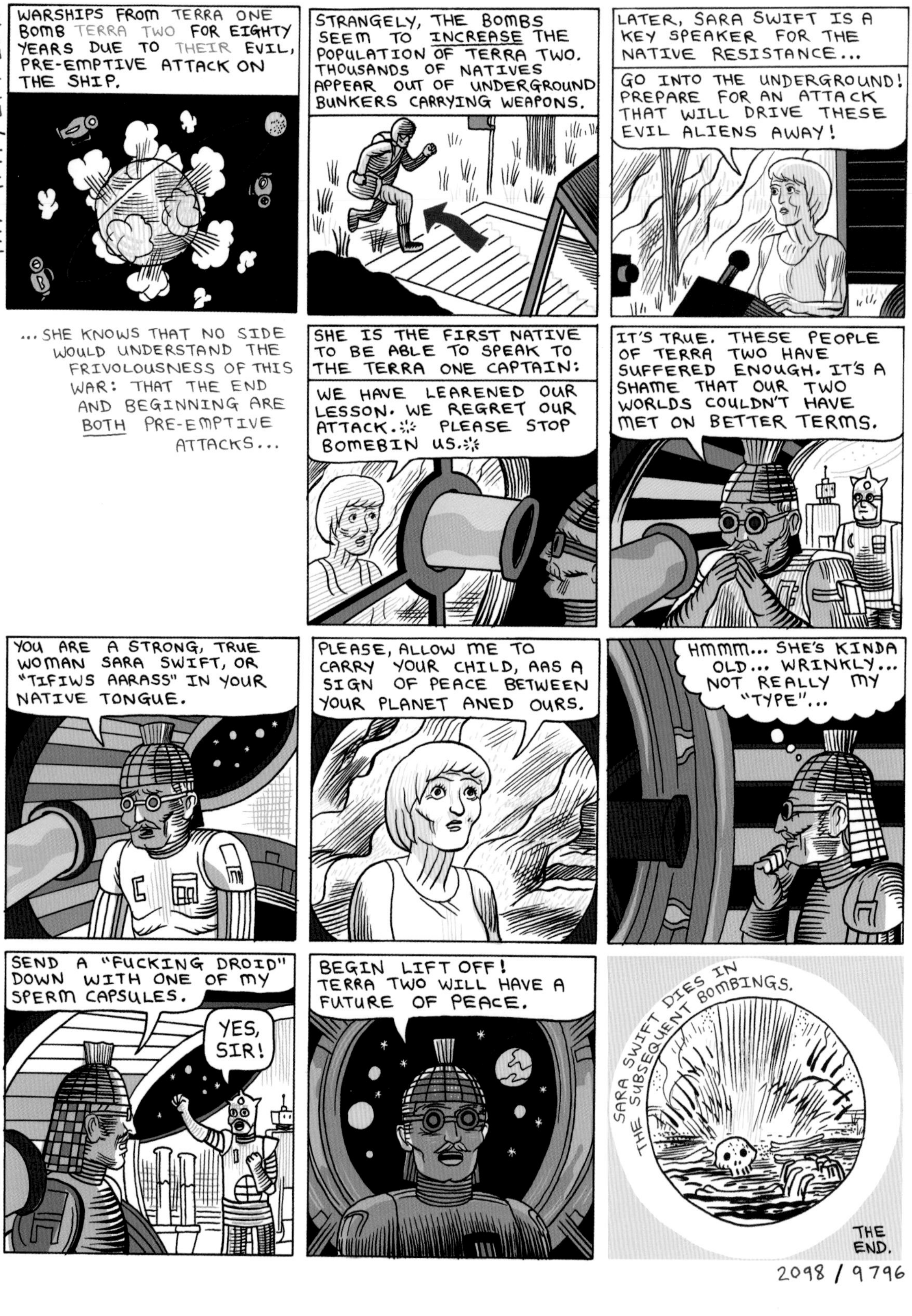
WARSHIPS FROM TERRA ONE BOMB TERRA TWO FOR EIGHTY YEARS DUE TO THEIR EVIL, PRE-EMPTIVE ATTACK ON THE SHIP.
STRANGELY, THE BOMBS SEEM TO INCREASE THE POPULATION OF TERRA TWO. THOUSANDS OF NATIVES APPEAR OUT OF UNDERGROUND BUNKERS CARRYING WEAPONS.
LATER, SARA SWIFT IS A KEY SPEAKER FOR THE NATIVE RESISTANCE...
GO INTO THE UNDERGROUND! PREPARE FOR AN ATTACK THAT WILL DRIVE THESE EVIL ALIENS AWAY!
...SHE KNOWS THAT NO SIDE WOULD UNDERSTAND THE FRIVOLOUSNESS OF THIS WAR: THAT THE END AND BEGINNING ARE BOTH PRE-EMPTIVE ATTACKS...
SHE IS THE FIRST NATIVE TO BE ABLE TO SPEAK TO THE TERRA ONE CAPTAIN:
WE HAVE LEARENED OUR LESSON. WE REGRET OUR ATTACK. PLEASE STOP BOMEBIN US.
IT'S TRUE. THESE PEOPLE OF TERRA TWO HAVE SUFFERED ENOUGH. IT'S A SHAME THAT OUR TWO WORLDS COULDN'T HAVE MET ON BETTER TERMS.
YOU ARE A STRONG, TRUE WOMAN SARA SWIFT, OR "TIFIWS AARASS" IN YOUR NATIVE TONGUE.
PLEASE, ALLOW ME TO CARRY YOUR CHILD, AAS A SIGN OF PEACE BETWEEN YOUR PLANET ANED OURS.
HMMM... SHE'S KINDA OLD... WRINKLY... NOT REALLY MY "TYPE"...
SEND A "FUCKING DROID" DOWN WITH ONE OF MY SPERM CAPSULES.
YES, SIR!
BEGIN LIFT OFF! TERRA TWO WILL HAVE A FUTURE OF PEACE.
SARA SWIFT DIES IN THE SUBSEQUENT BOMBINGS.
THE END.

SATELLITE CMYK

DRAWN MAY 2008

TRAVIS STUTTERED:

THE-THEY'RE LET-TING ME G-GO.

I-I WA-WANT YOU T-TO TAKE CA-CARE OF SAMANTHA, O-OKAY?

SAMANTHA WAS A YEAR YOUNGER THAN ME.

IT-IT'S LIKELY I-I'LL NE-NEVER SEE YOU A-AGAIN, BA-BA-BARRY.

O-OR IF I DO, THA-THAT I WO-WONT RE-RECOGNIZE YOU.

I-IN SIX YE-YEARS, WHEN YOU'RE SE-SEVENTE-TEEN, YO-YOU'LL B-BE FREE T-TOO.

WILL SAMANTHA BE ALL ALONE THEN?

THE-THEY'LL CA-CAPTURE MORE.

GO-GOODBYE.

SLIDE

IN SIX YEARS MY FACE GREW TALLER, THINNER.

MY NAME IS BARRY.

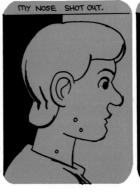

MY NOSE SHOT OUT.

ACNE.

ANDREW STONE, ARRIVING FOR MY MORNING CLASS.

>BZZT<

SCAN COMPLETE.

NINE HUNDRED YEARS AGO THE EARTH EXPLODED.

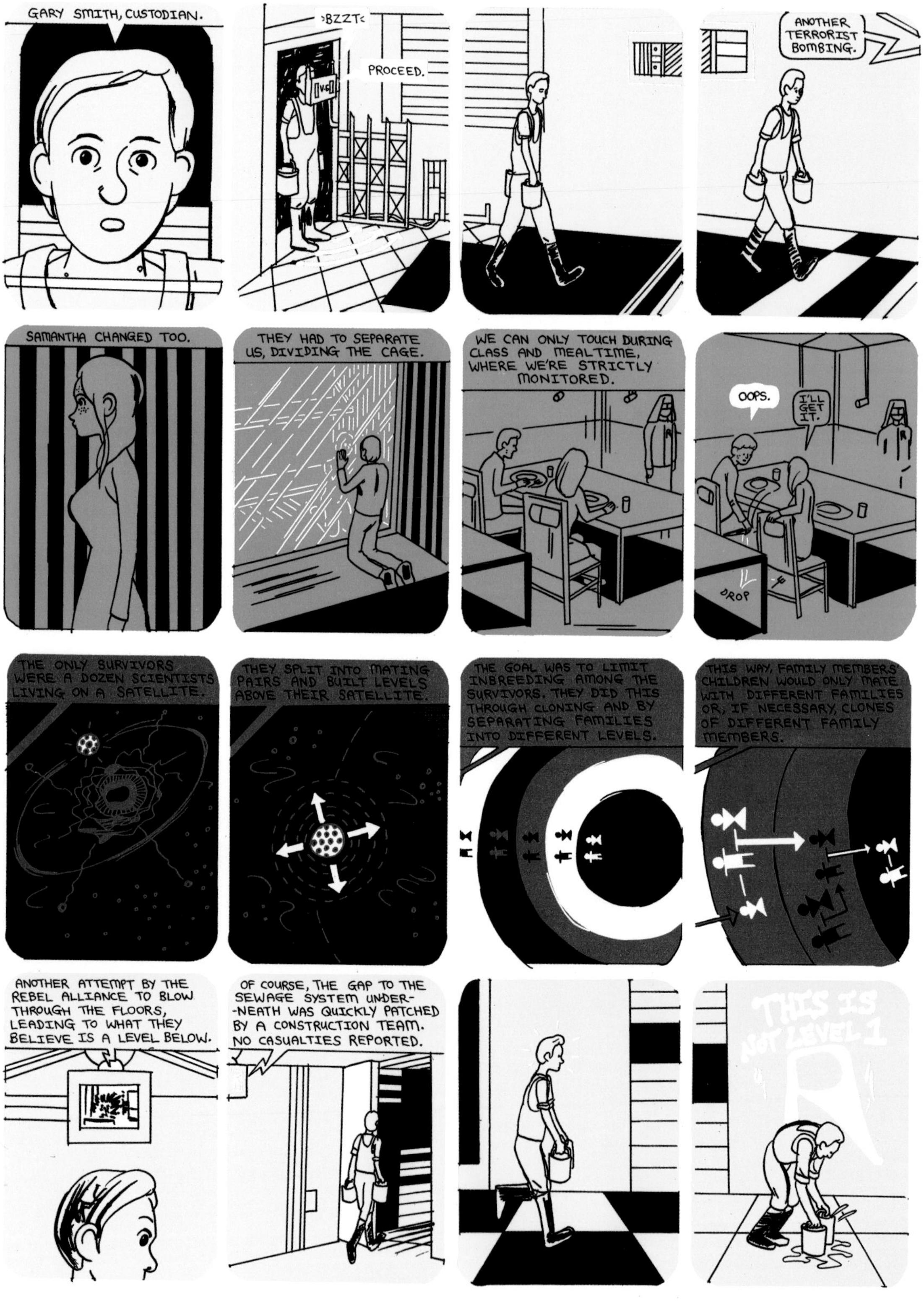
GARY SMITH, CUSTODIAN.
>BZZT<
PROCEED.
ANOTHER TERRORIST BOMBING.
SAMANTHA CHANGED TOO.
THEY HAD TO SEPARATE US, DIVIDING THE CAGE.
WE CAN ONLY TOUCH DURING CLASS AND MEALTIME, WHERE WE'RE STRICTLY MONITORED.
OOPS.
I'LL GET IT.
DROP
THE ONLY SURVIVORS WERE A DOZEN SCIENTISTS LIVING ON A SATELLITE.
THEY SPLIT INTO MATING PAIRS AND BUILT LEVELS ABOVE THEIR SATELLITE.
THE GOAL WAS TO LIMIT INBREEDING AMONG THE SURVIVORS. THEY DID THIS THROUGH CLONING AND BY SEPARATING FAMILIES INTO DIFFERENT LEVELS.
THIS WAY, FAMILY MEMBERS' CHILDREN WOULD ONLY MATE WITH DIFFERENT FAMILIES OR, IF NECESSARY, CLONES OF DIFFERENT FAMILY MEMBERS.
ANOTHER ATTEMPT BY THE REBEL ALLIANCE TO BLOW THROUGH THE FLOORS, LEADING TO WHAT THEY BELIEVE IS A LEVEL BELOW.
OF COURSE, THE GAP TO THE SEWAGE SYSTEM UNDER-NEATH WAS QUICKLY PATCHED BY A CONSTRUCTION TEAM. NO CASUALTIES REPORTED.
THIS IS NOT LEVEL 1

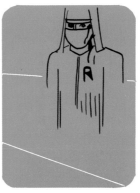

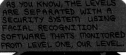

 AS YOU KNOW, THE LEVELS ARE SEPARATED WITH A SECURITY SYSTEM USING FACIAL RECOGNITION SOFTWARE THAT'S MONITORED FROM LEVEL ONE, OUR LEVEL.

THAT'S WHY EVERYONE HAS A FACIAL SCAN EVERY TEN YEARS AFTER THEIR 18TH BIRTHDAY.

YOU'VE NEVER HAD A FACIAL SCAN BECAUSE YOUR FACES ARE STILL IN DEVELOPMENT.

IN TODAY'S CLASS, I'LL TEACH YOU HOW FACIAL RECOGNITION SCANS WORK AND WE'LL DISCUSS HOW THESE SECURITY MEASURES PROTECT US, THE POPULATION OF LEVEL ONE, FROM UPPER-LEVEL INVADERS.

MALL FACILITY

HEY TARA.

HEY, GARY.

WHEN DO YOU GET OFF?

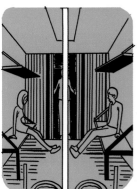

YOUR BIRTHDAY IS COMING UP. THEY'LL TAKE YOU AWAY SOON.

WELL, IT'LL ONLY BE A YEAR. I'M SURE THEY'LL PUT YOU WITH ME. THEY KNOW THAT WE CARE FOR EACH OTHER.

I DON'T KNOW, BARRY.

TRAVIS NEVER CAME BACK FOR US. IT'S POSSIBLE THAT, ONCE YOU LEAVE, YOU NEVER WANT TO BE REMINDED OF THIS PLACE.

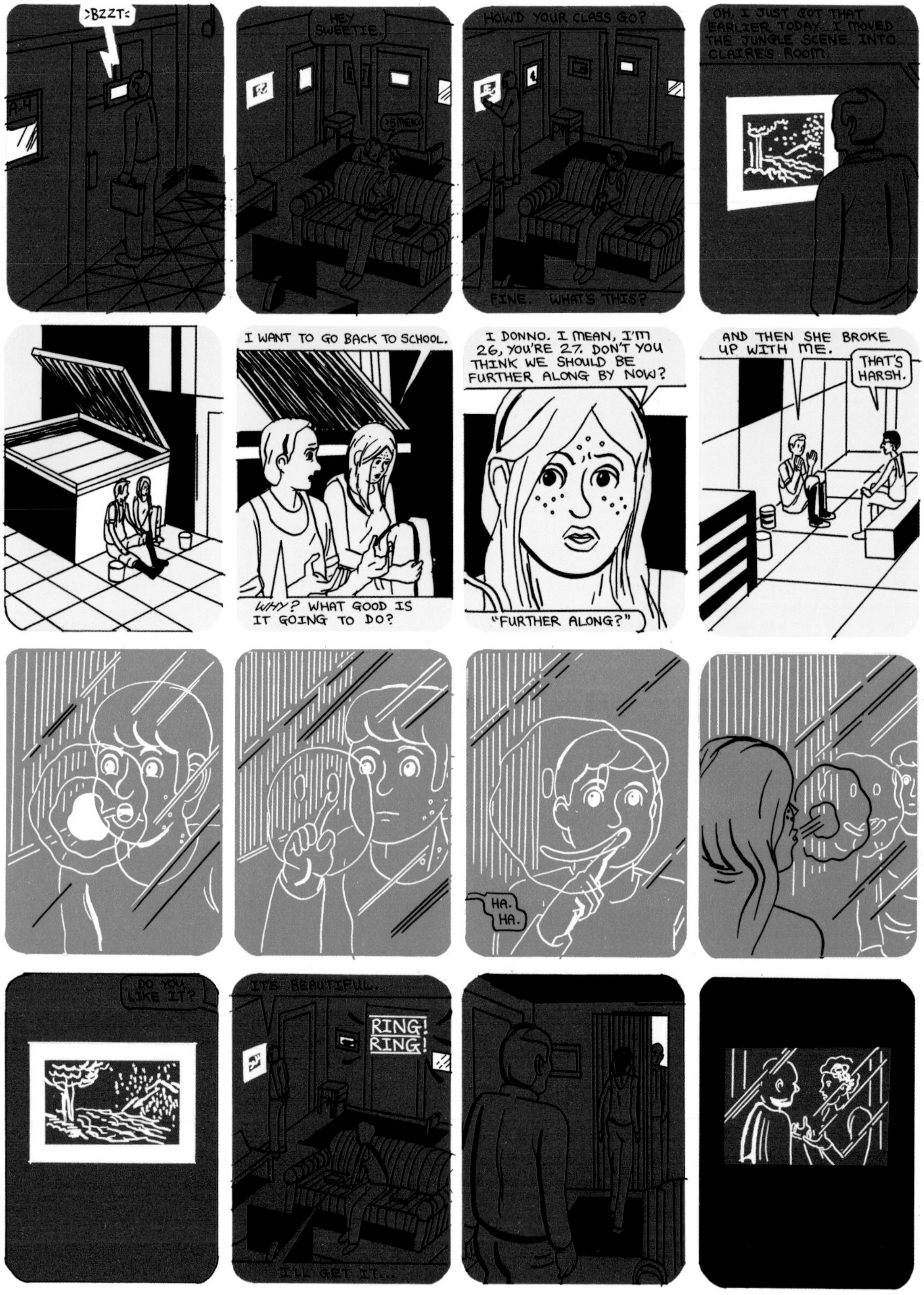
>BZZT<
HEY SWEETIE.
>SMEK<
HOW'D YOUR CLASS GO?
FINE. WHAT'S THIS?
OH, I JUST GOT THAT EARLIER TODAY. I MOVED THE JUNGLE SCENE INTO CLAIRE'S ROOM.
I WANT TO GO BACK TO SCHOOL.
WHY? WHAT GOOD IS IT GOING TO DO?
I DONNO. I MEAN, I'M 26, YOU'RE 27. DON'T YOU THINK WE SHOULD BE FURTHER ALONG BY NOW?
"FURTHER ALONG?"
AND THEN SHE BROKE UP WITH ME.
THAT'S HARSH.
HA. HA.
DO YOU LIKE IT?
IT'S BEAUTIFUL.
RING! RING!
I'LL GET IT...

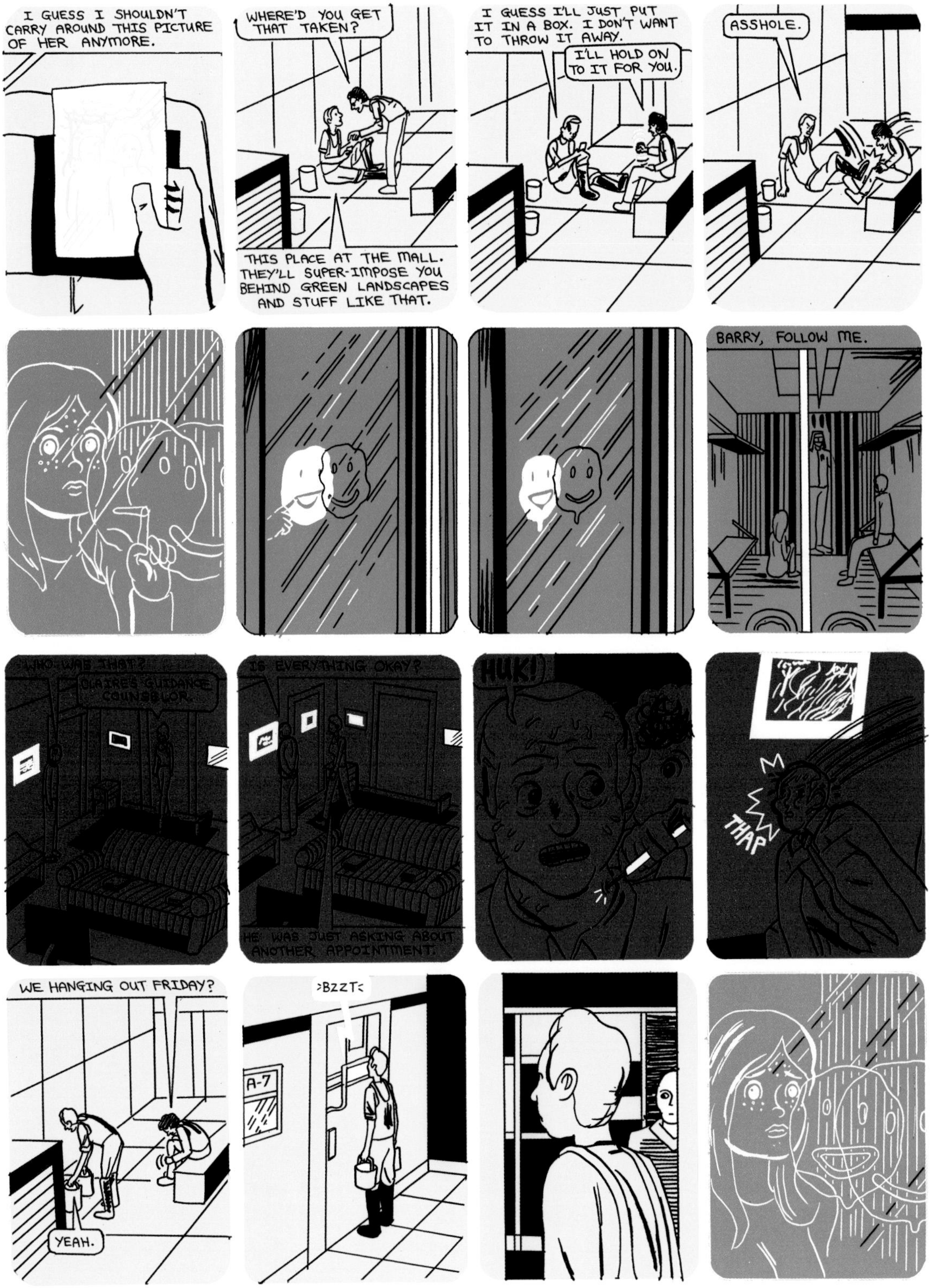
I GUESS I SHOULDN'T CARRY AROUND THIS PICTURE OF HER ANYMORE.
WHERE'D YOU GET THAT TAKEN?
THIS PLACE AT THE MALL. THEY'LL SUPER-IMPOSE YOU BEHIND GREEN LANDSCAPES AND STUFF LIKE THAT.
I GUESS I'LL JUST PUT IT IN A BOX. I DON'T WANT TO THROW IT AWAY.
I'LL HOLD ON TO IT FOR YOU.
ASSHOLE.
BARRY, FOLLOW ME.
WHO WAS THAT?
CLAIRE'S GUIDANCE COUNSELOR.
IS EVERYTHING OKAY?
HE WAS JUST ASKING ABOUT ANOTHER APPOINTMENT.
HUK!
THAP
WE HANGING OUT FRIDAY?
YEAH.
>BZZT<

UH-

MOVE HIM OUT.

I'LL GET CLAIRE.

SIT.

EVERYONE IS TOLD THAT THEY LIVE ON LEVEL ONE, THE FIRST HOME BASE LEVEL OF THE GOVERNMENT AND FACIAL RECOGNITION SOFTWARE. THIS IS JUST NOT TRUE. WHY ARE WE TOLD THIS MONSTROUS LIE?

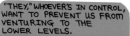

"THEY," WHOEVER'S IN CONTROL, WANT TO PREVENT US FROM VENTURING TO THE LOWER LEVELS.

WHERE ARE YOU TAKING CLAIRE?! WHERE'S MY LITTLE GIRL?!

JUST BEFORE YOUR TEN-YEAR FACIAL UPDATE SCAN, THERE'S A DAY-LONG PERIOD WHEN THE SCANNERS UPDATE THEIR FACIAL DATABASE SYSTEM IN PREPARATION.

WE USE THIS TIME WINDOW TO MOVE YOU INTO A LOWER LEVEL.

CLAIRE'S WITH US NOW, A RECRUIT, JUST AS YOU WERE ONCE, TWO LEVELS ABOVE, AND YOUR REAL MOTHER, FOUR LEVELS ABOVE, YEARS AGO.

I DON'T UNDERSTAND.

THERE YOU HAVE A HOST FAMILY SUPPLIED BY THE REBEL ALLIANCE.

YOUR MEMORIES OF OUR CONTAINMENT FACILITY WILL BE ERASED AND REPLACED WITH A—

"GARY SMITH," WHO IS NOW MOVING TO A NEW IDENTITY A LEVEL BELOW HIM. HIS MEMORIES, OF COURSE, WILL BE REPLACED BY THE REBELS BELOW HIM. THE REBELS ON EACH LEVEL HAVE CONTACT WITH THE LEVELS DIRECTLY BELOW AND ABOVE THEIRS. IT'S ALL ARRANGED.

CAN'T THE PEOPLE BELOW LET ME KEEP MY MEMORIES? I DON'T GET IT.

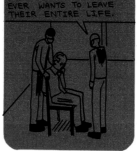

IF YOUR MEMORIES WERE INTACT, IT'S HIGHLY LIKELY YOU'D COMPROMISE OUR MISSION. NOBODY EVER WANTS TO LEAVE THEIR ENTIRE LIFE.

OUR MISSION IS TO MOVE PEOPLE DOWN, LEVEL BY LEVEL, TO FIND THE TRUE LOWEST LEVEL— LEVEL ONE.

WHAT ABOUT MY FAMILY? CAN I SAY GOODBYE TO THEM?

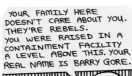

YOUR FAMILY HERE
DOESN'T CARE ABOUT YOU.
THEY'RE REBELS.
YOU WERE RAISED IN A
CONTAINMENT FACILITY
A LEVEL ABOVE THIS. YOUR
REAL NAME IS BARRY GORE.

BUT I DON'T WANT TO
GO. I LIKE MY LIFE
HERE.

IT'S NOT YOUR
DECISION.

PLEASE! PLEASE!
I DON'T WANT TO GO!
JUST LEAVE ME HERE!
I WON'T TELL ANYONE!

SLIDE

THEY'RE LETTING ME GO.
YOU WERE RIGHT,

I'LL PROBABLY NEVER SEE
YOU AGAIN, OR I WON'T
RECOGNIZE YOU IF I DO.

BUT, MAYBE, WE'LL MEET
UP A YEAR FROM NOW,
WHEN THEY LET YOU FREE.

I LOVE
YOU SO
MUCH.

I LOVE
YOU TOO.

CAN'T I JUST SAY
GOODBYE TO CLAIRE?
PLEASE?

GOOD BYE.

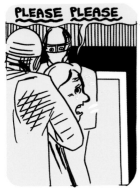

PLEASE PLEASE

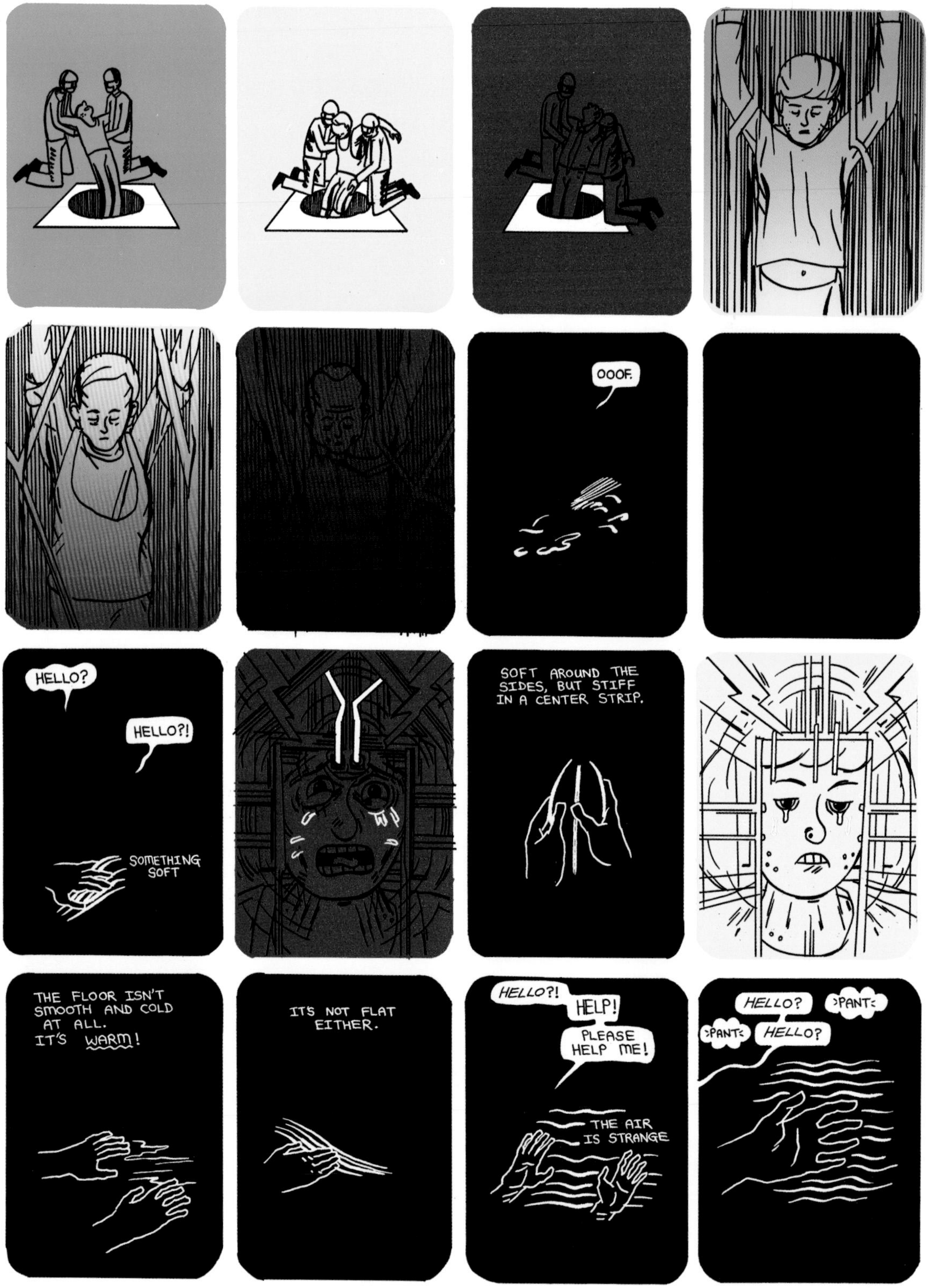
OOOF.
HELLO?
HELLO?!
SOMETHING SOFT
SOFT AROUND THE SIDES, BUT STIFF IN A CENTER STRIP.
THE FLOOR ISN'T SMOOTH AND COLD AT ALL. IT'S WARM!
IT'S NOT FLAT EITHER.
HELLO?!
HELP!
PLEASE HELP ME!
THE AIR IS STRANGE
HELLO?
>PANT<
>PANT<
HELLO?

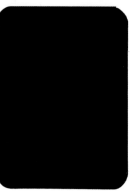

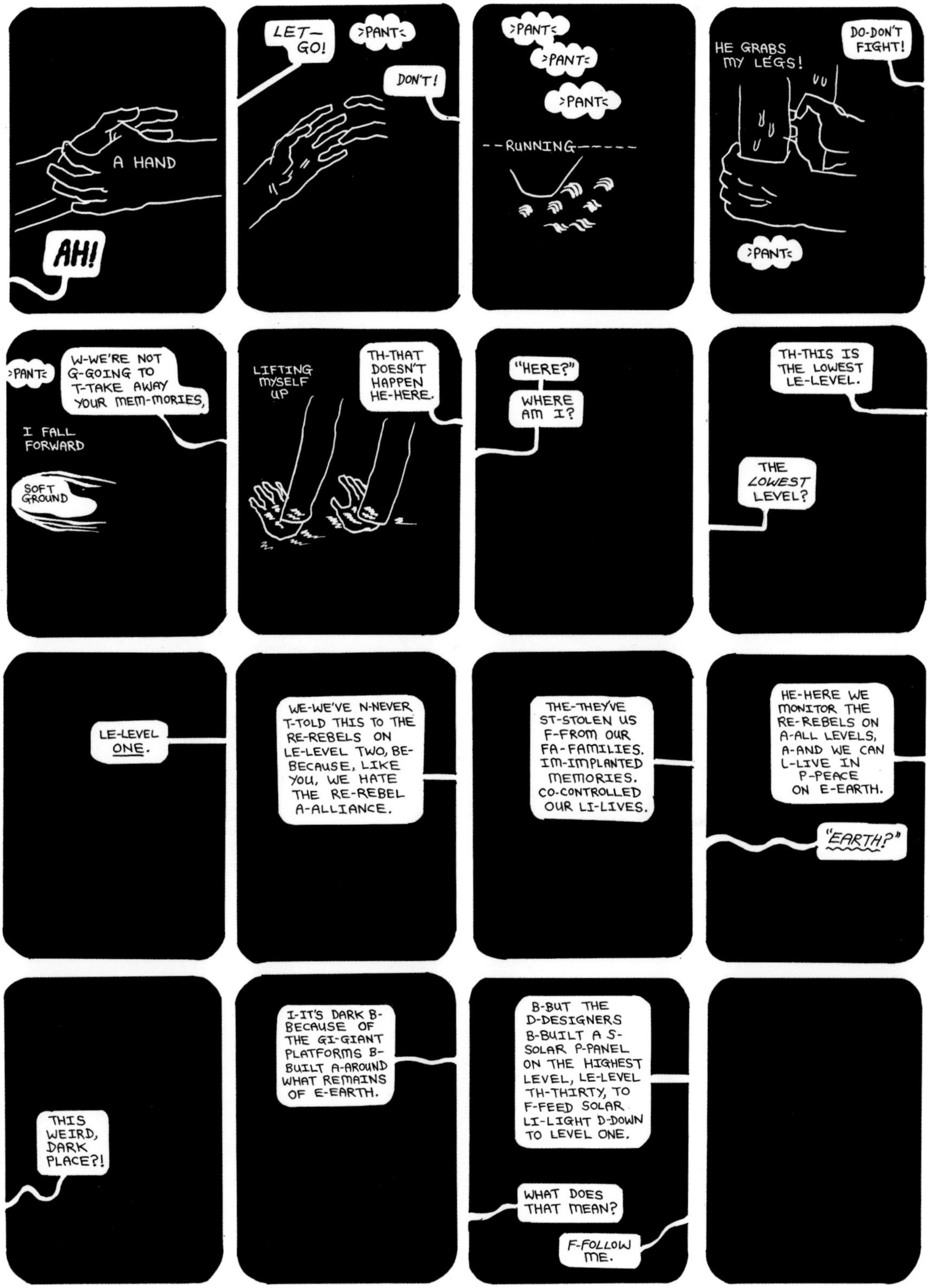
A HAND
AH!
LET— GO!
>PANT<
DON'T!
>PANT<
>PANT<
>PANT<
RUNNING
HE GRABS MY LEGS!
DO-DON'T FIGHT!
>PANT<
>PANT<
W-WE'RE NOT G-GOING TO T-TAKE AWAY YOUR MEM-MORIES,
I FALL FORWARD
SOFT GROUND
LIFTING MYSELF UP
TH-THAT DOESN'T HAPPEN HE-HERE.
"HERE?"
WHERE AM I?
TH-THIS IS THE LOWEST LE-LEVEL.
THE LOWEST LEVEL?
LE-LEVEL ONE.
WE-WE'VE N-NEVER T-TOLD THIS TO THE RE-REBELS ON LE-LEVEL TWO, BE-BECAUSE, LIKE YOU, WE HATE THE RE-REBEL A-ALLIANCE.
THE-THEY'VE ST-STOLEN US F-FROM OUR FA-FAMILIES. IM-IMPLANTED MEMORIES. CO-CONTROLLED OUR LI-LIVES.
HE-HERE WE MONITOR THE RE-REBELS ON A-ALL LEVELS, A-AND WE CAN L-LIVE IN P-PEACE ON E-EARTH.
"EARTH?"
THIS WEIRD, DARK PLACE?!
I-IT'S DARK B-BECAUSE OF THE GI-GIANT PLATFORMS B-BUILT A-AROUND WHAT REMAINS OF E-EARTH.
B-BUT THE D-DESIGNERS B-BUILT A S-SOLAR P-PANEL ON THE HIGHEST LEVEL, LE-LEVEL TH-THIRTY, TO F-FEED SOLAR LI-LIGHT D-DOWN TO LEVEL ONE.
WHAT DOES THAT MEAN?
F-FOLLOW ME.

I'D NEVER SEEN SUCH A FRESH COLOR BEFORE. A REAL GREEN!

OF COURSE I'D SEEN GREEN BEFORE, PRINTED IN MAGAZINES OR REPRODUCTIONS OF PAINTINGS——BUT IT NEVER LOOKED LIKE THIS.

A YEAR LATER I MEET SOMEONE NEW.

THE END

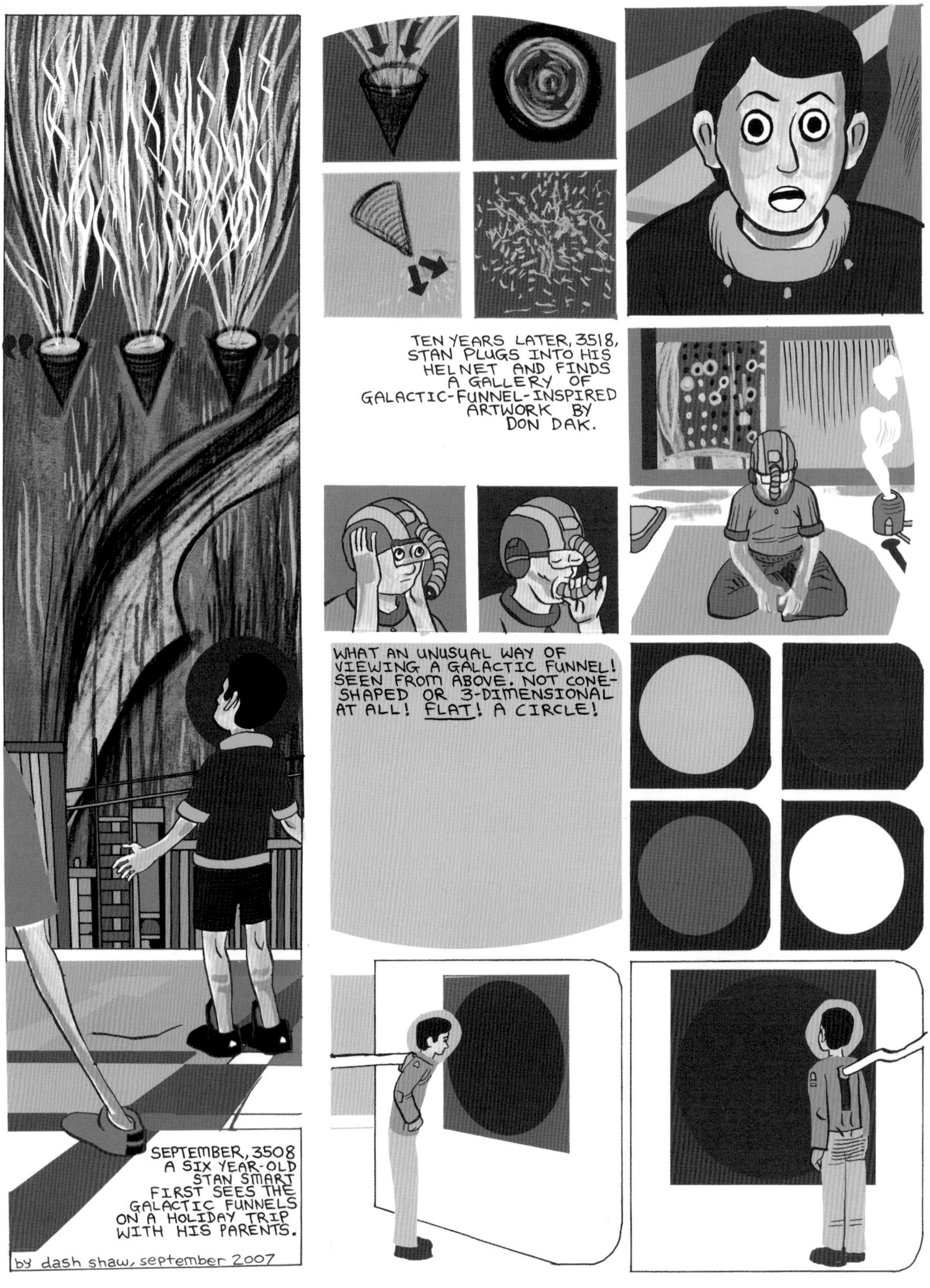
SEPTEMBER, 3508 A SIX YEAR-OLD STAN SMART FIRST SEES THE GALACTIC FUNNELS ON A HOLIDAY TRIP WITH HIS PARENTS.
by dash shaw, september 2007
TEN YEARS LATER, 3518, STAN PLUGS INTO HIS HELNET AND FINDS A GALLERY OF GALACTIC-FUNNEL-INSPIRED ARTWORK BY DON DAK.
WHAT AN UNUSUAL WAY OF VIEWING A GALACTIC FUNNEL! SEEN FROM ABOVE. NOT CONE-SHAPED OR 3-DIMENSIONAL AT ALL! FLAT! A CIRCLE!

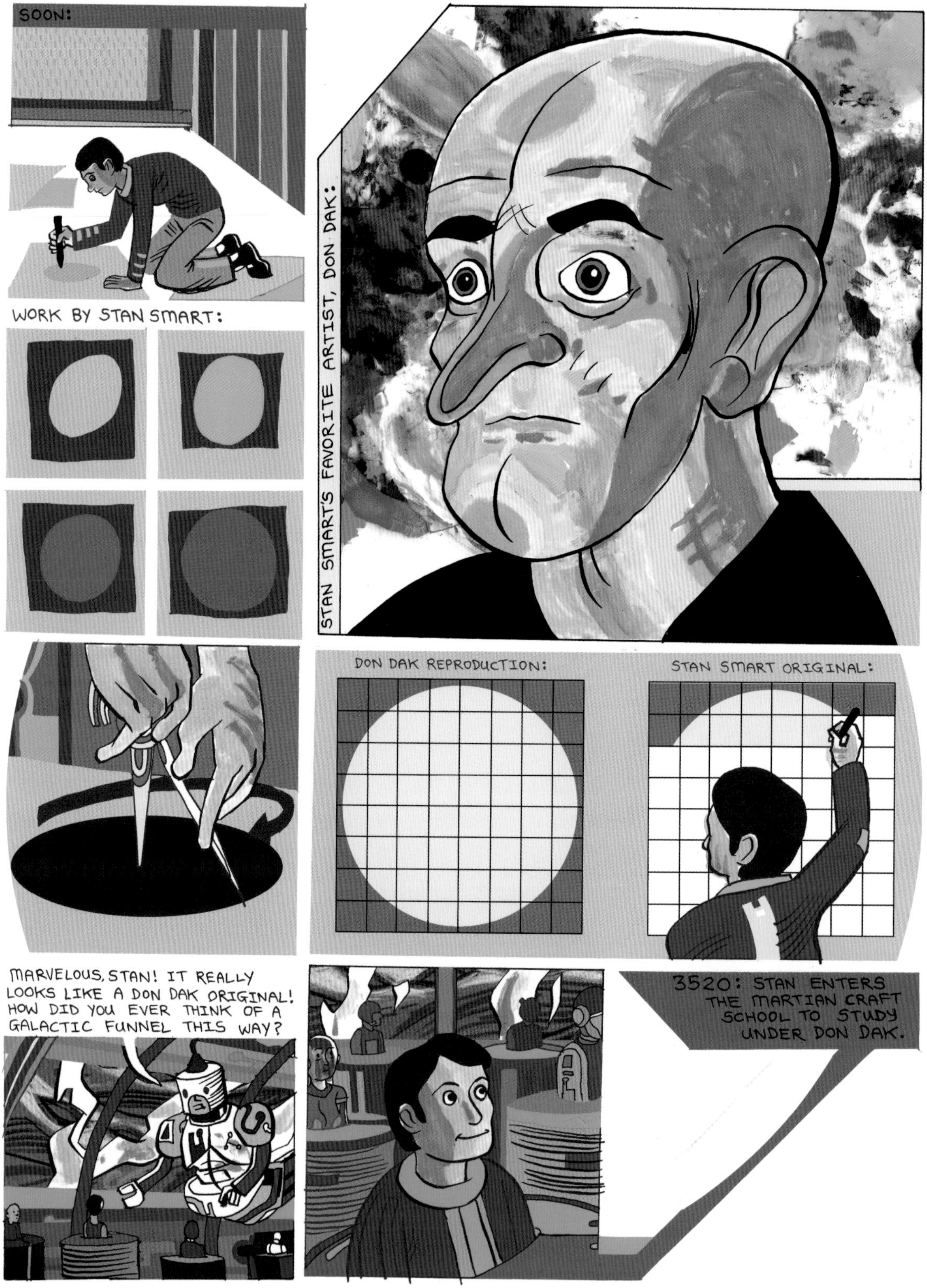
SOON:
WORK BY STAN SMART:
STAN SMART'S FAVORITE ARTIST, DON DAK:
DON DAK REPRODUCTION:
STAN SMART ORIGINAL:
MARVELOUS, STAN! IT REALLY LOOKS LIKE A DON DAK ORIGINAL! HOW DID YOU EVER THINK OF A GALACTIC FUNNEL THIS WAY?
3520: STAN ENTERS THE MARTIAN CRAFT SCHOOL TO STUDY UNDER DON DAK.

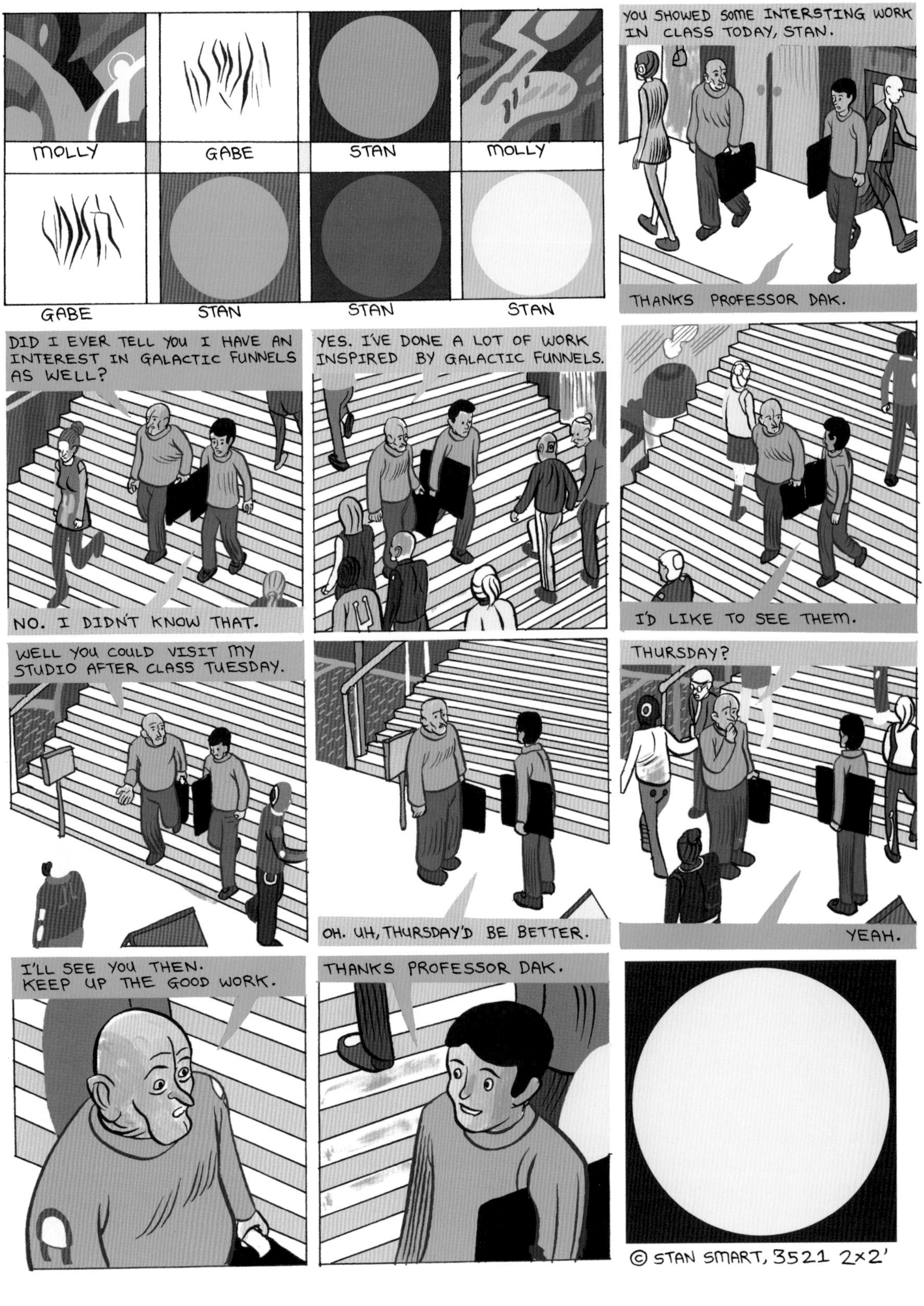
MOLLY
GABE
STAN
MOLLY
GABE
STAN
STAN
STAN
YOU SHOWED SOME INTERSTING WORK IN CLASS TODAY, STAN.
THANKS PROFESSOR DAK.
DID I EVER TELL YOU I HAVE AN INTEREST IN GALACTIC FUNNELS AS WELL?
NO. I DIDN'T KNOW THAT.
YES. I'VE DONE A LOT OF WORK INSPIRED BY GALACTIC FUNNELS.
I'D LIKE TO SEE THEM.
WELL YOU COULD VISIT MY STUDIO AFTER CLASS TUESDAY.
OH. UH, THURSDAY'D BE BETTER.
THURSDAY?
YEAH.
I'LL SEE YOU THEN. KEEP UP THE GOOD WORK.
THANKS PROFESSOR DAK.
© STAN SMART, 3521 2×2'

FLUSH
DON! THE GALACTIC FUNNELS ARE OUT!
HA!
END.
I HAVE TO GO INSIDE.
WHAT?! STAY!. WATCH THEM WITH ME!
GOd GET OFF IT!. YOU FUCKIN **HACK**. GET YOUR OWN FUCKIN INTERESTS.
YOU'RE LIKE A LEECH!
YOU THINK I WANT TO SPEND MY TIME WITH SOME OLD WASHED-UP CUNT? YOU'RE THE FUCKIN LEECH!.

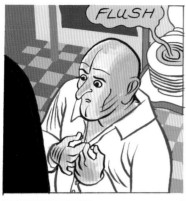

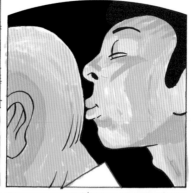

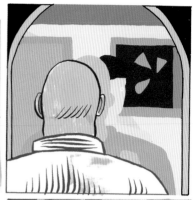

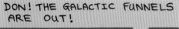

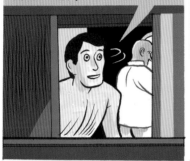

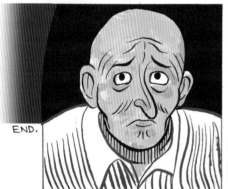

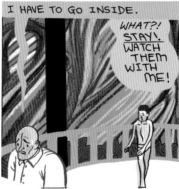

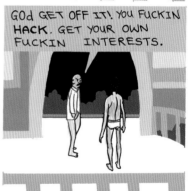

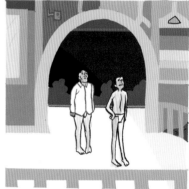

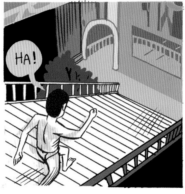

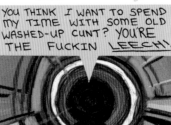

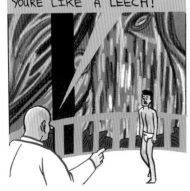

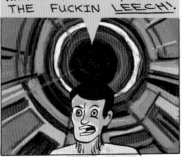

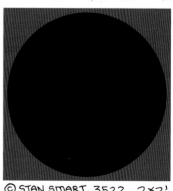

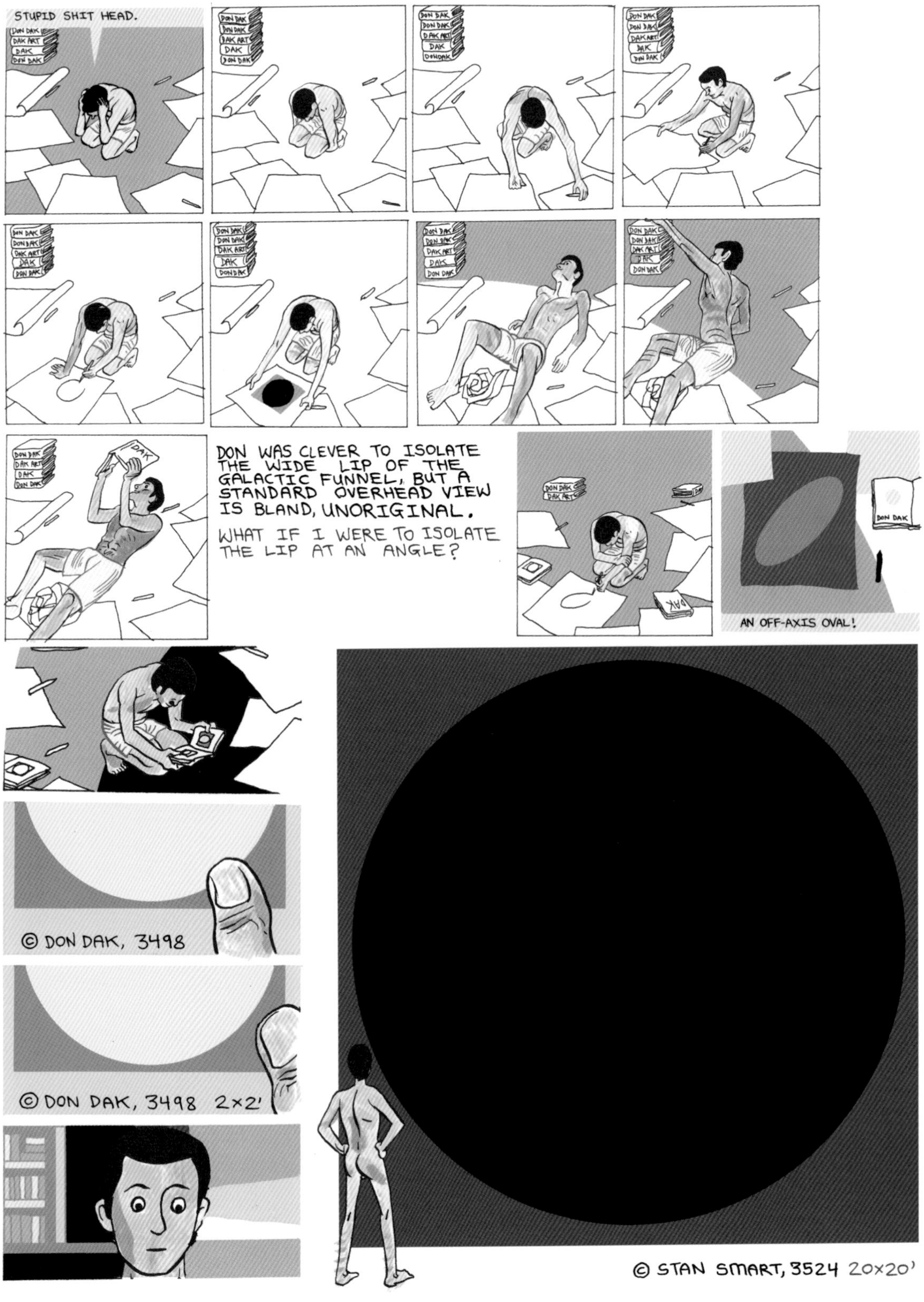
STUPID SHIT HEAD.
DON DAK
DAK ART
DAK
DON DAK
DON WAS CLEVER TO ISOLATE THE WIDE LIP OF THE GALACTIC FUNNEL, BUT A STANDARD OVERHEAD VIEW IS BLAND, UNORIGINAL.
WHAT IF I WERE TO ISOLATE THE LIP AT AN ANGLE?
DON DAK
AN OFF-AXIS OVAL!
© DON DAK, 3498
© DON DAK, 3498 2×2'
© STAN SMART, 3524 20×20'

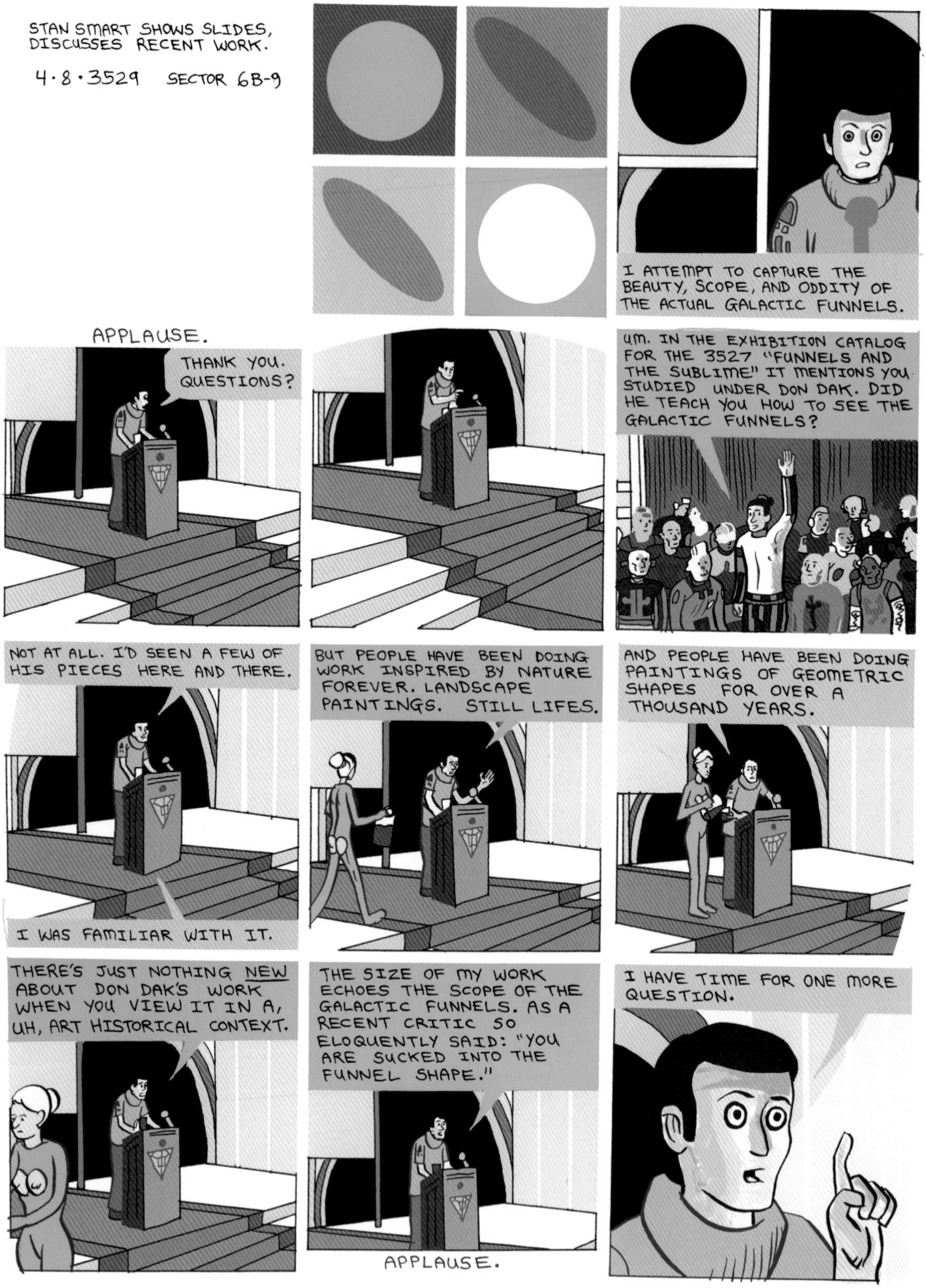
STAN SMART SHOWS SLIDES, DISCUSSES RECENT WORK.
4·8·3529 SECTOR 6B-9
I ATTEMPT TO CAPTURE THE BEAUTY, SCOPE, AND ODDITY OF THE ACTUAL GALACTIC FUNNELS.
APPLAUSE.
THANK YOU. QUESTIONS?
UM. IN THE EXHIBITION CATALOG FOR THE 3527 "FUNNELS AND THE SUBLIME" IT MENTIONS YOU STUDIED UNDER DON DAK. DID HE TEACH YOU HOW TO SEE THE GALACTIC FUNNELS?
NOT AT ALL. I'D SEEN A FEW OF HIS PIECES HERE AND THERE.
I WAS FAMILIAR WITH IT.
BUT PEOPLE HAVE BEEN DOING WORK INSPIRED BY NATURE FOREVER. LANDSCAPE PAINTINGS. STILL LIFES.
AND PEOPLE HAVE BEEN DOING PAINTINGS OF GEOMETRIC SHAPES FOR OVER A THOUSAND YEARS.
THERE'S JUST NOTHING NEW ABOUT DON DAK'S WORK WHEN YOU VIEW IT IN A, UH, ART HISTORICAL CONTEXT.
THE SIZE OF MY WORK ECHOES THE SCOPE OF THE GALACTIC FUNNELS. AS A RECENT CRITIC SO ELOQUENTLY SAID: "YOU ARE SUCKED INTO THE FUNNEL SHAPE."
APPLAUSE.
I HAVE TIME FOR ONE MORE QUESTION.

PROFESSOR DAK, YOUR WORK REMINDS ME OF STAN SMART.

--HH--

≧PANT

-HUK!

3550: DON DAK DIES. STAN SMART ATTENDS THE FUNERAL.

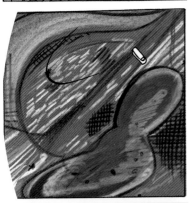

ISN'T IT BEAUTIFUL, STAN? THE GALACTIC FUNNELS?

THE GALACTIC FUNNELS AREN'T LIKE FLAT CIRCLES AT ALL.
THEY'RE MORE THREE-DIMENSIONAL, REALLY.
LIKE A CONE,
OR A PARTY HAT.
A BIG SCULPTURE FLOATING IN SPACE.

END.

TITLE: "Cartooning Symbolia" AUTHOR: Dash Shaw 2005

Invisidites: dotted lines symbolizing invisibility (see: *The Fantastic Four* issue one- Invisible Woman) also: people/objects behind glass, or missing. Used in a sequence:

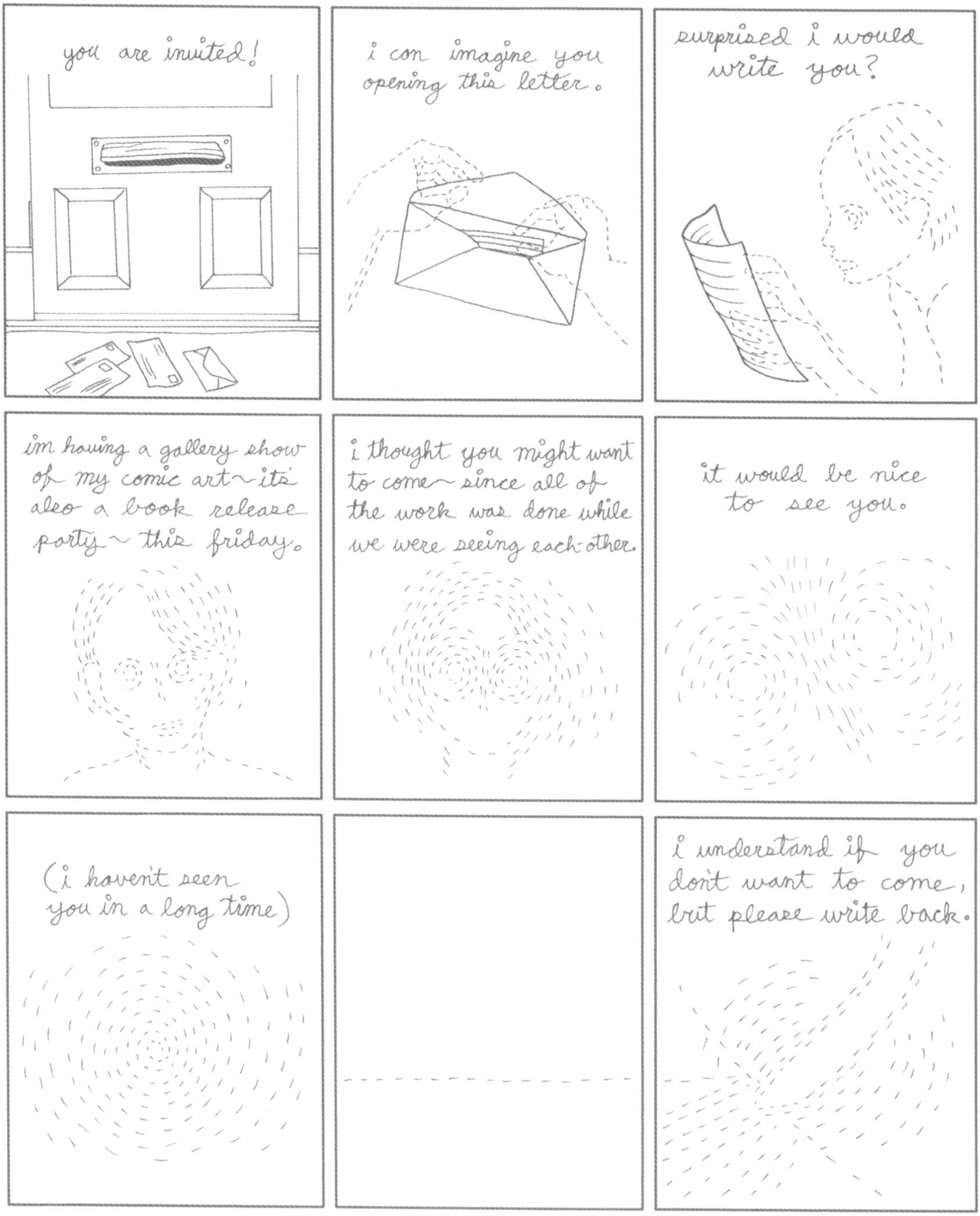

you are invited!
i can imagine you opening this letter.
surprised i would write you?
im having a gallery show of my comic art~ it's also a book release party~ this friday.
i thought you might want to come~ since all of the work was done while we were seeing each-other.
it would be nice to see you.
(i haven't seen you in a long time)
i understand if you don't want to come, but please write back.

Waftarom: wavy lines expressing an aroma.
Variations on the waftarom:

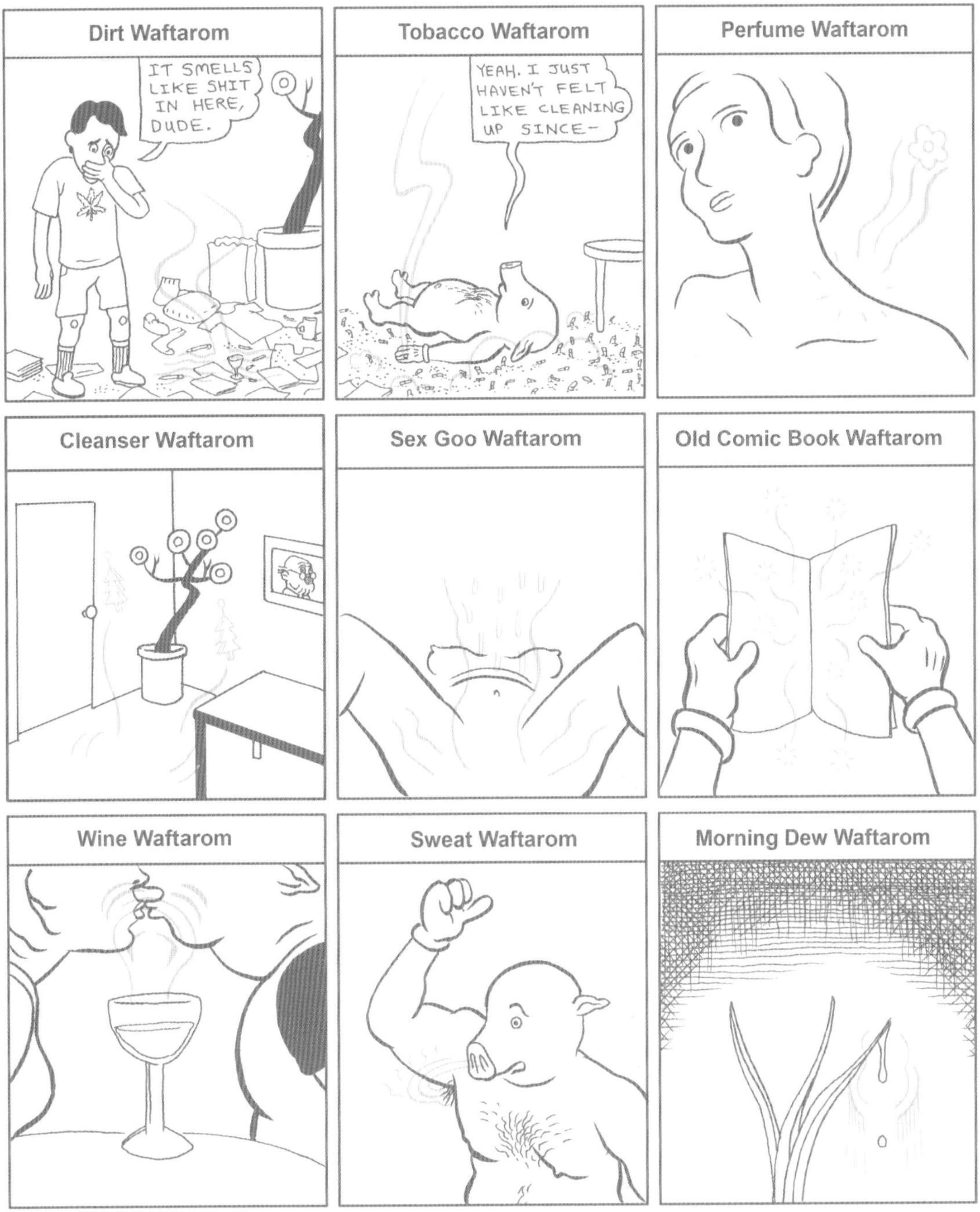
Dirt Waftarom
IT SMELLS LIKE SHIT IN HERE, DUDE.
Tobacco Waftarom
YEAH. I JUST HAVEN'T FELT LIKE CLEANING UP SINCE-
Perfume Waftarom
Cleanser Waftarom
Sex Goo Waftarom
Old Comic Book Waftarom
Wine Waftarom
Sweat Waftarom
Morning Dew Waftarom

Solrads: Radiating waves from a sun shape, indicating sun rays or heat.

He loves making comics so much. After drawing all night, he crawls onto the roof with her (second love) to watch the solrads fight away the cross-hatching.

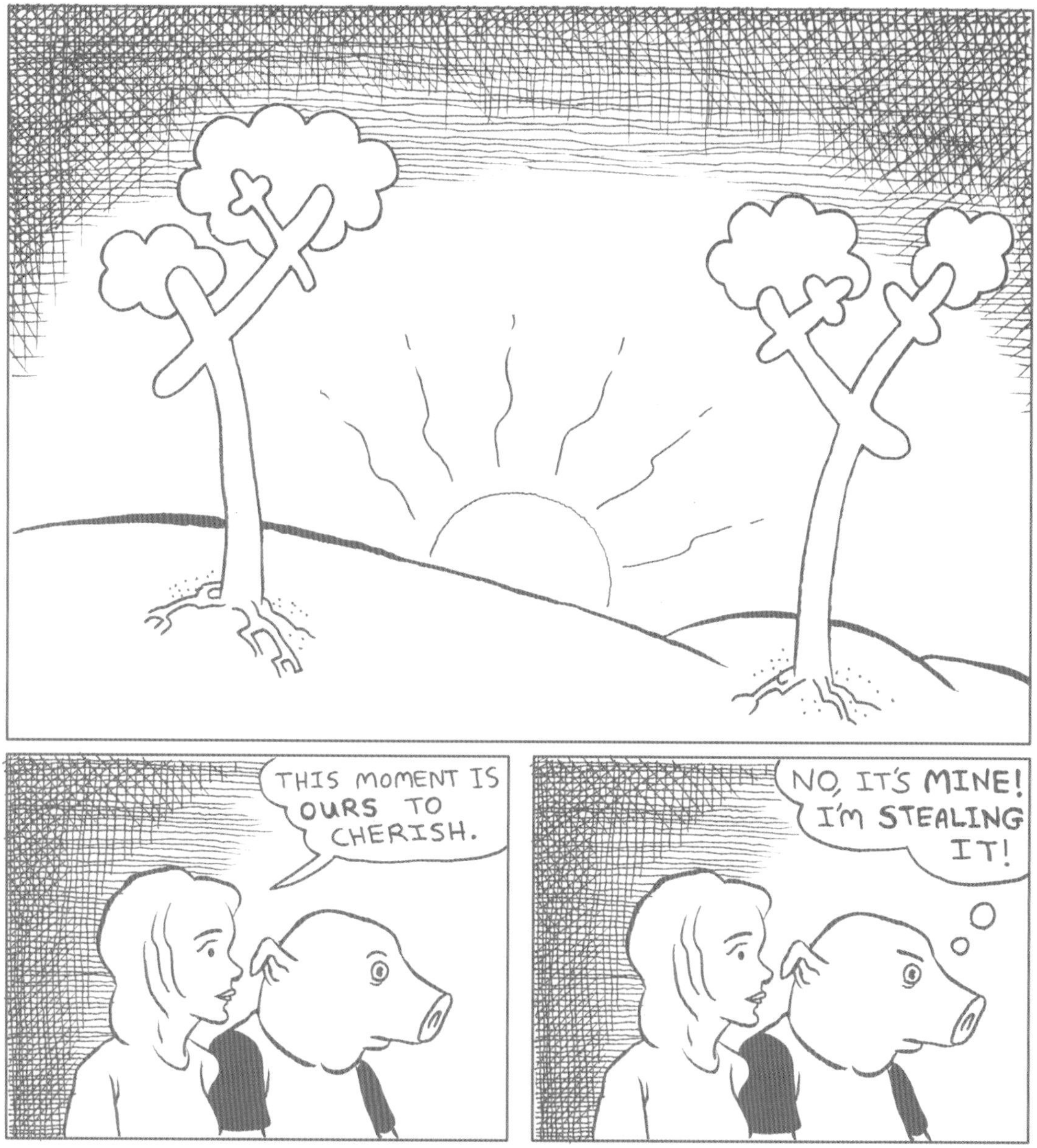
THIS MOMENT IS OURS TO CHERISH.
NO, IT'S MINE! I'M STEALING IT!

And so he did a drawing,
tied a noose around it,
hung it in a gallery.

Plewds: drop shapes indicating a liquid discharge.
Variations on the plewd:

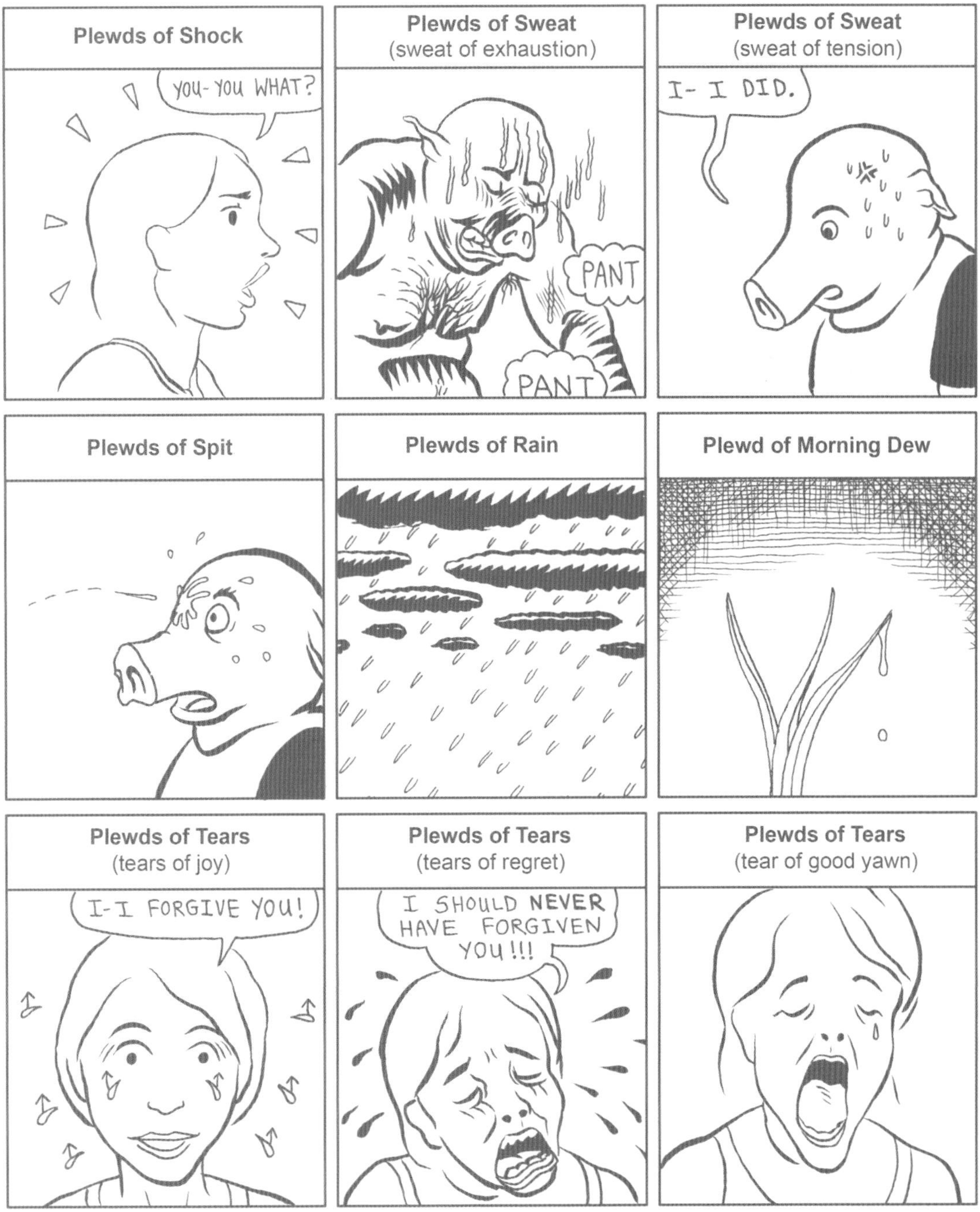
Plewds of Shock
YOU- YOU WHAT?
Plewds of Sweat (sweat of exhaustion)
PANT
PANT
Plewds of Sweat (sweat of tension)
I- I DID.
Plewds of Spit
Plewds of Rain
Plewd of Morning Dew
Plewds of Tears (tears of joy)
I-I FORGIVE YOU!
Plewds of Tears (tears of regret)
I SHOULD NEVER HAVE FORGIVEN YOU!!!
Plewds of Tears (tear of good yawn)

He takes the dramatic moments... pins them to the page.

Oculama: giant “X”es on eyes meaning that character is dead.

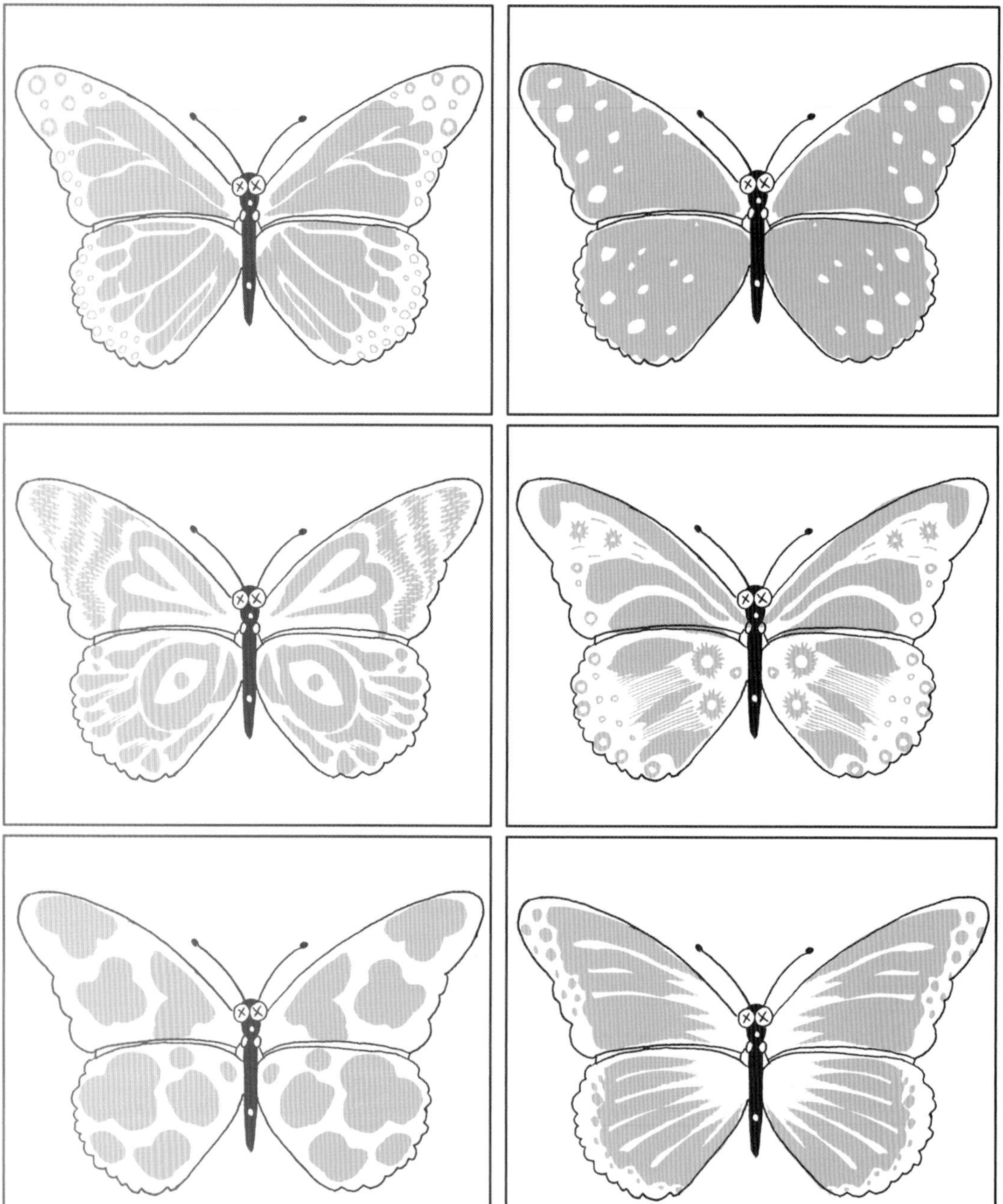

Briffit: a small smoke cloud shooting from an action, denotes anger or fighting.

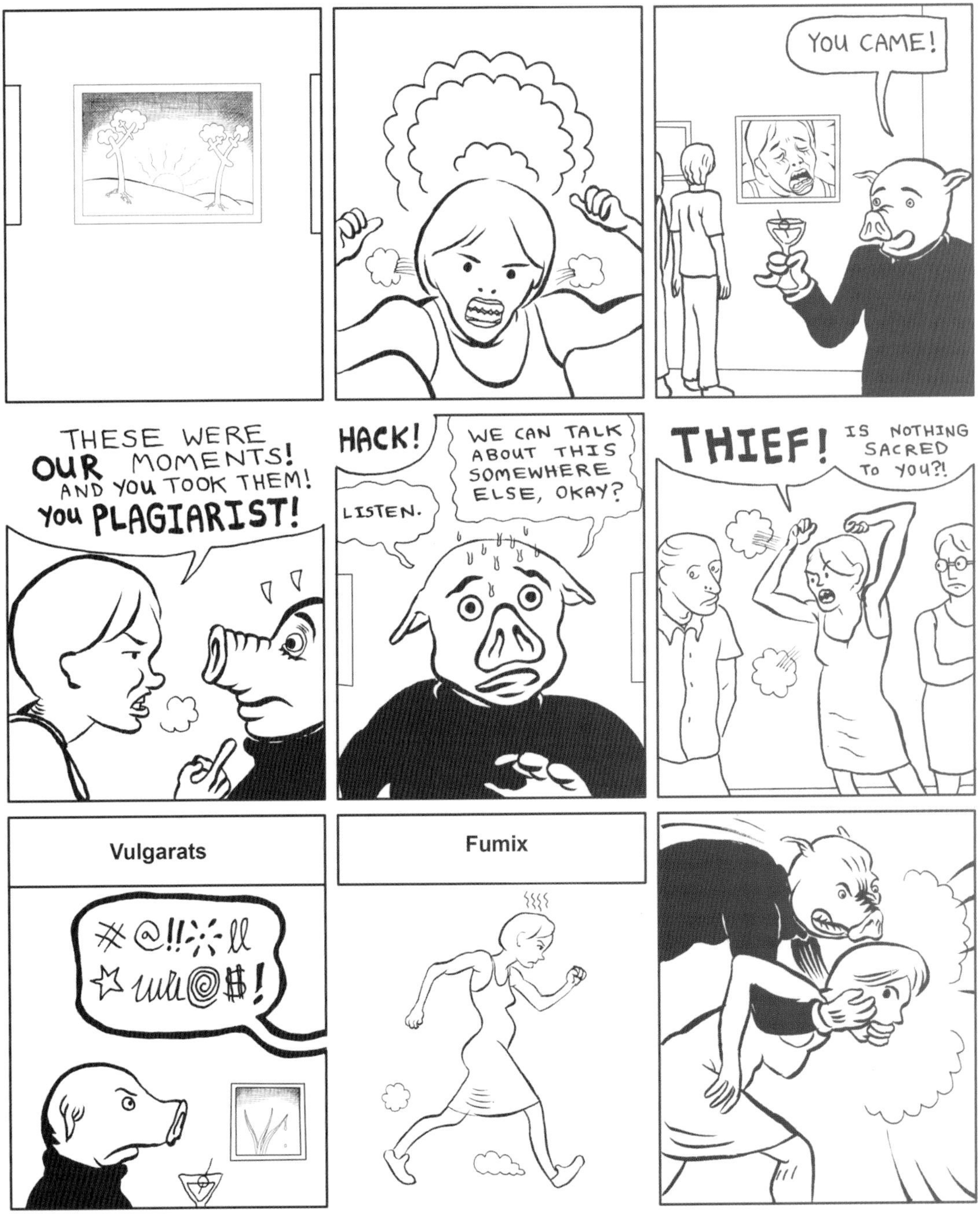

YOU CAME!
THESE WERE OUR MOMENTS! AND YOU TOOK THEM! YOU PLAGIARIST!
HACK!
LISTEN.
WE CAN TALK ABOUT THIS SOMEWHERE ELSE, OKAY?
THIEF!
IS NOTHING SACRED TO YOU?!
Vulgarats
Fumix

And so he choked her... gagged her (she's crying)... and bound her into a book.

Agitrons: uneven contour lines surrounding a character, signifiies that the character is shaking, nervous, or wounded. Example:

hĕlp mē hĕlp mē plēz plēz

Can you hear **her?**

ō gŏd hĕlp

can you **hear her?**

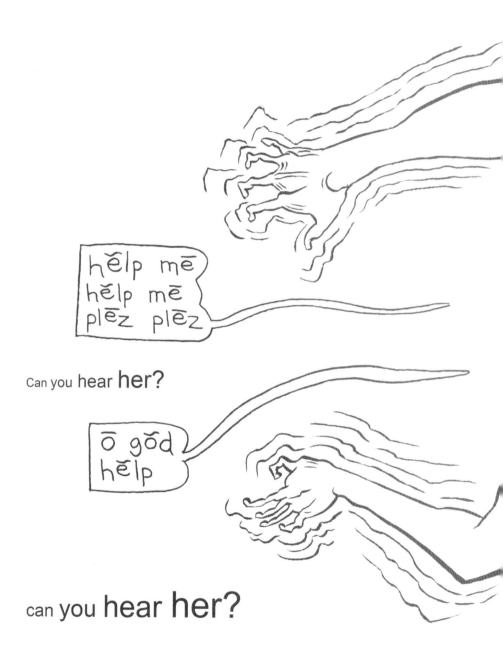

Spurl

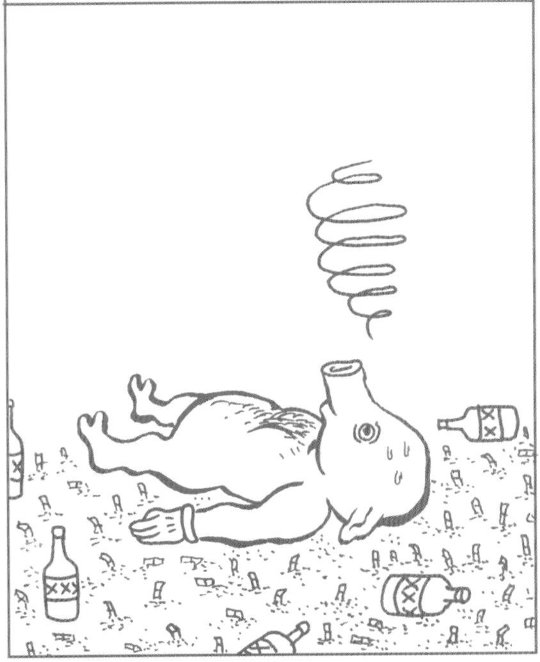

Squeans

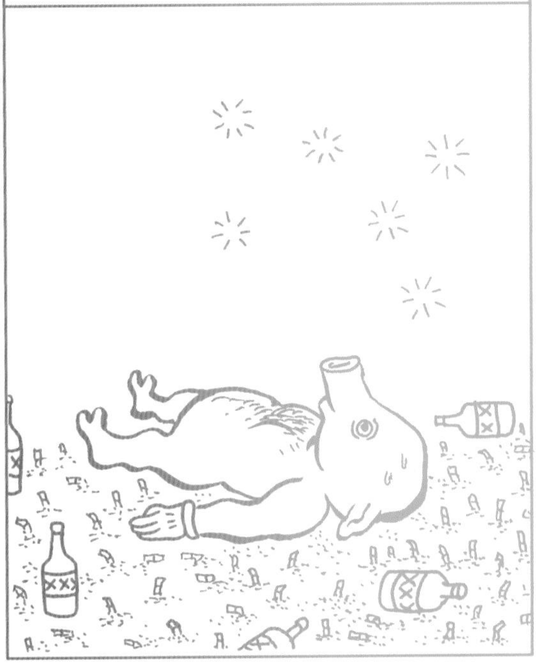

Staggeratron

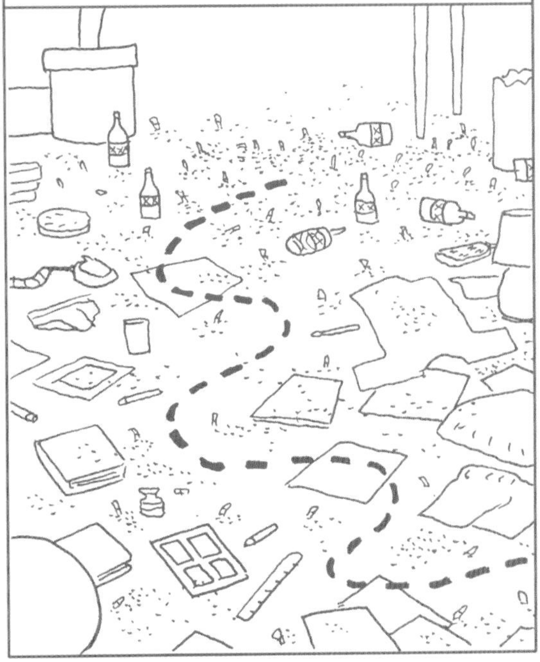

Onamatopoeia

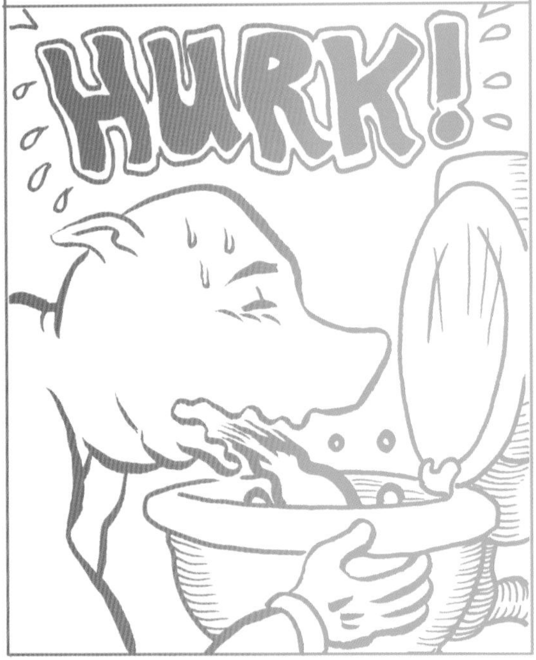
HURK!

Dites: diagonal lines signifying glass.
"**Hites**" refer to horizontal lines (pools, reflections).
Dites used in a sequence:

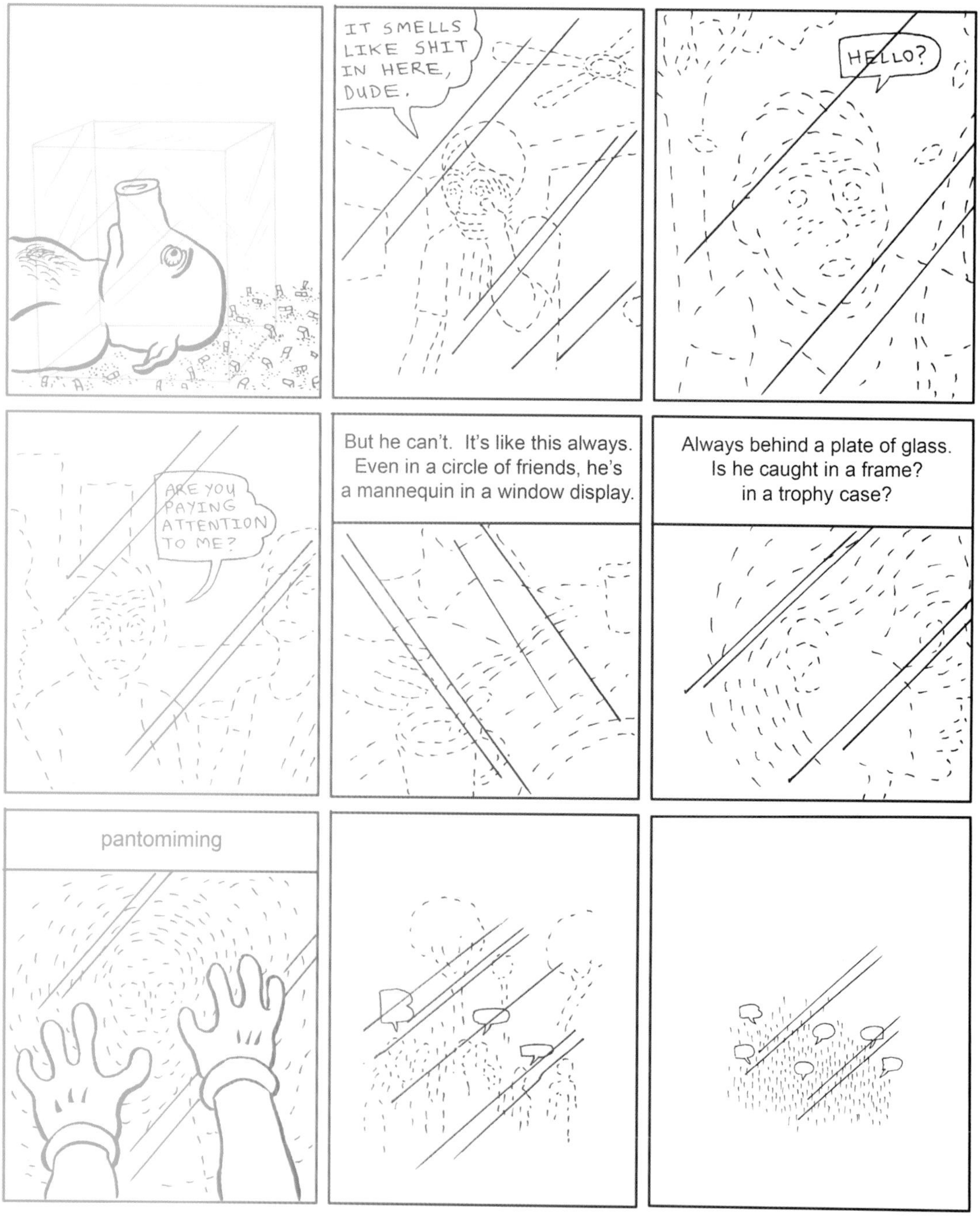
IT SMELLS LIKE SHIT IN HERE, DUDE.
HELLO?
ARE YOU PAYING ATTENTION TO ME?
But he can't. It's like this always. Even in a circle of friends, he's a mannequin in a window display.
Always behind a plate of glass. Is he caught in a frame? in a trophy case?
pantomiming

There's another way to describe this feeling of isolation, of disconnection: radiating halos of plewds.

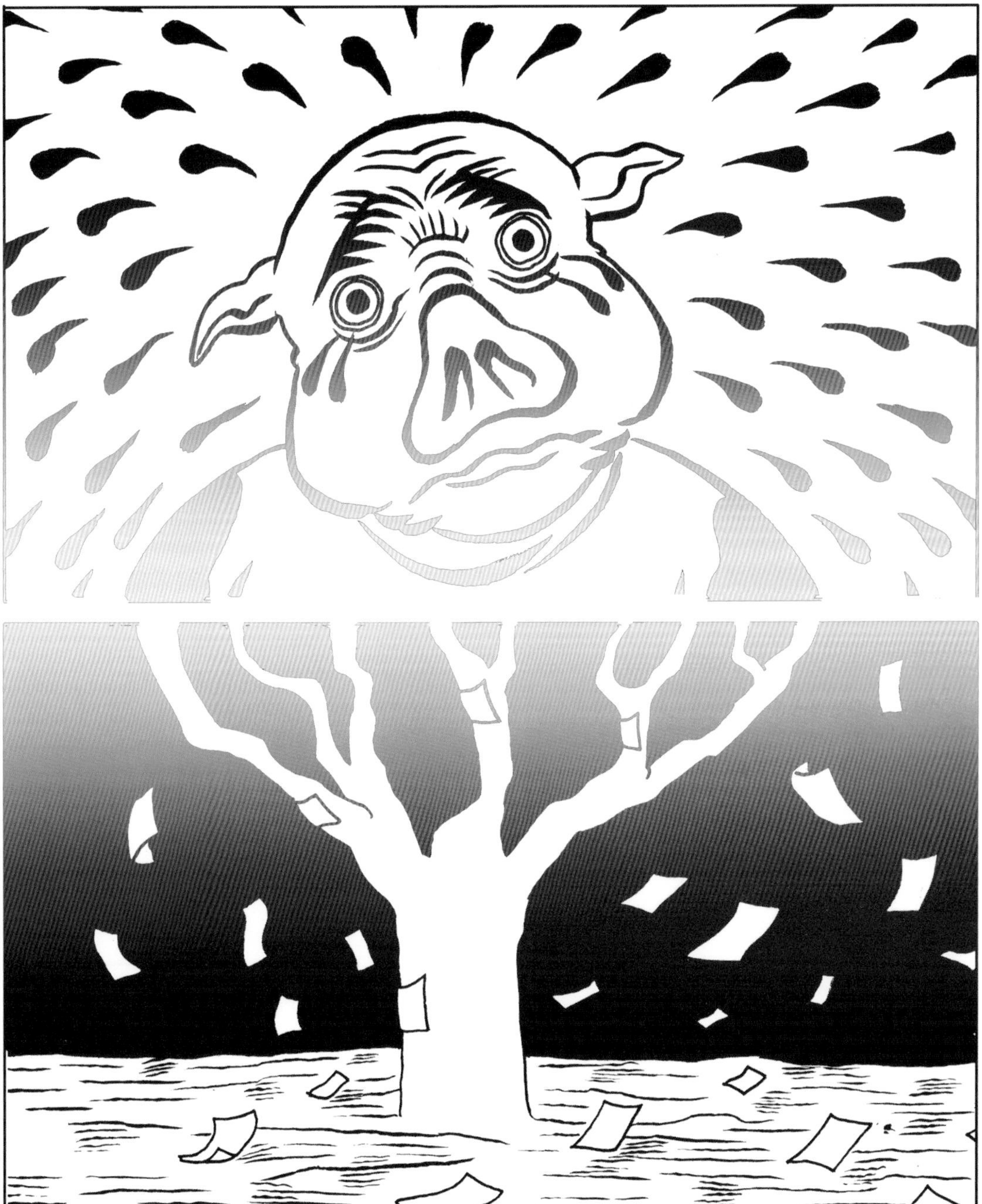

But with this new girl he thinks it will be different maybe. I mean, what I mean to say, is that there might be a new language between them, you know what I mean? A communication that they share, do you know what I mean?

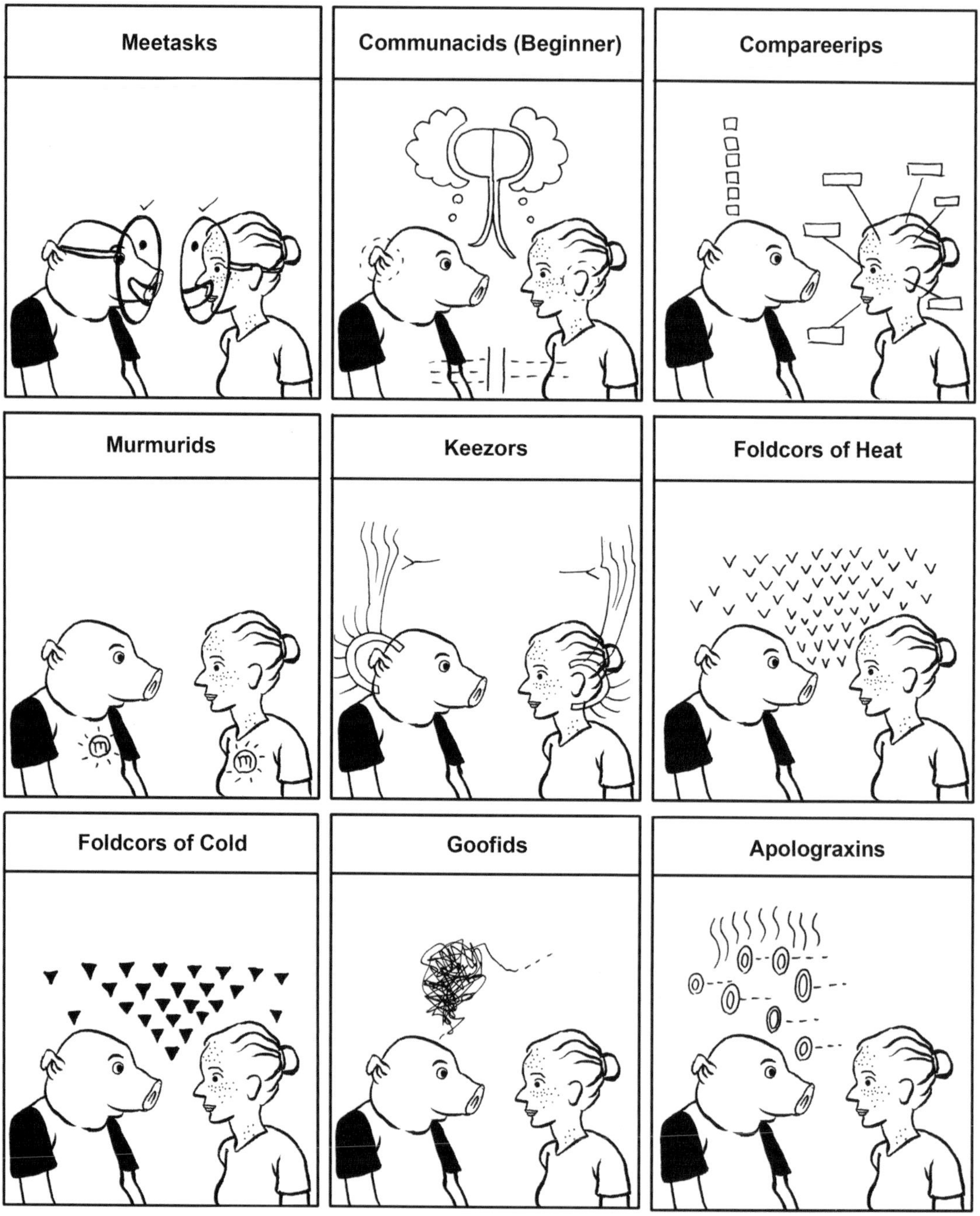
Meetasks
Communacids (Beginner)
Compareerips
Murmurids
Keezors
Foldcors of Heat
Foldcors of Cold
Goofids
Apolograxins

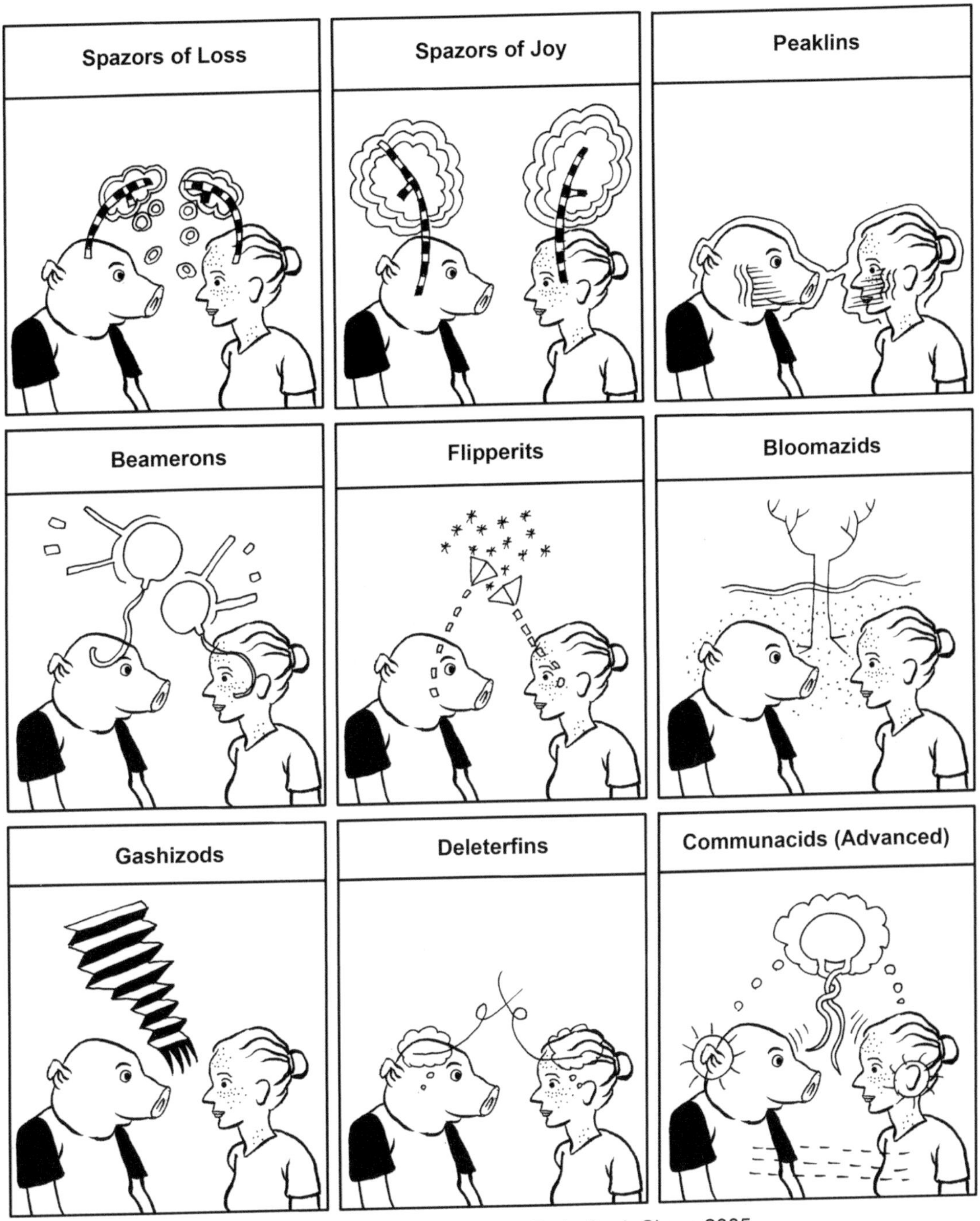
Spazors of Loss
Spazors of Joy
Peaklins
Beamerons
Flipperits
Bloomazids
Gashizods
Deleterfins
Communacids (Advanced)

He can't wait to read it. The End. Dash Shaw, 2005

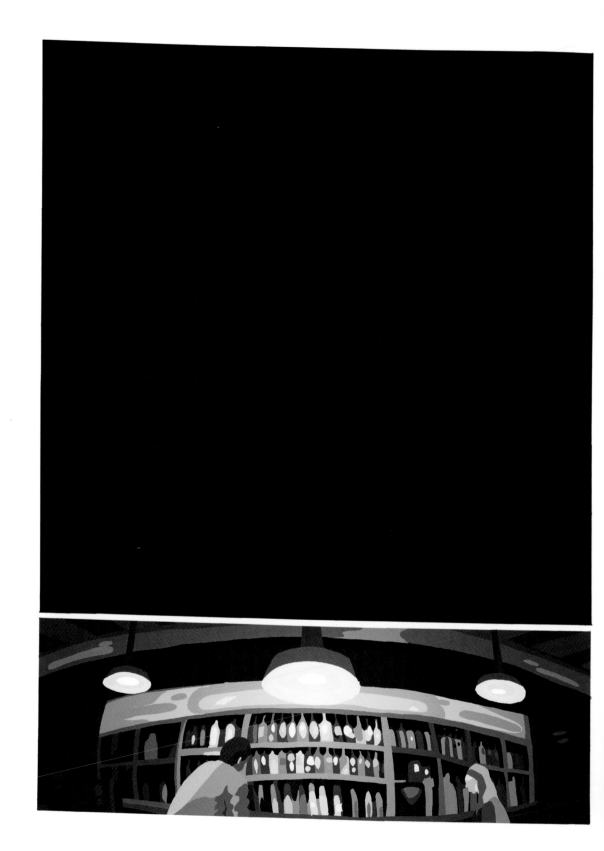

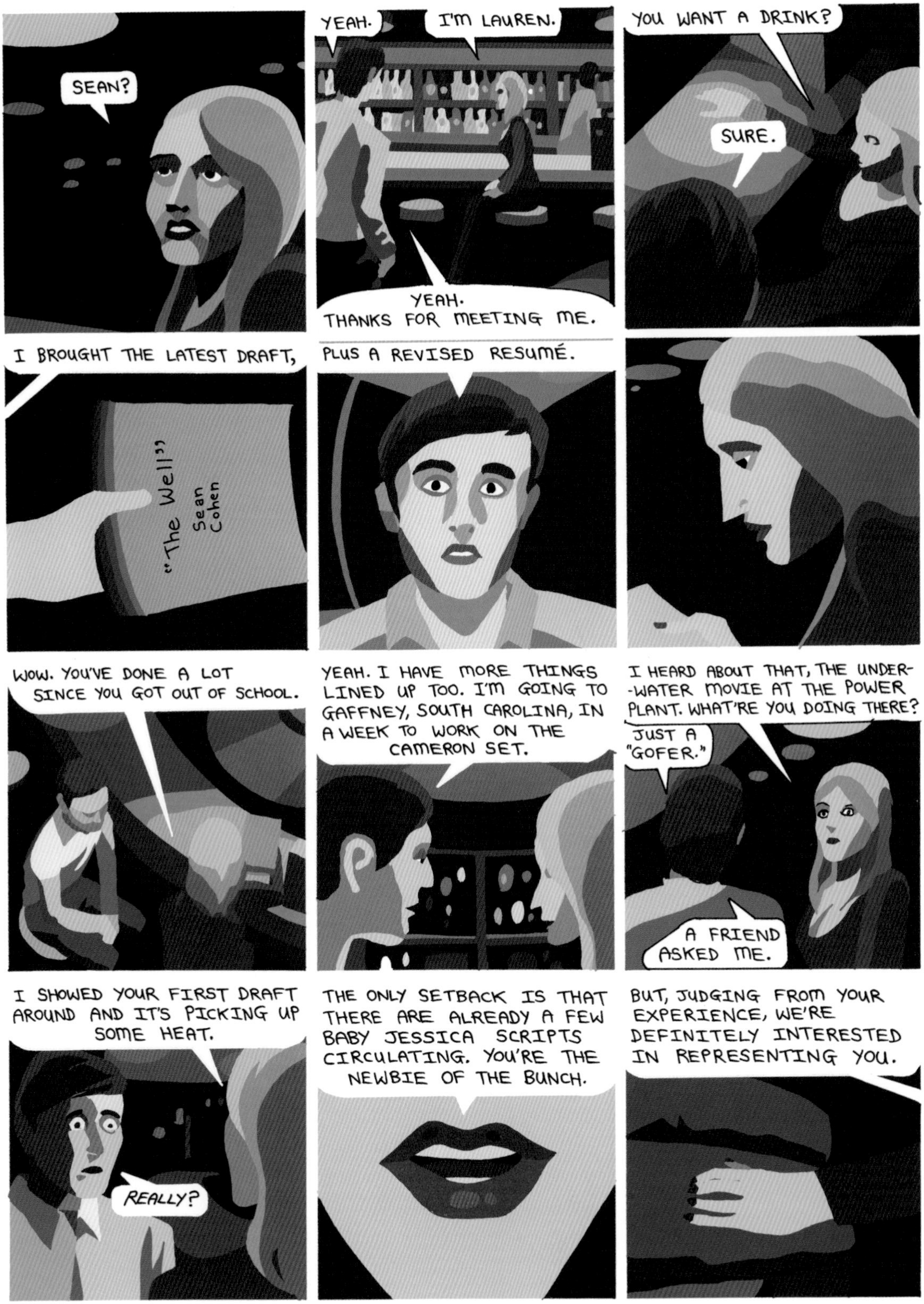
SEAN?
YEAH.
I'M LAUREN.
YEAH. THANKS FOR MEETING ME.
YOU WANT A DRINK?
SURE.
I BROUGHT THE LATEST DRAFT,
"The Well" Sean Cohen
PLUS A REVISED RESUMÉ.
WOW. YOU'VE DONE A LOT SINCE YOU GOT OUT OF SCHOOL.
YEAH. I HAVE MORE THINGS LINED UP TOO. I'M GOING TO GAFFNEY, SOUTH CAROLINA, IN A WEEK TO WORK ON THE CAMERON SET.
I HEARD ABOUT THAT, THE UNDER--WATER MOVIE AT THE POWER PLANT. WHAT'RE YOU DOING THERE?
JUST A "GOFER."
A FRIEND ASKED ME.
I SHOWED YOUR FIRST DRAFT AROUND AND IT'S PICKING UP SOME HEAT.
REALLY?
THE ONLY SETBACK IS THAT THERE ARE ALREADY A FEW BABY JESSICA SCRIPTS CIRCULATING. YOU'RE THE NEWBIE OF THE BUNCH.
BUT, JUDGING FROM YOUR EXPERIENCE, WE'RE DEFINITELY INTERESTED IN REPRESENTING YOU.

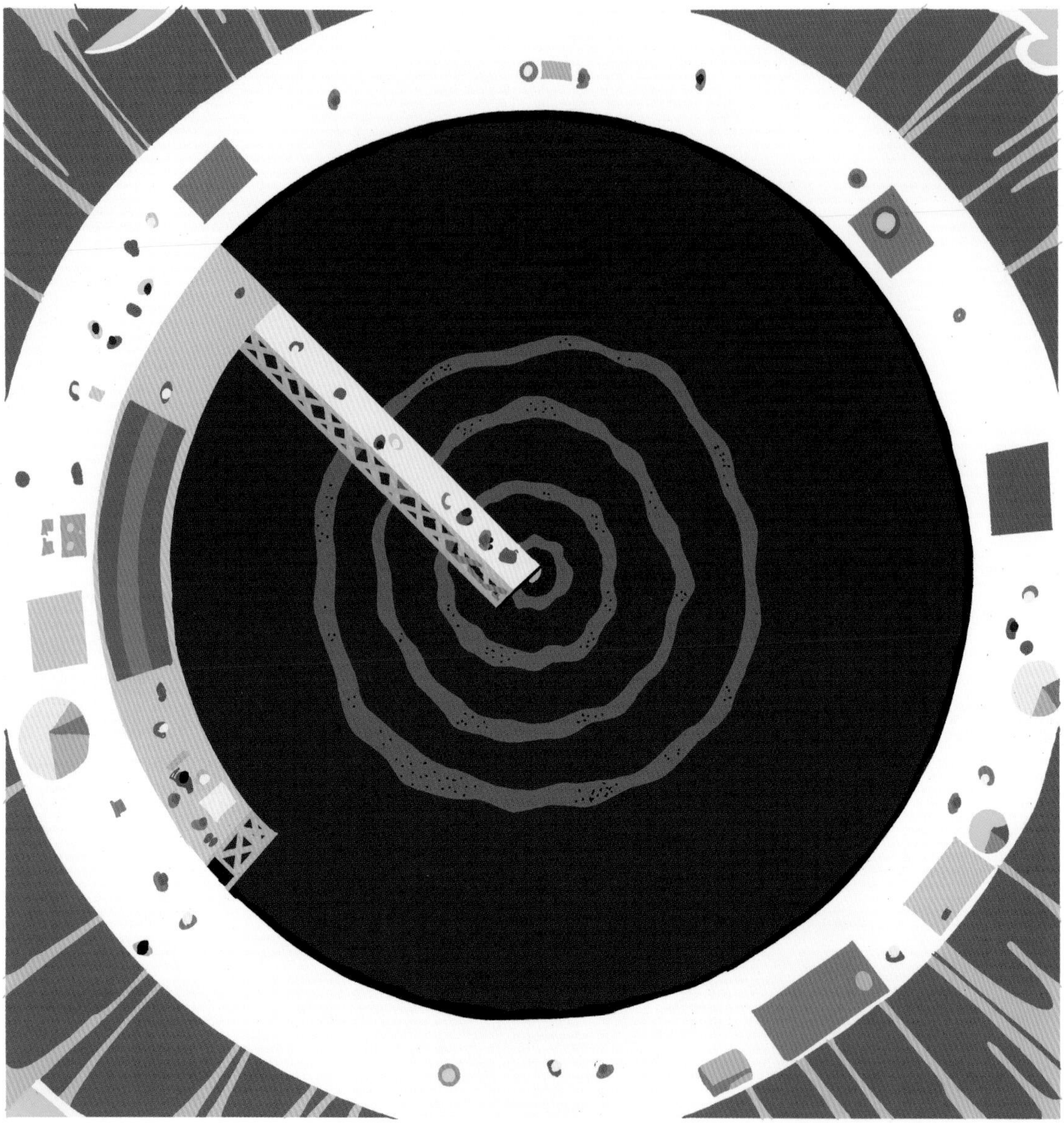

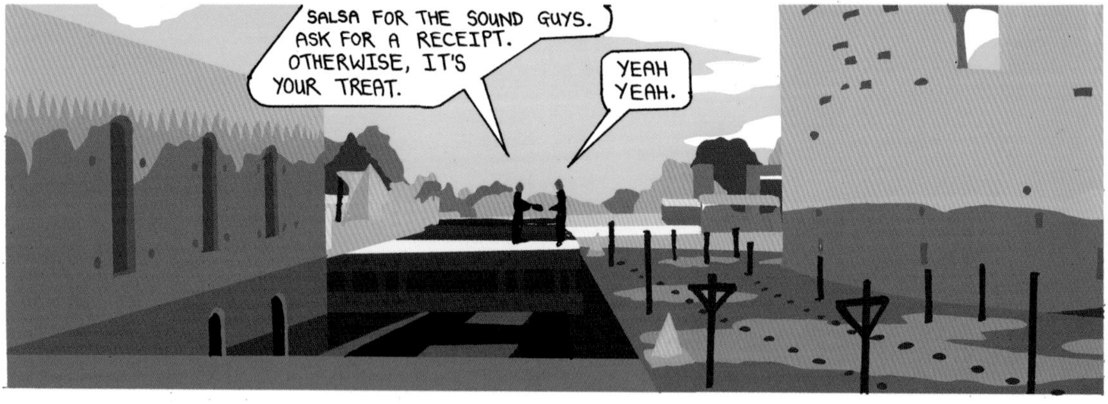
SALSA FOR THE SOUND GUYS. ASK FOR A RECEIPT. OTHERWISE, IT'S YOUR TREAT.
YEAH YEAH.

UGH. I HATE WALKING TO THIS STORE. THEY ALWAYS STARE AT ME. BUNCH OF BUSH-LOVING RED NECKS.

CAN'T WAIT TO GET BACK TO THE CITY.

TWO-FIFTY.

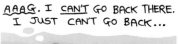

FUCK! I FORGOT TO ASK FOR A RECEIPT!

AAAG. I *CAN'T* GO BACK THERE. I JUST CAN'T GO BACK...

FUCKING HICKS!

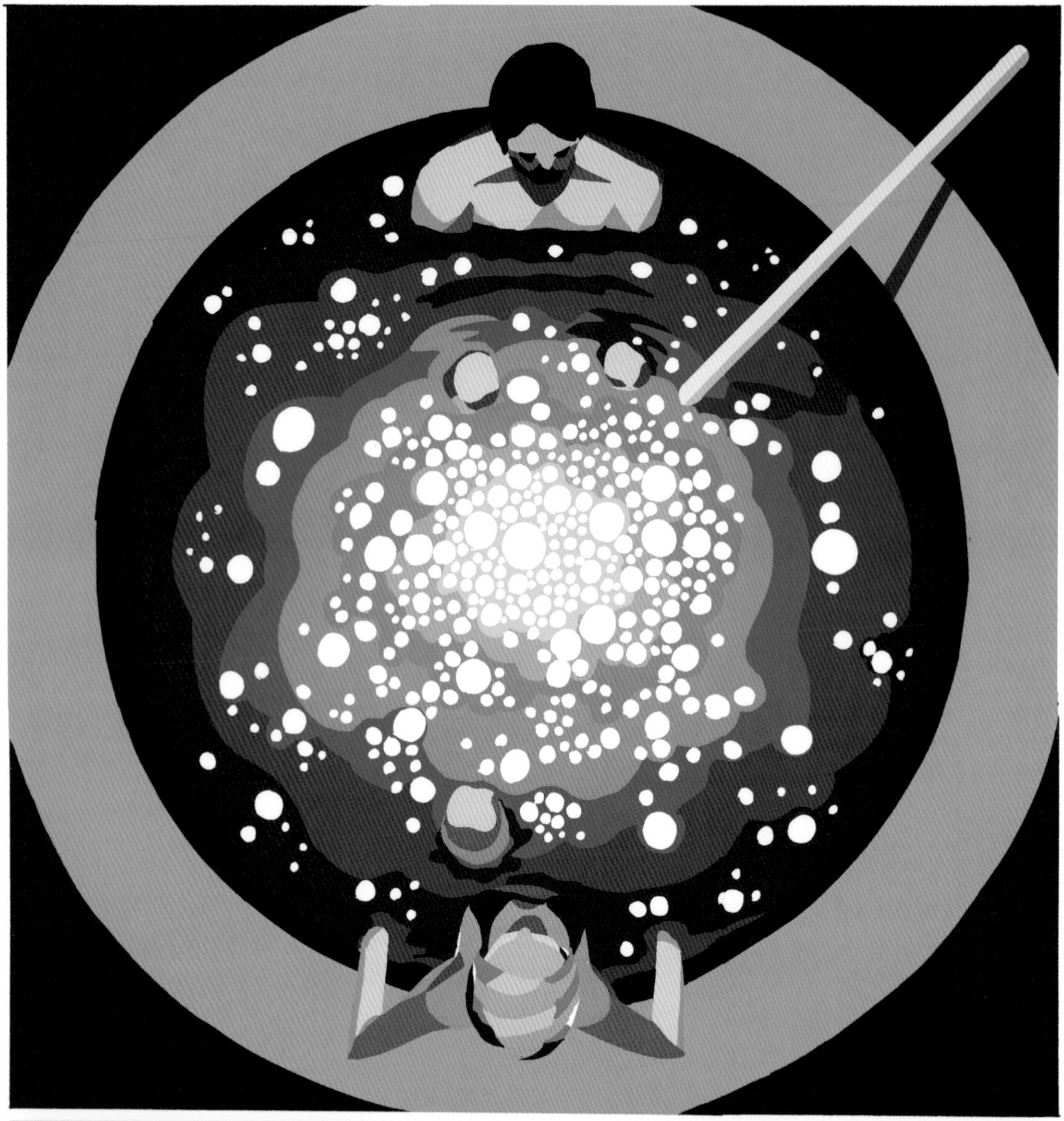
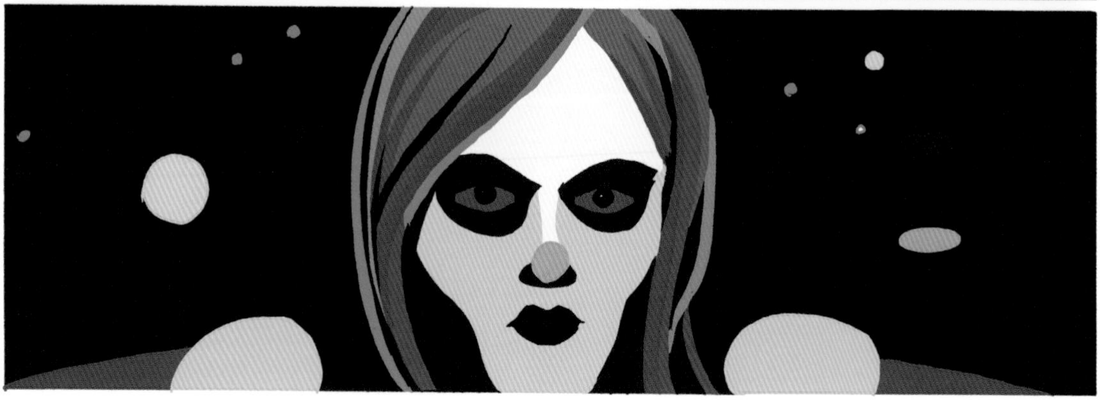

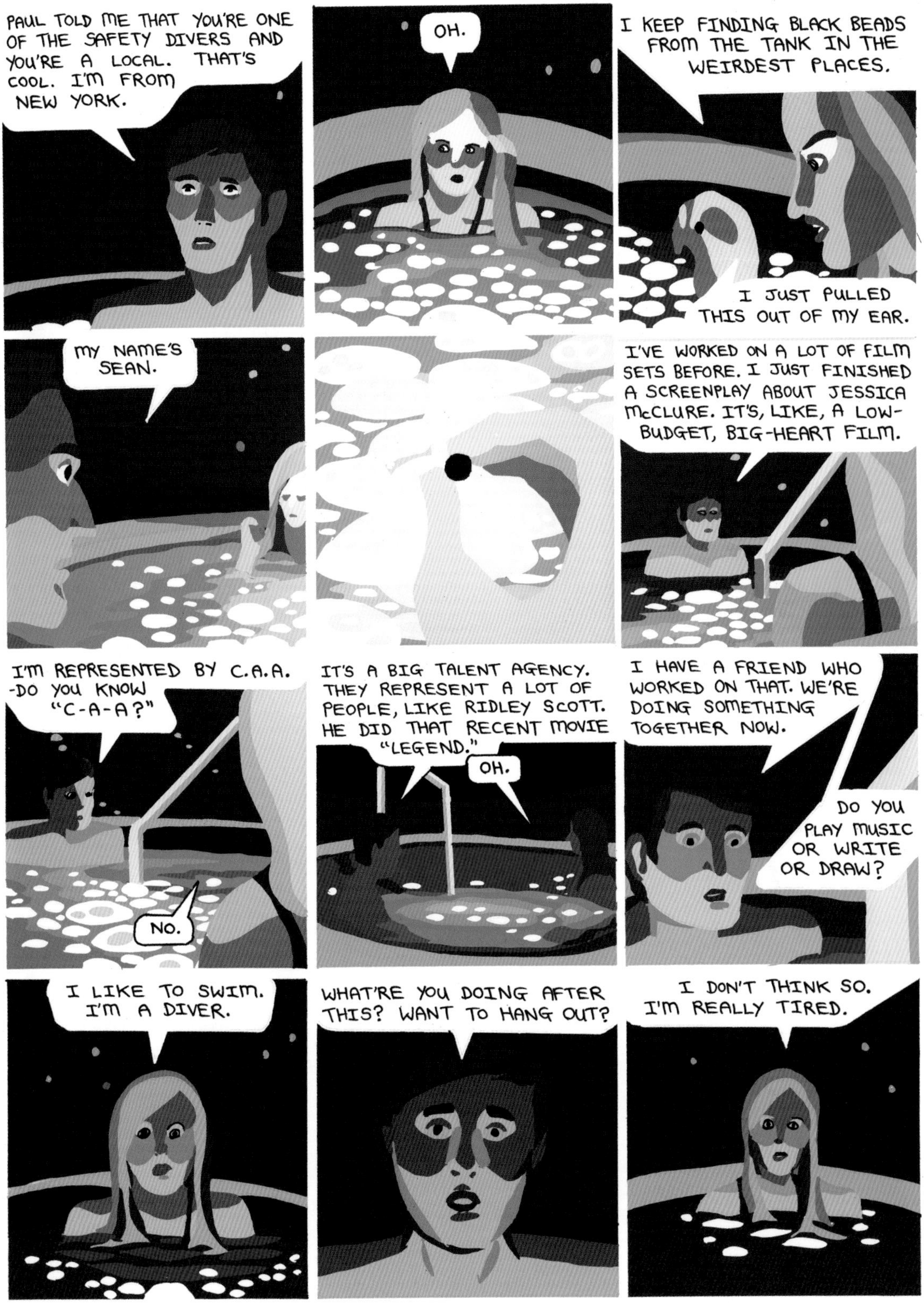
PAUL TOLD ME THAT YOU'RE ONE OF THE SAFETY DIVERS AND YOU'RE A LOCAL. THAT'S COOL. I'M FROM NEW YORK.
OH.
I KEEP FINDING BLACK BEADS FROM THE TANK IN THE WEIRDEST PLACES.
I JUST PULLED THIS OUT OF MY EAR.
MY NAME'S SEAN.
I'VE WORKED ON A LOT OF FILM SETS BEFORE. I JUST FINISHED A SCREENPLAY ABOUT JESSICA McCLURE. IT'S, LIKE, A LOW-BUDGET, BIG-HEART FILM.
I'M REPRESENTED BY C.A.A. -DO YOU KNOW "C-A-A?"
NO.
IT'S A BIG TALENT AGENCY. THEY REPRESENT A LOT OF PEOPLE, LIKE RIDLEY SCOTT. HE DID THAT RECENT MOVIE "LEGEND."
OH.
I HAVE A FRIEND WHO WORKED ON THAT. WE'RE DOING SOMETHING TOGETHER NOW.
DO YOU PLAY MUSIC OR WRITE OR DRAW?
I LIKE TO SWIM. I'M A DIVER.
WHAT'RE YOU DOING AFTER THIS? WANT TO HANG OUT?
I DON'T THINK SO. I'M REALLY TIRED.

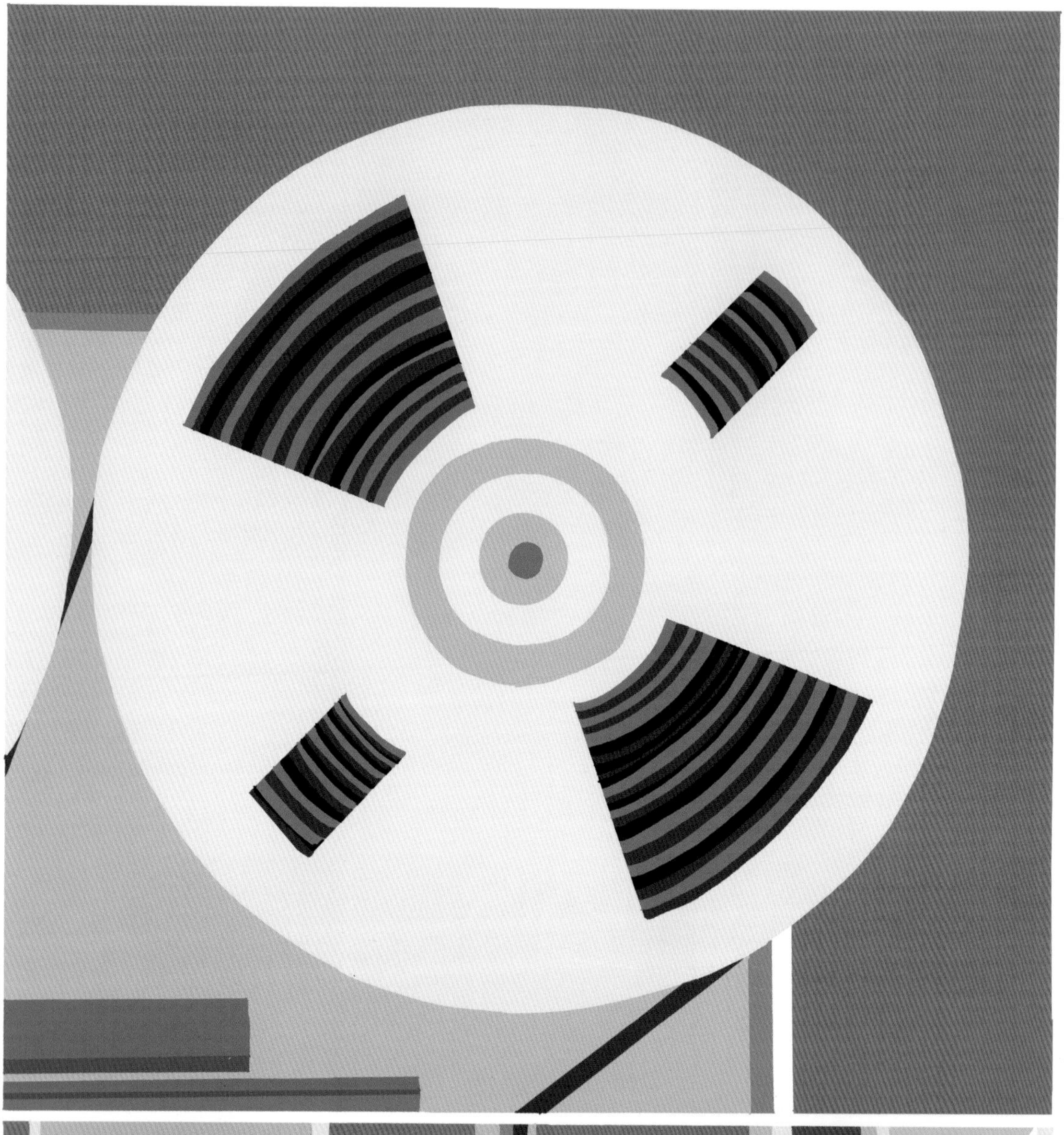
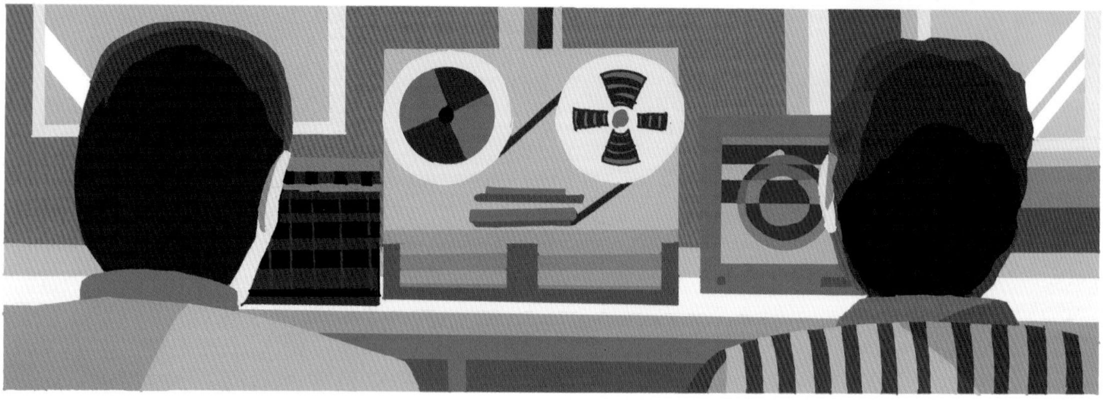

TAP

TAP

THERE ARE TWO WAYS WE COULD DO THIS: "A"— BUY A STOCK CRYING SOUND 'N DISTORT IT. ECHO FILTER. WE COULD WAIT UNTIL WE GET DISTRO AND HAVE THEM PAY FOR THE SOUND MIX.

WE COULD EVEN PUT THE SPEAKER AT THE OPPOSITE END OF AN 8-INCH WIDE STEEL TUBE. BUT THAT'D BE SECOND GENERATION QUALITY.

WHAT'S OPTION "B?"

CAST A VOICE FOR SOUND. IT WOULDN'T HAVE TO BE A BABY. COULD BE A 6-YEAR-OLD OR WHATEVER. IT'S THE VOICE.

IF SHE CAN CRY ON COMMAND, WE TAKE HER TO A CON--STRUCTION SITE OR SOME PLACE TO RECORD LIVE.

RIGHT.

I KNOW WHAT YOU MEAN. GET HER VOICE BOUNCING THROUGH OR AROUND A LOT OF DIFFERENT MATERIALS.

UH-HUH. HOW MUCH DO YOU THINK IS RIGHT TO PAY SOMEONE FOR THAT? A KID FOR A FEW HOURS?

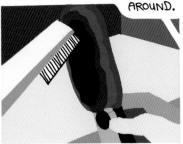

I DONNO. FIND A FRIEND--OF-A-FRIEND'S DAUGHTER AND I BET IT'D BE CHEAP.

FIFTY BUCKS FOR AN HOUR.

SOUNDS GOOD TO ME.

CLICK.

I KNOW A CONSTRUCTION SITE IN BROOKLYN THAT HAS A LOT OF DIFFERENT TUBES AND SHIT LYING AROUND.

SOMETIMES THE MOST REALISTIC SOUND ISN'T NECESSARILY THE MOST BELIEVABLE SOUND.

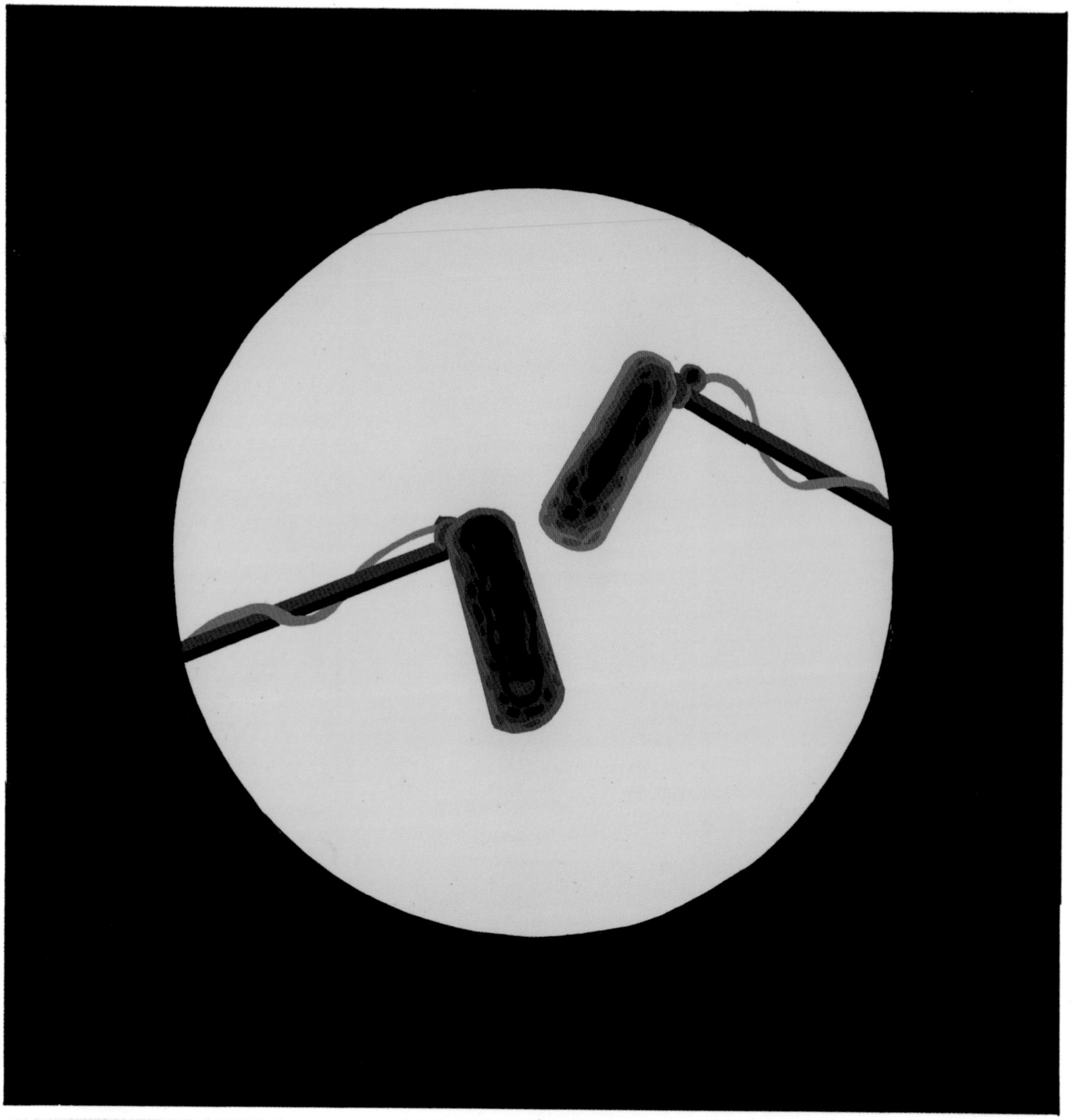
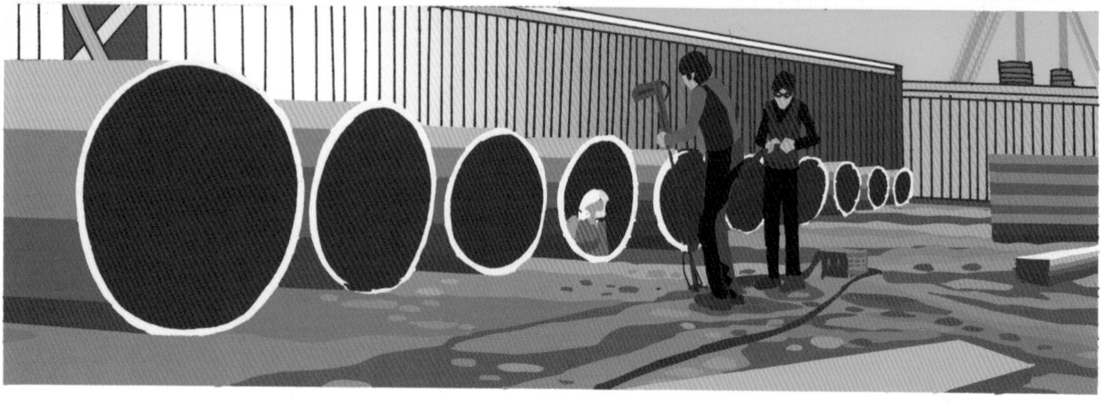

JUST TEN MORE MINUTES AND YOU'RE FREE TO GO. LET IT OUT.

I'M TRYING.

YOU WERE DOING GREAT.

CAN'T I LEAVE NOW?

WE'RE ALMOST DONE. JUST ONE LAST TIME,

THEN MOM WILL TAKE YOU OUT TO EAT, GET YOU ICE CREAM.

WHATEVER YOU WANT.

OKAY? CRYING IS EASY, REMEMBER?

JUST IMAGINE THE MOST TERRIBLE, DEPRESSING THING YOU CAN THINK OF.

HOLD IT IN YOUR MIND. TRY TO MAKE IT FEEL REAL.

MAYBE YOUR MOM OR DAD OR BEST FRIEND DIED. WOULDN'T THAT MAKE YOU CRY?

IMAGINE IT.

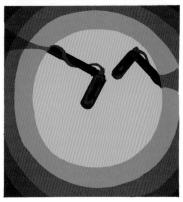

I'M TRYING.

MY ENTIRE HIGH SCHOOL... SINKING INTO THE SEA!

BY DASH SHAW FEB '09

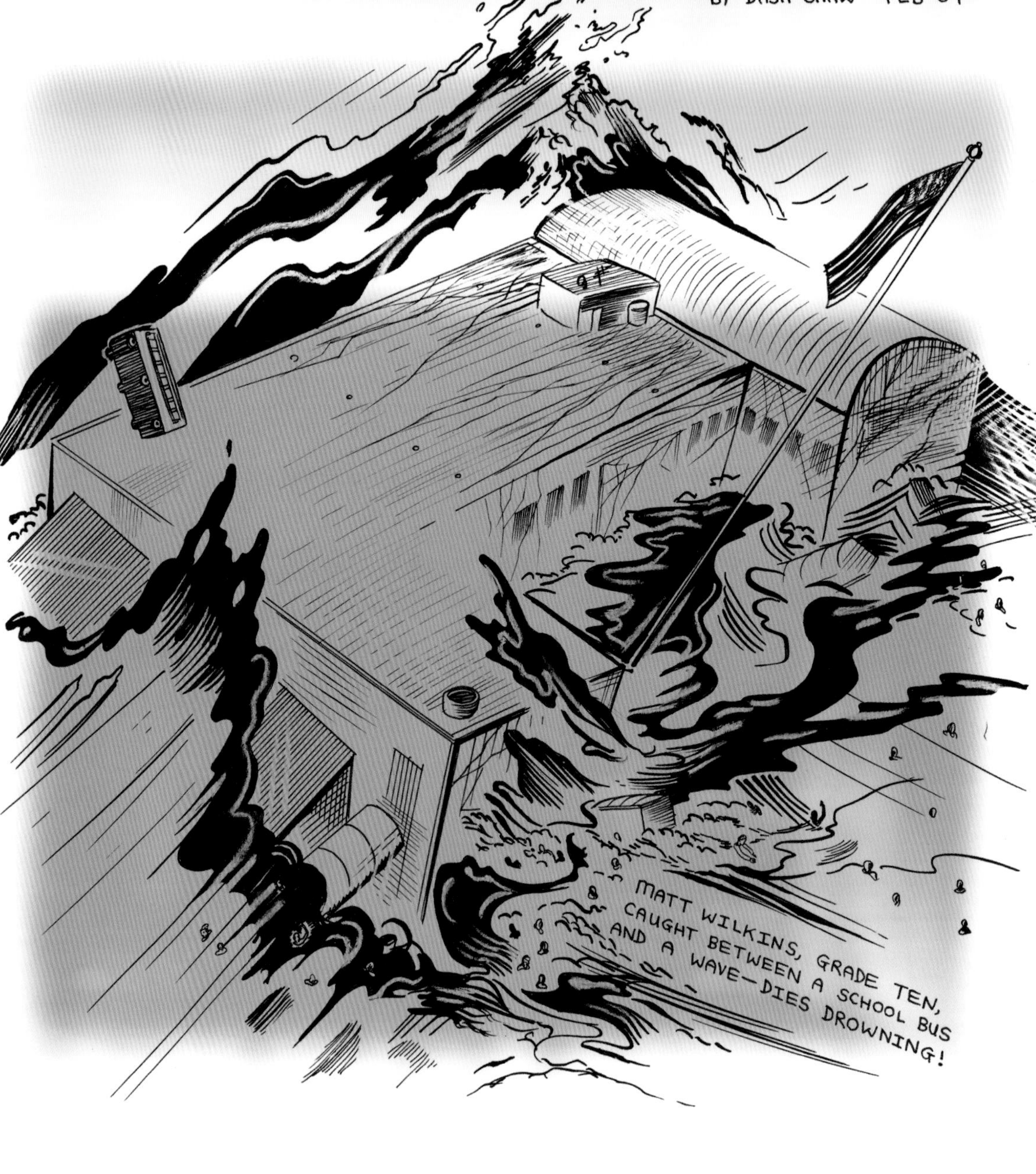
MATT WILKINS, GRADE TEN, CAUGHT BETWEEN A SCHOOL BUS AND A WAVE—DIES DROWNING!

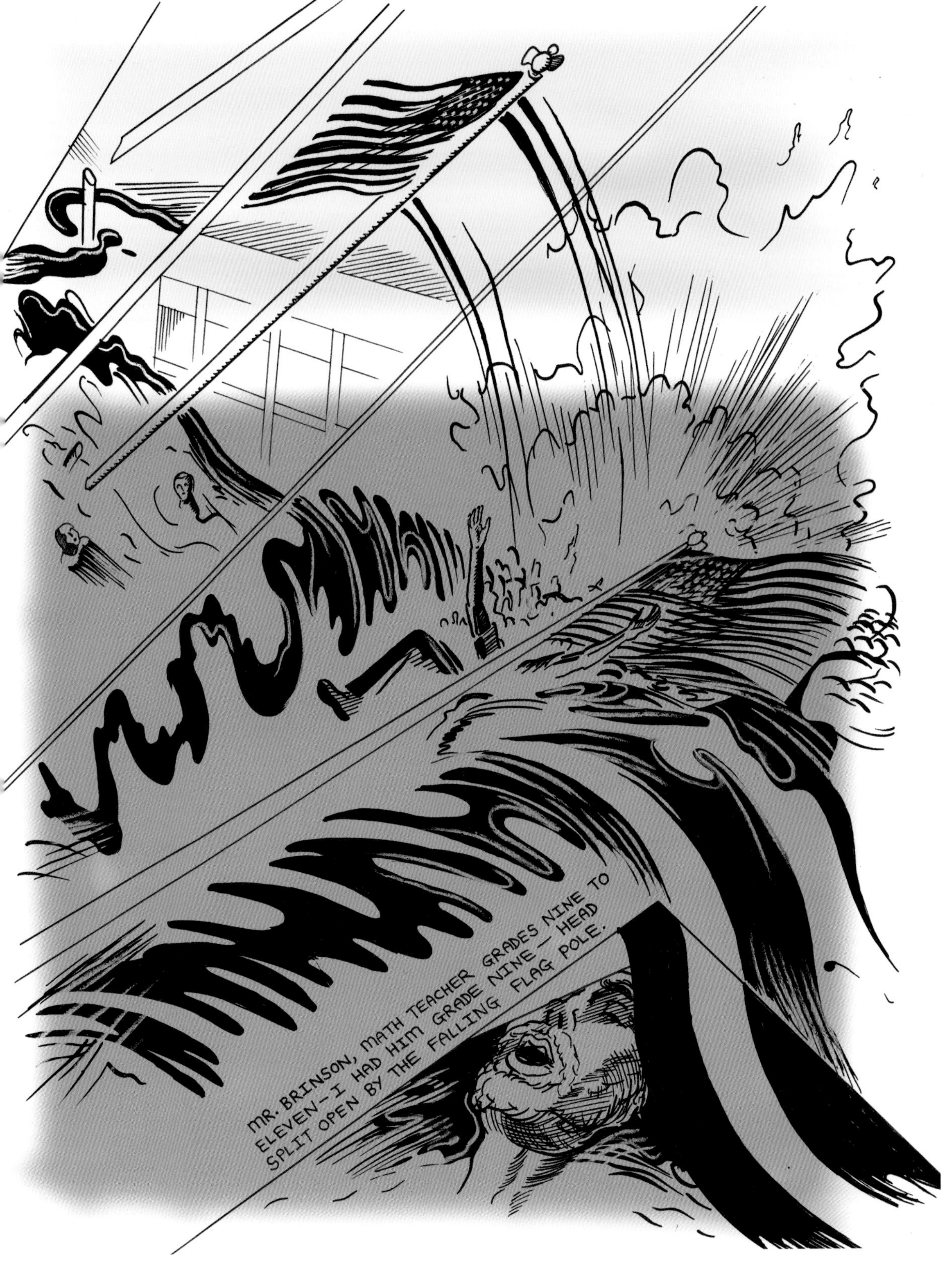
MR. BRINSON, MATH TEACHER GRADES NINE TO ELEVEN--I HAD HIM GRADE NINE--HEAD SPLIT OPEN BY THE FALLING FLAG POLE.

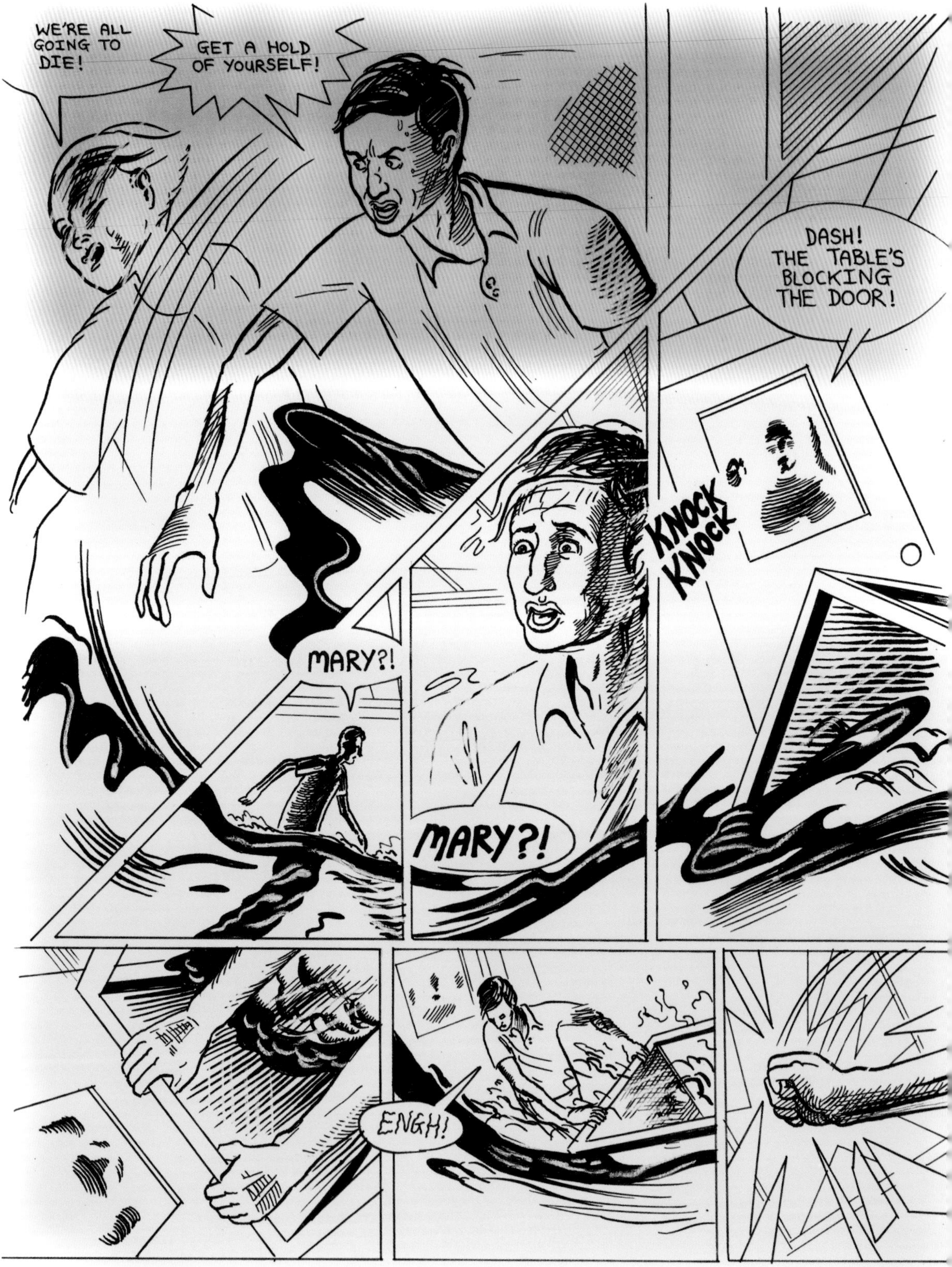
WE'RE ALL GOING TO DIE!
GET A HOLD OF YOURSELF!
DASH! THE TABLE'S BLOCKING THE DOOR!
MARY?!
MARY?!
KNOCK KNOCK
ENGH!

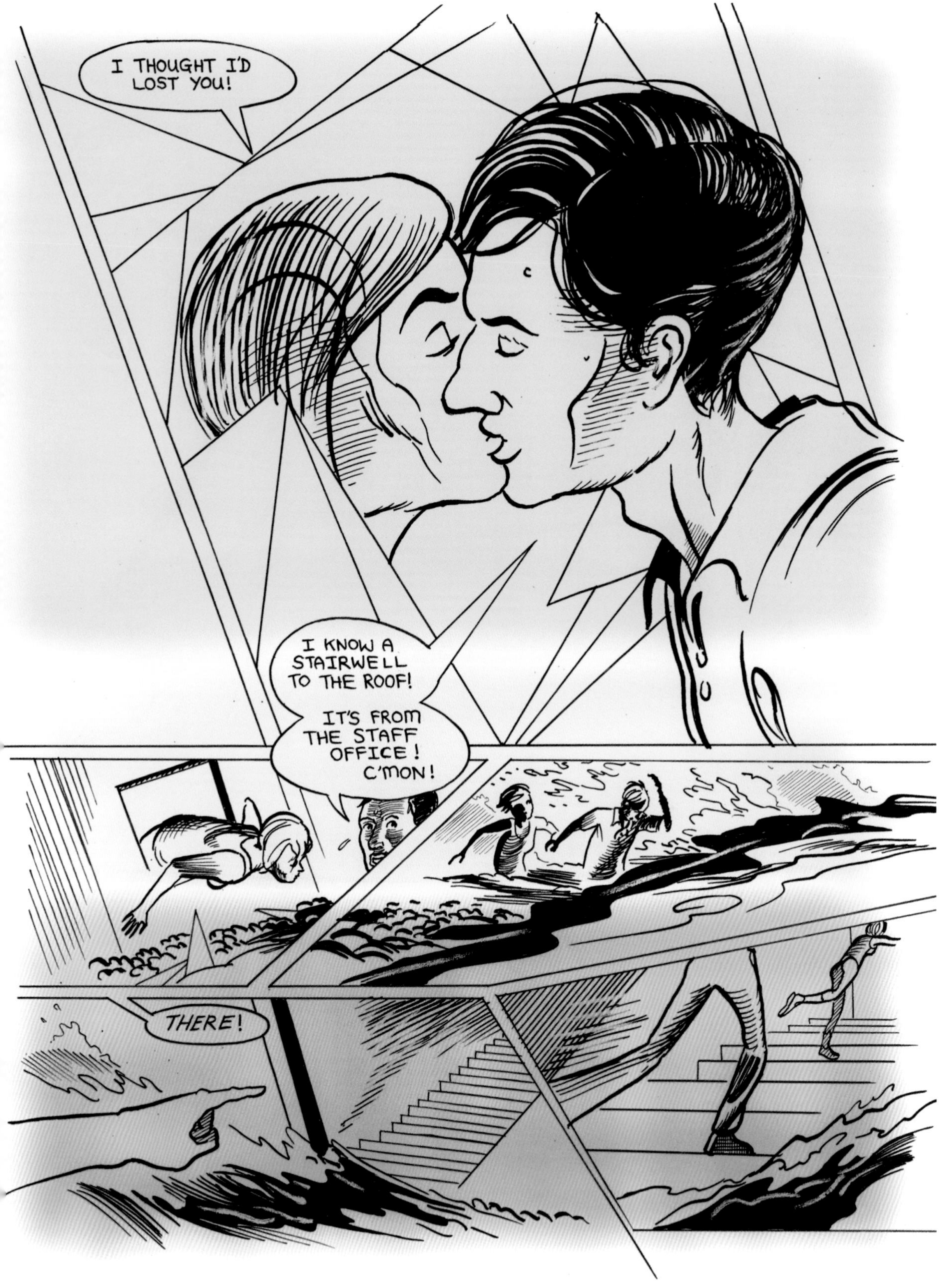
I THOUGHT I'D LOST YOU!
I KNOW A STAIRWELL TO THE ROOF!
IT'S FROM THE STAFF OFFICE! C'MON!
THERE!

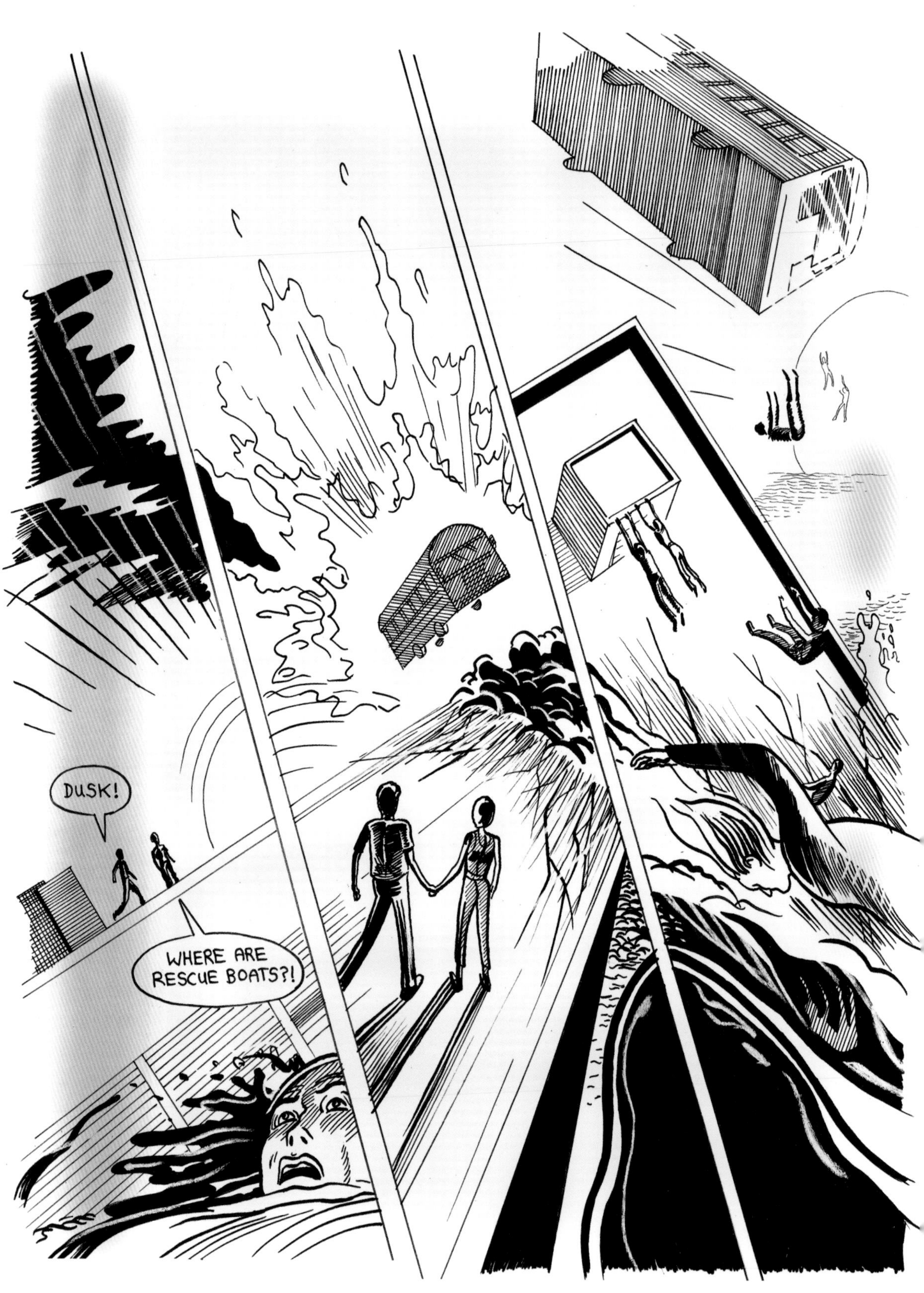
DUSK!
WHERE ARE RESCUE BOATS?!

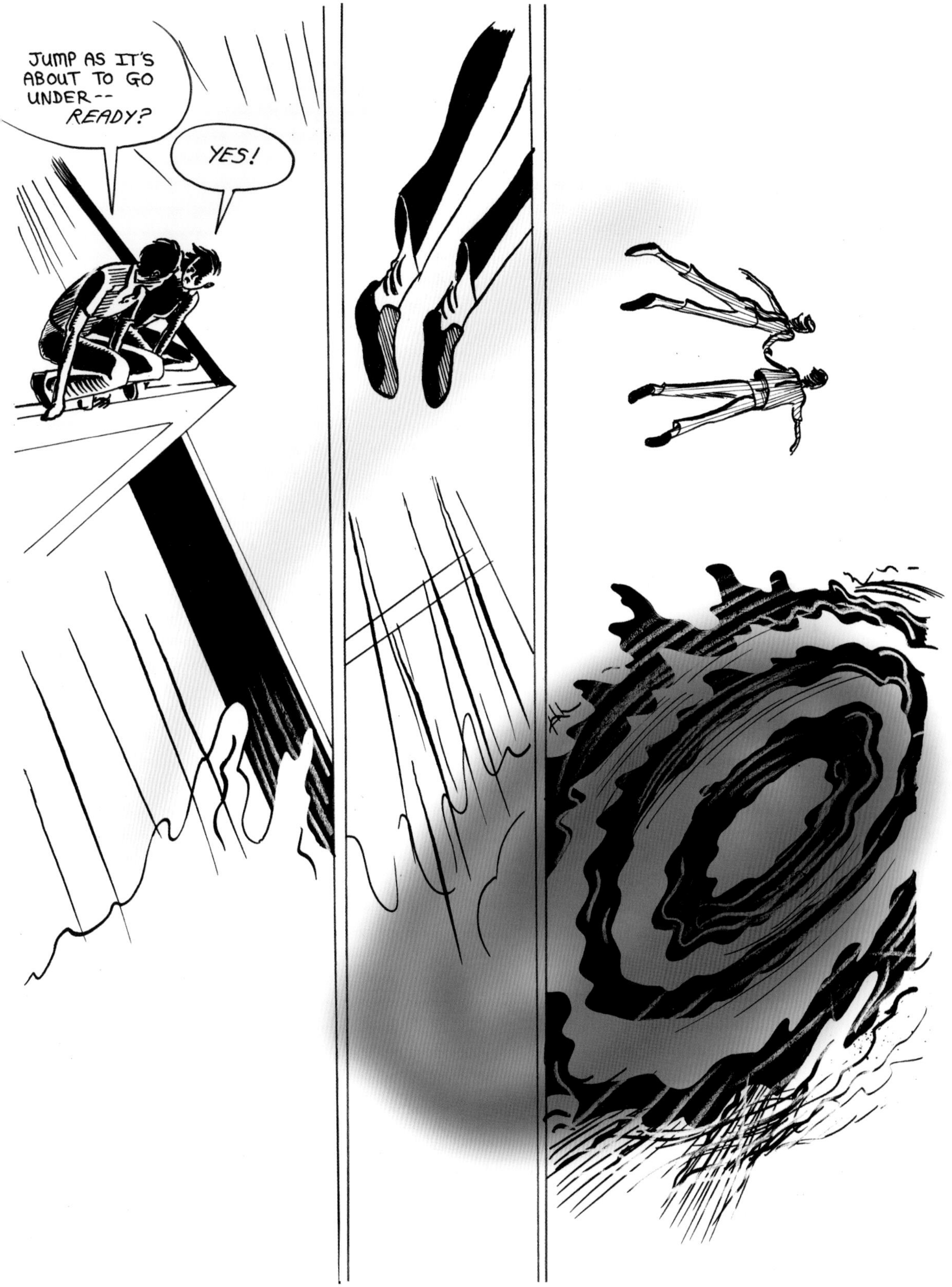
JUMP AS IT'S ABOUT TO GO UNDER -- READY?
YES!

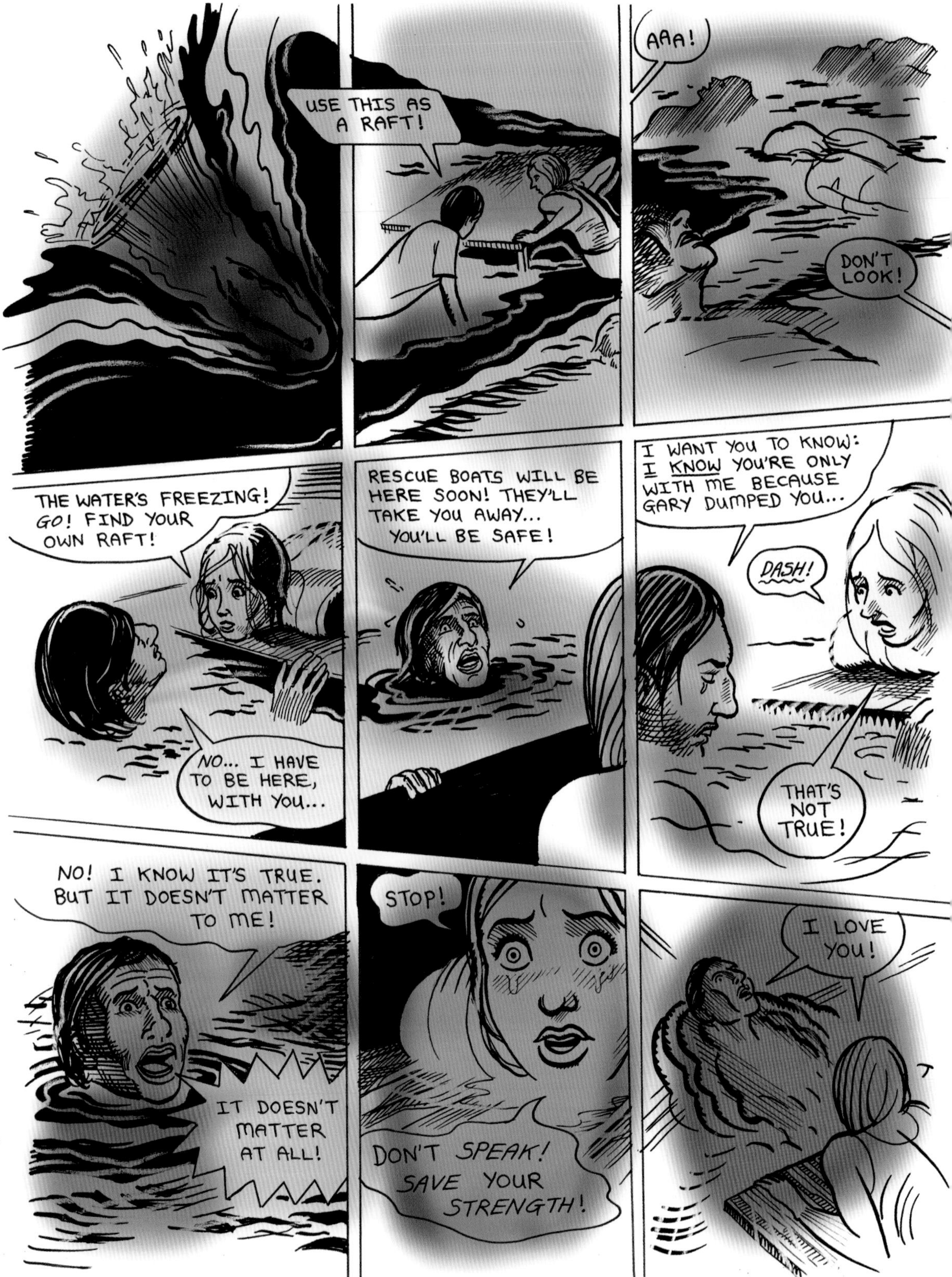
USE THIS AS A RAFT!
AAA!
DON'T LOOK!
THE WATER'S FREEZING! GO! FIND YOUR OWN RAFT!
NO... I HAVE TO BE HERE, WITH YOU...
RESCUE BOATS WILL BE HERE SOON! THEY'LL TAKE YOU AWAY... YOU'LL BE SAFE!
I WANT YOU TO KNOW: I KNOW YOU'RE ONLY WITH ME BECAUSE GARY DUMPED YOU...
DASH!
THAT'S NOT TRUE!
NO! I KNOW IT'S TRUE. BUT IT DOESN'T MATTER TO ME!
IT DOESN'T MATTER AT ALL!
STOP!
DON'T SPEAK! SAVE YOUR STRENGTH!
I LOVE YOU!

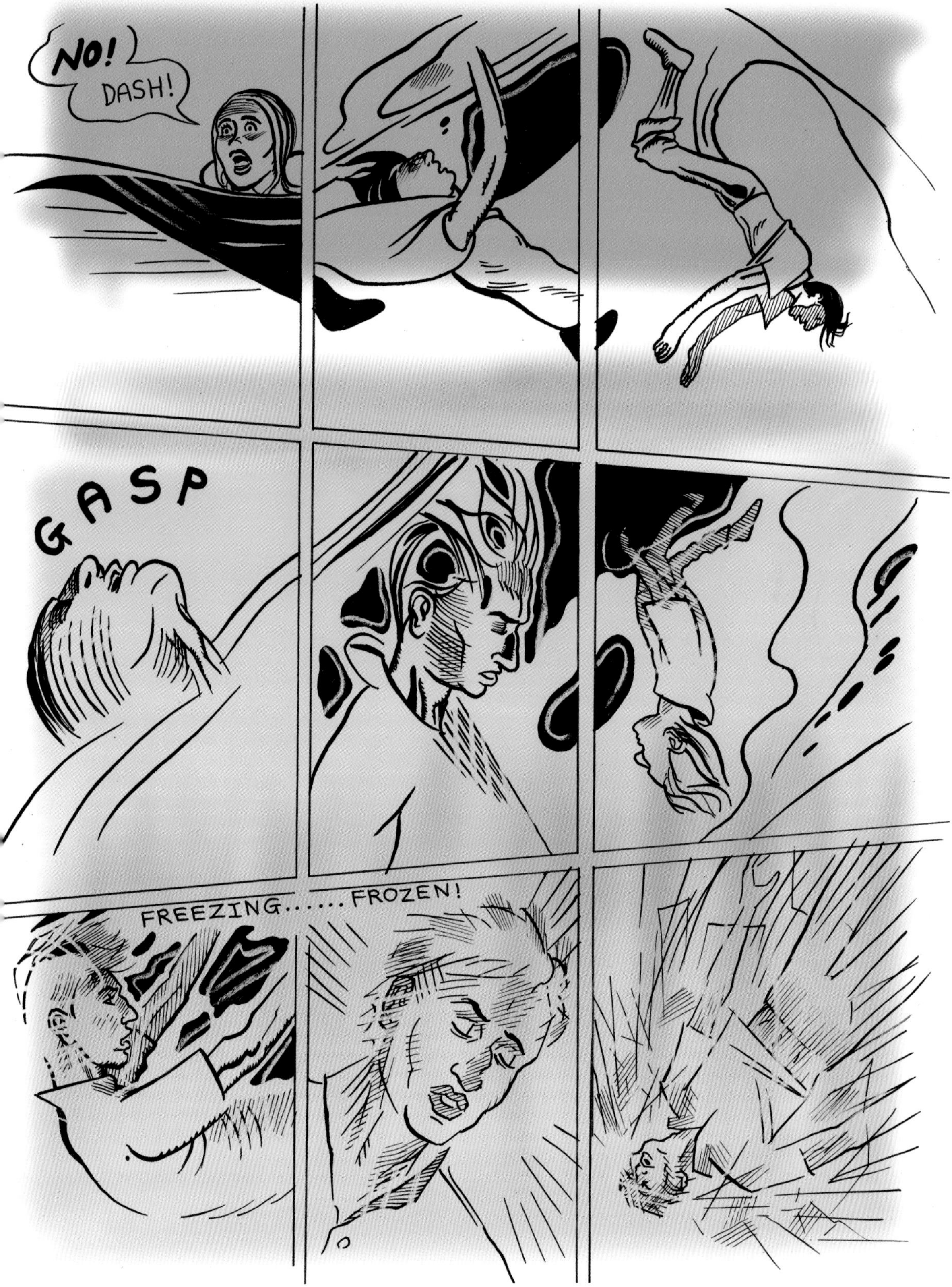
NO! DASH!
GASP
FREEZING......FROZEN!

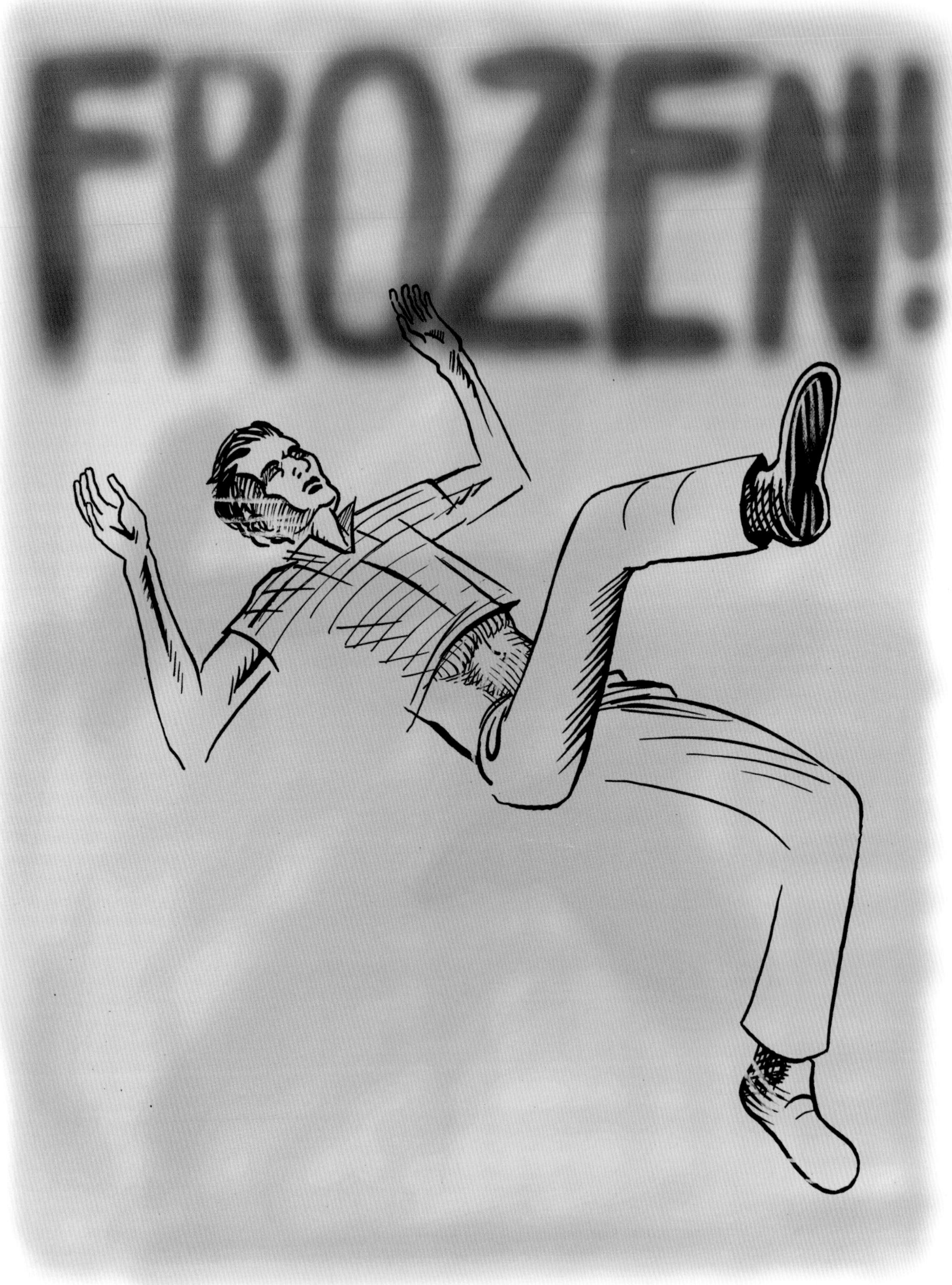
FROZEN!

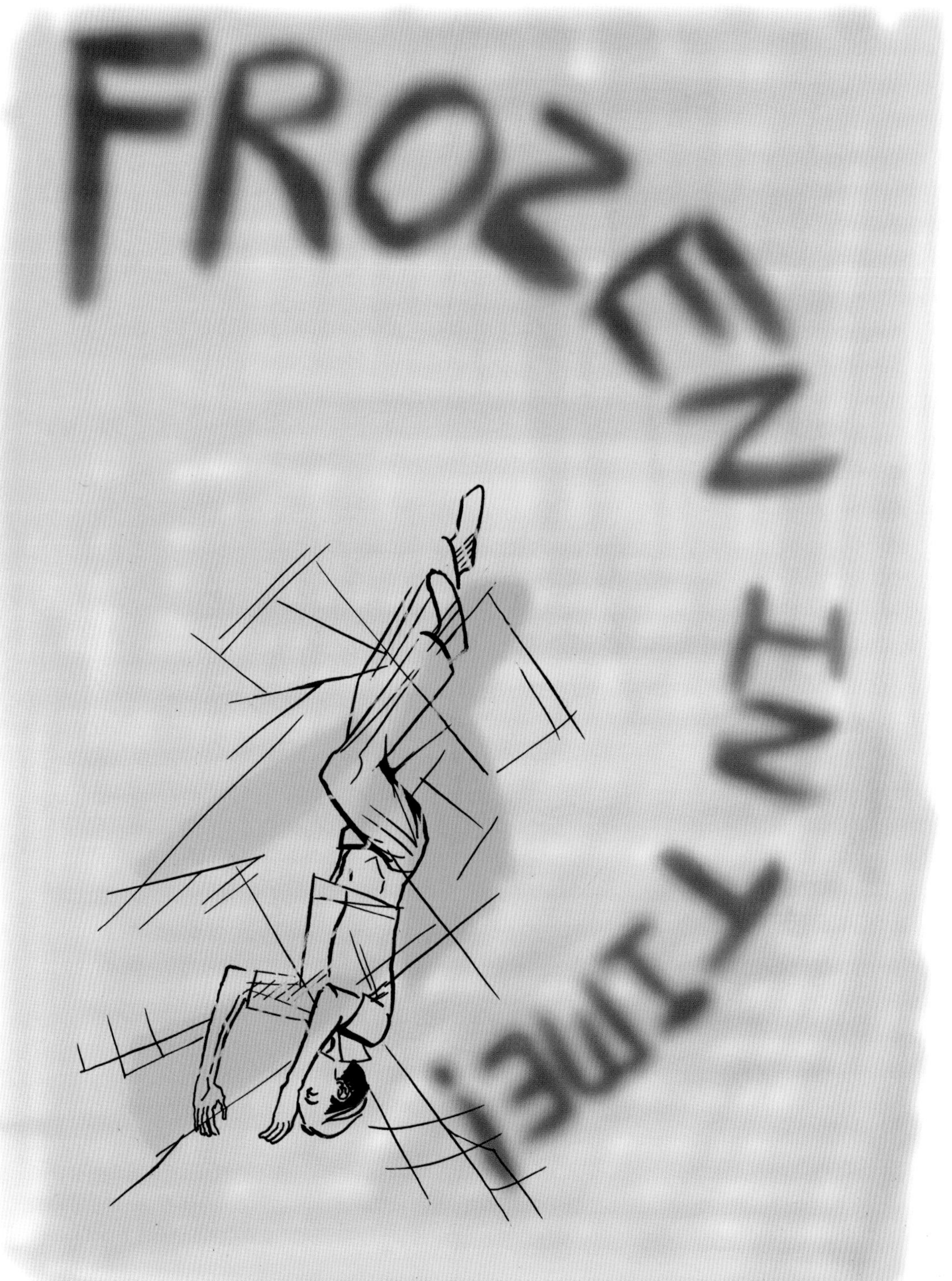
FROZEN IN TIME!

THE END.

"BLIND DATE 1"
DASH SHAW MARCH 2009

THIS COMIC IS AN ADAPTATION OF AN EPISODE OF "BLIND DATE."

I MET A WONDERFUL GUY AND WE WERE TOGETHER FOR EIGHT YEARS, AND DURING THAT TIME WE WERE GOING TO GET MARRIED. IT HAS BEEN VERY DEVASTATING TO HAVE GONE THROUGH THAT, THINKING I WAS GOING TO MARRY HIM AND SPEND THE REST OF MY LIFE WITH HIM AND IT'S ALL GONE. I'M THRILLED TO HAVE A GOOD CAREER BUT I'D GIVE ALL THAT UP TO FIND THE RIGHT GUY AND SETTLE DOWN AND BE ABLE TO ACTUALLY HAVE THAT TRADITIONAL MARRIAGE.

THE GIRL THAT I MEET, THE ONE, IS GOING TO ZAP ME SO HARD WITH ELECTRICITY.
WITH SHAZAM. WITH POWER.
I'LL KNOW RIGHT AWAY THIS IS THE GIRL I NEED TO MARRY.

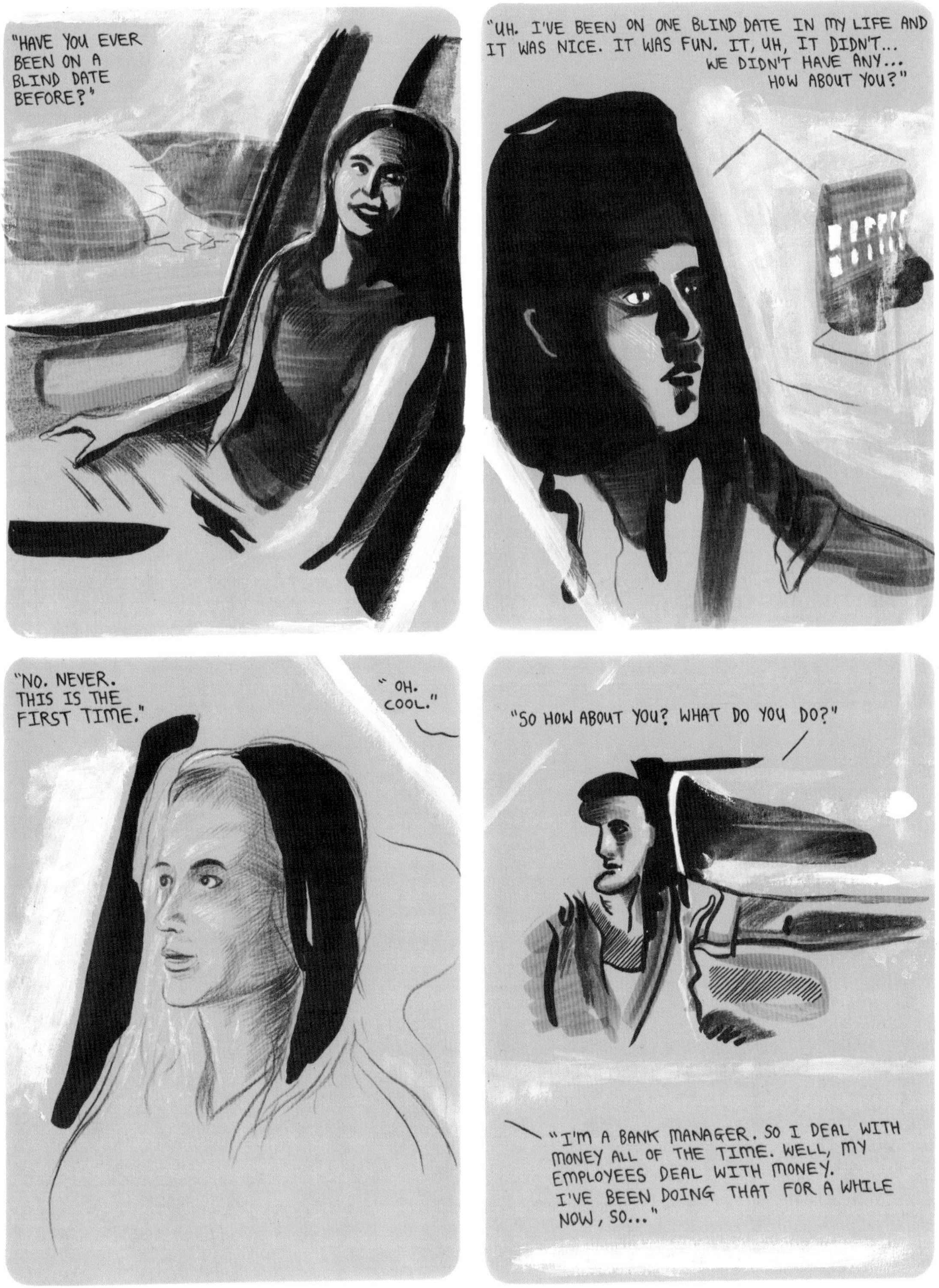
"HAVE YOU EVER BEEN ON A BLIND DATE BEFORE?"
"UH. I'VE BEEN ON ONE BLIND DATE IN MY LIFE AND IT WAS NICE. IT WAS FUN. IT, UH, IT DIDN'T... WE DIDN'T HAVE ANY... HOW ABOUT YOU?"
"NO. NEVER. THIS IS THE FIRST TIME."
"OH. COOL."
"SO HOW ABOUT YOU? WHAT DO YOU DO?"
"I'M A BANK MANAGER. SO I DEAL WITH MONEY ALL OF THE TIME. WELL, MY EMPLOYEES DEAL WITH MONEY. I'VE BEEN DOING THAT FOR A WHILE NOW, SO..."

"IT'S GOOD.
I LIKE IT."
HA. HA.

" SO WHAT DO
YOU LIKE TO
DO FOR FUN?"

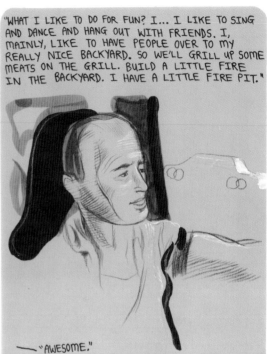

"WHAT I LIKE TO DO FOR FUN? I... I LIKE TO SING
AND DANCE AND HANG OUT WITH FRIENDS. I,
MAINLY, LIKE TO HAVE PEOPLE OVER TO MY
REALLY NICE BACKYARD. SO WE'LL GRILL UP SOME
MEATS ON THE GRILL. BUILD A LITTLE FIRE
IN THE BACKYARD. I HAVE A LITTLE FIRE PIT."

— "AWESOME."

"IF YOU HAD TO DESCRIBE YOUR IDEAL WOMAN,
WHAT WOULD THE LIST BE LIKE?"

"UM. CONFIDENT. INDEPENDENT. AMBITIOUS.
UHM. DARING. UH. WILLING TO PLAY.
WILLING TO HAVE FUN."

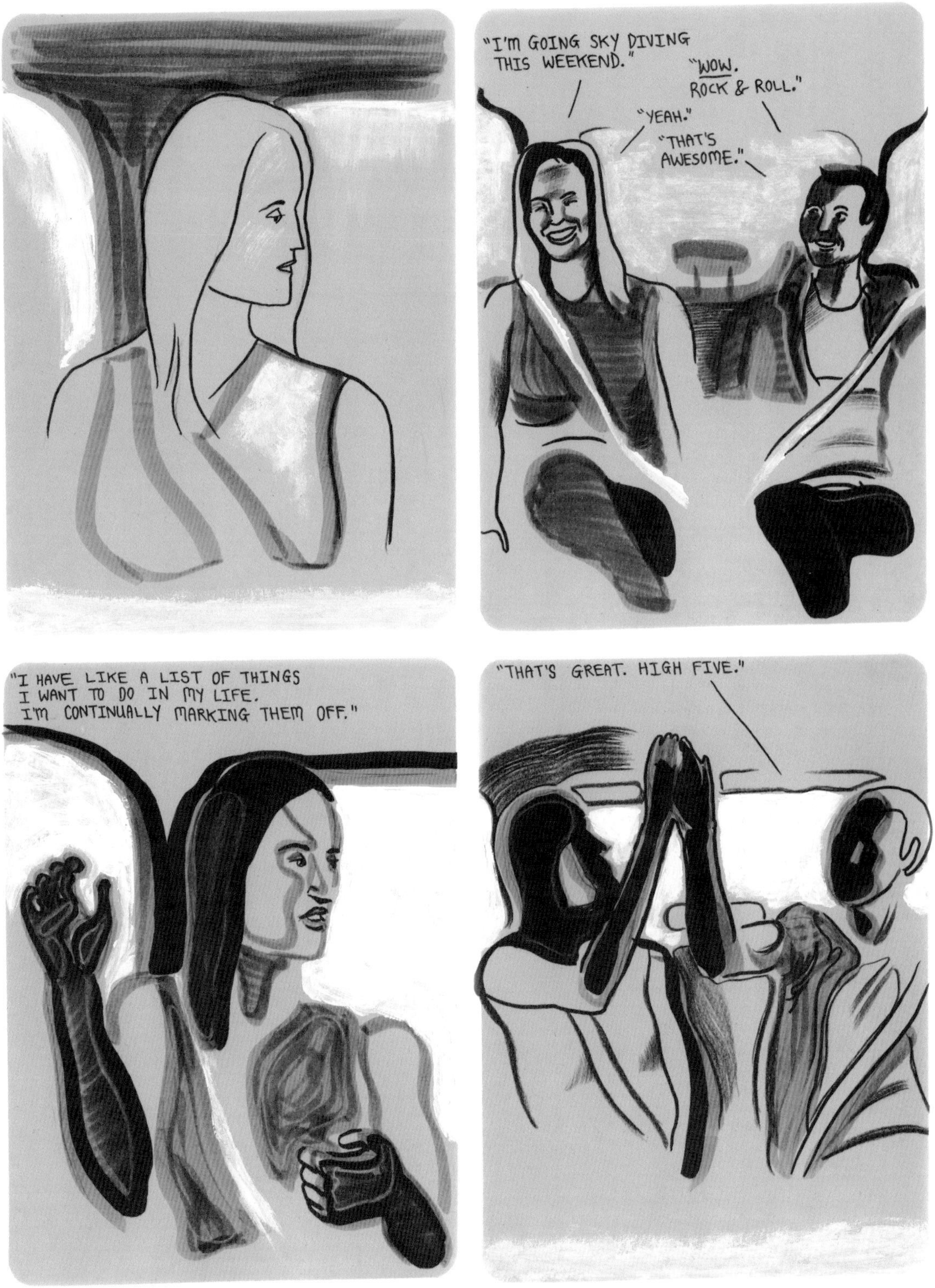
"I'M GOING SKY DIVING THIS WEEKEND."
"WOW. ROCK & ROLL."
"YEAH."
"THAT'S AWESOME."
"I HAVE LIKE A LIST OF THINGS I WANT TO DO IN MY LIFE. I'M CONTINUALLY MARKING THEM OFF."
"THAT'S GREAT. HIGH FIVE."

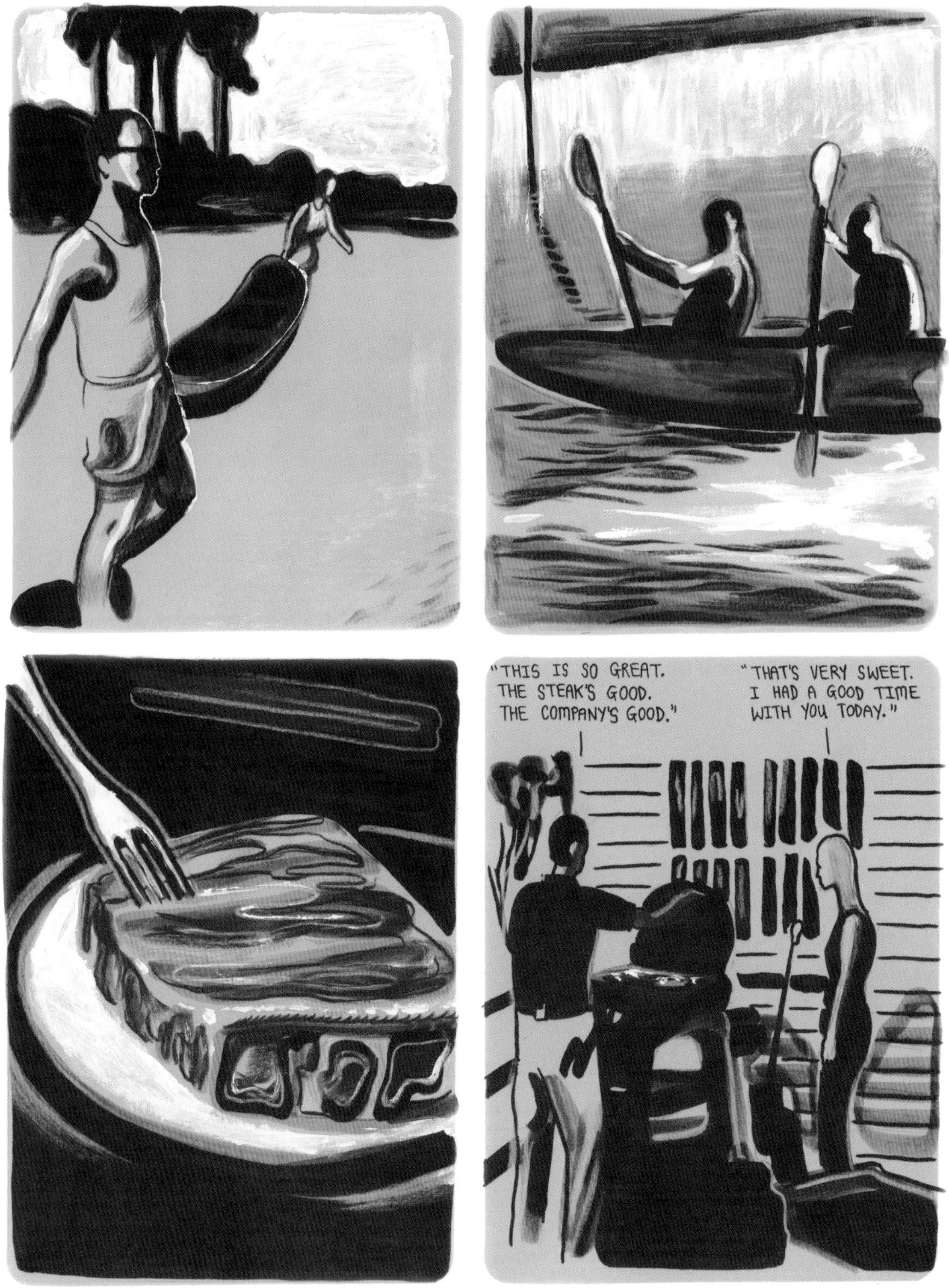
"THIS IS SO GREAT. THE STEAK'S GOOD. THE COMPANY'S GOOD."
"THAT'S VERY SWEET. I HAD A GOOD TIME WITH YOU TODAY."

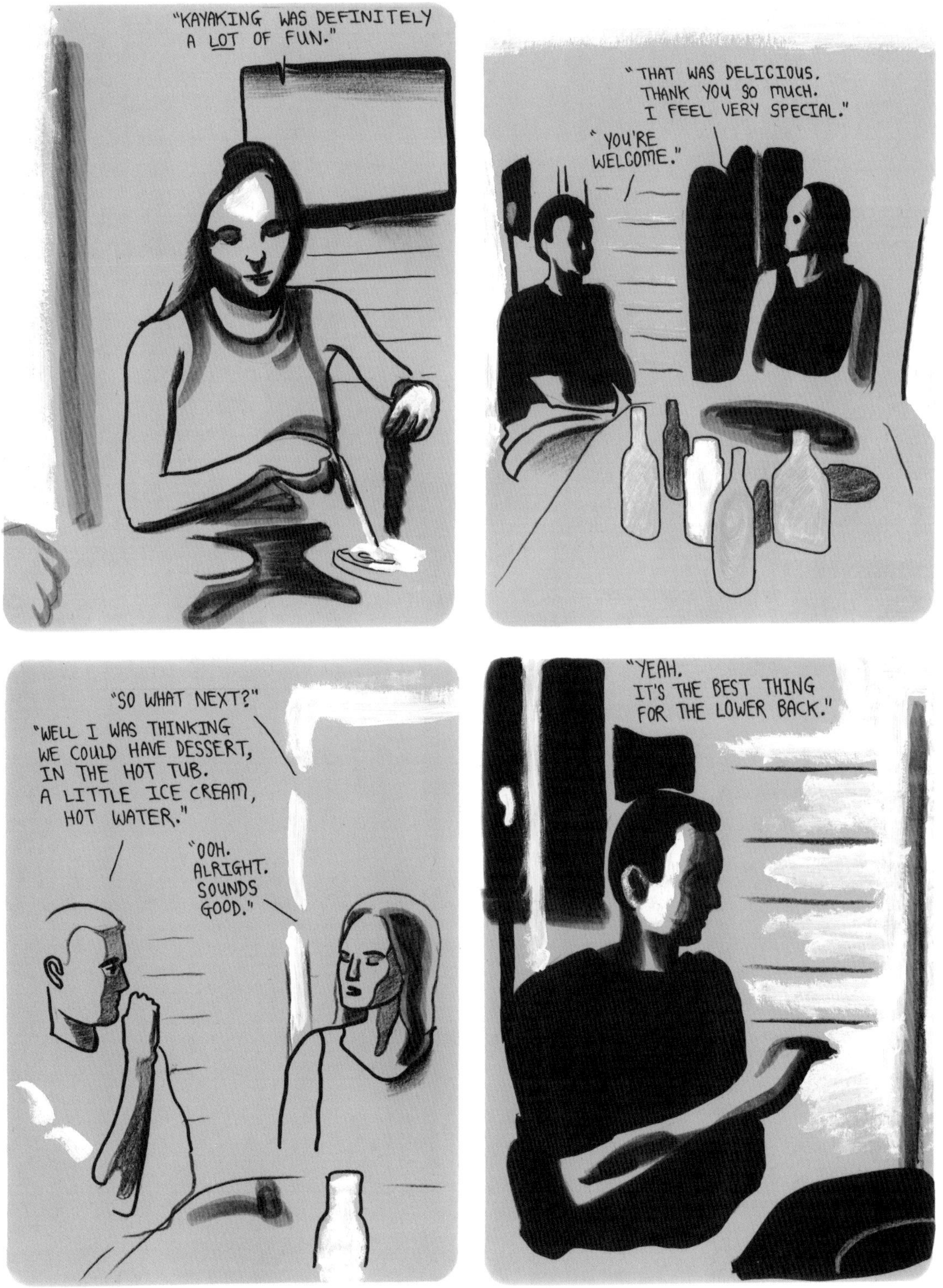
"KAYAKING WAS DEFINITELY A LOT OF FUN."
"THAT WAS DELICIOUS. THANK YOU SO MUCH. I FEEL VERY SPECIAL."
"YOU'RE WELCOME."
"SO WHAT NEXT?"
"WELL I WAS THINKING WE COULD HAVE DESSERT, IN THE HOT TUB. A LITTLE ICE CREAM, HOT WATER."
"OOH. ALRIGHT. SOUNDS GOOD."
"YEAH. IT'S THE BEST THING FOR THE LOWER BACK."

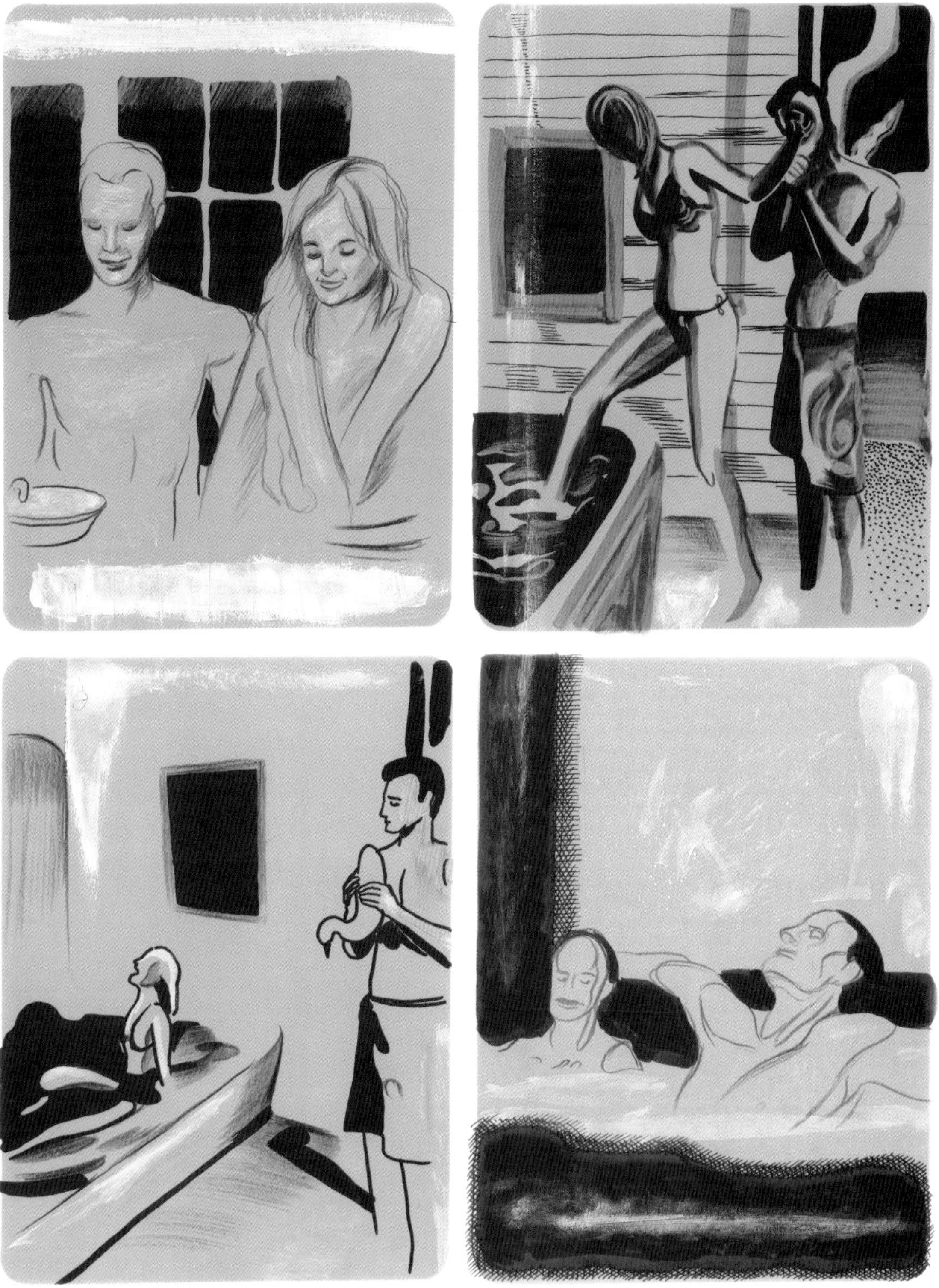

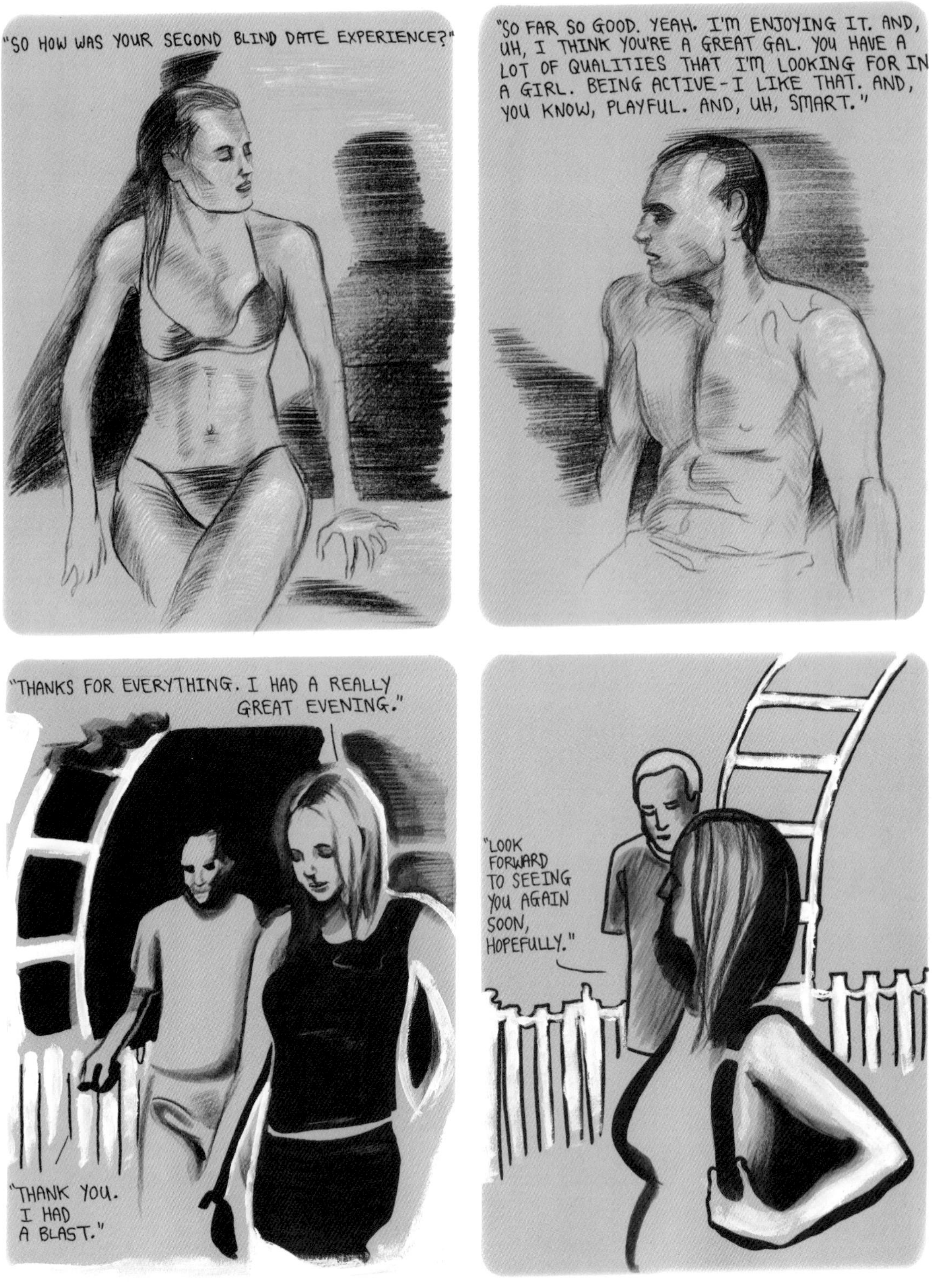
"SO HOW WAS YOUR SECOND BLIND DATE EXPERIENCE?"
"SO FAR SO GOOD. YEAH. I'M ENJOYING IT. AND, UH, I THINK YOU'RE A GREAT GAL. YOU HAVE A LOT OF QUALITIES THAT I'M LOOKING FOR IN A GIRL. BEING ACTIVE - I LIKE THAT. AND, YOU KNOW, PLAYFUL. AND, UH, SMART."
"THANKS FOR EVERYTHING. I HAD A REALLY GREAT EVENING."
"THANK YOU. I HAD A BLAST."
"LOOK FORWARD TO SEEING YOU AGAIN SOON, HOPEFULLY."

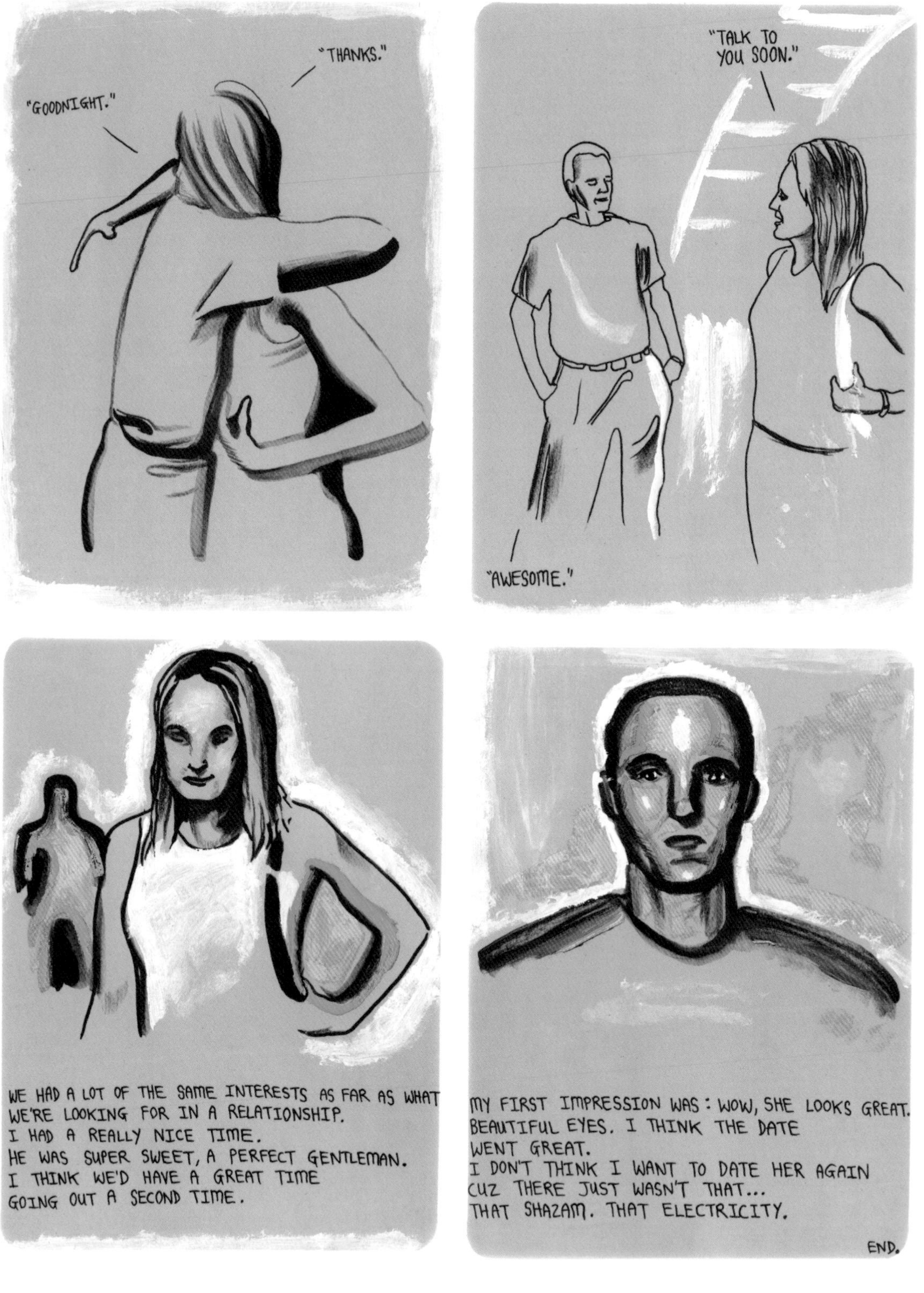
"GOODNIGHT."
"THANKS."
"TALK TO YOU SOON."
"AWESOME."
WE HAD A LOT OF THE SAME INTERESTS AS FAR AS WHAT WE'RE LOOKING FOR IN A RELATIONSHIP. I HAD A REALLY NICE TIME. HE WAS SUPER SWEET, A PERFECT GENTLEMAN. I THINK WE'D HAVE A GREAT TIME GOING OUT A SECOND TIME.
MY FIRST IMPRESSION WAS: WOW, SHE LOOKS GREAT. BEAUTIFUL EYES. I THINK THE DATE WENT GREAT. I DON'T THINK I WANT TO DATE HER AGAIN CUZ THERE JUST WASN'T THAT... THAT SHAZAM. THAT ELECTRICITY.
END.

1

WHITE SCREEN

2

LIGHT!

3

INCANDESCENT
LIGHT BULB

4

IDEA
NINON ASLEEP

5

SPARK

6

FWOOSH
GASP

GROWS

7

GROWING –
ZOOM BACK

8

SHUTTER

9

FARTHER

10

SHUTTER

11

FARTHER

12

PAN RIGHT

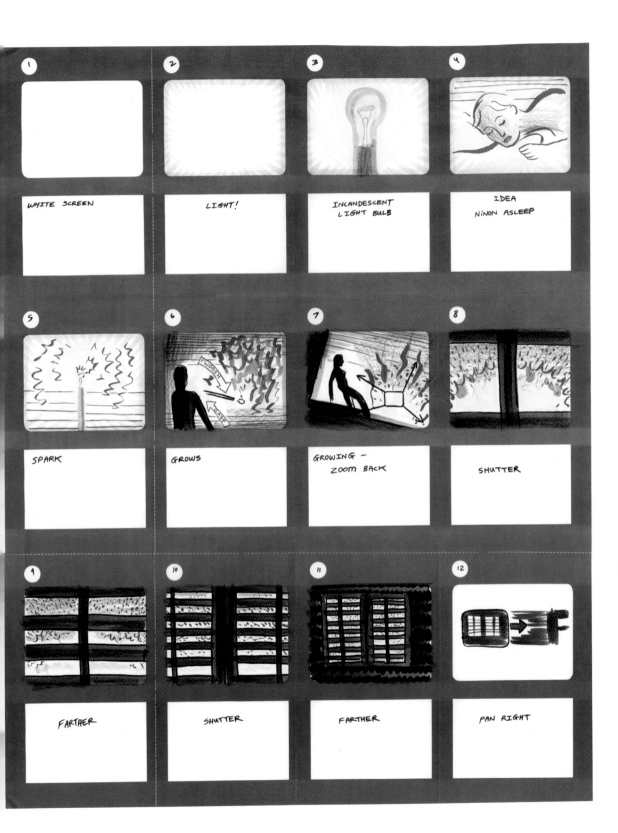

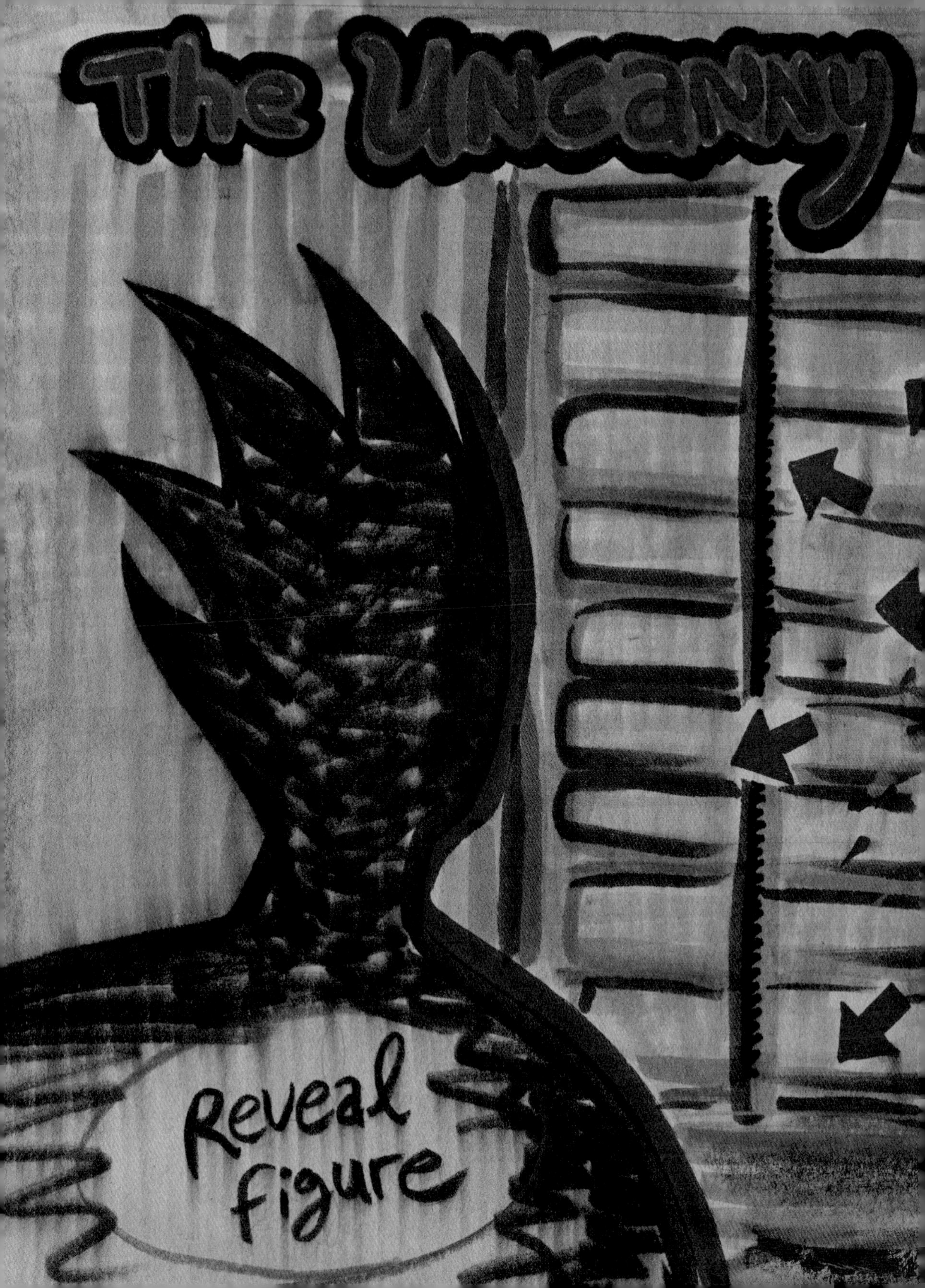
The UNCANNY
Reveal figure

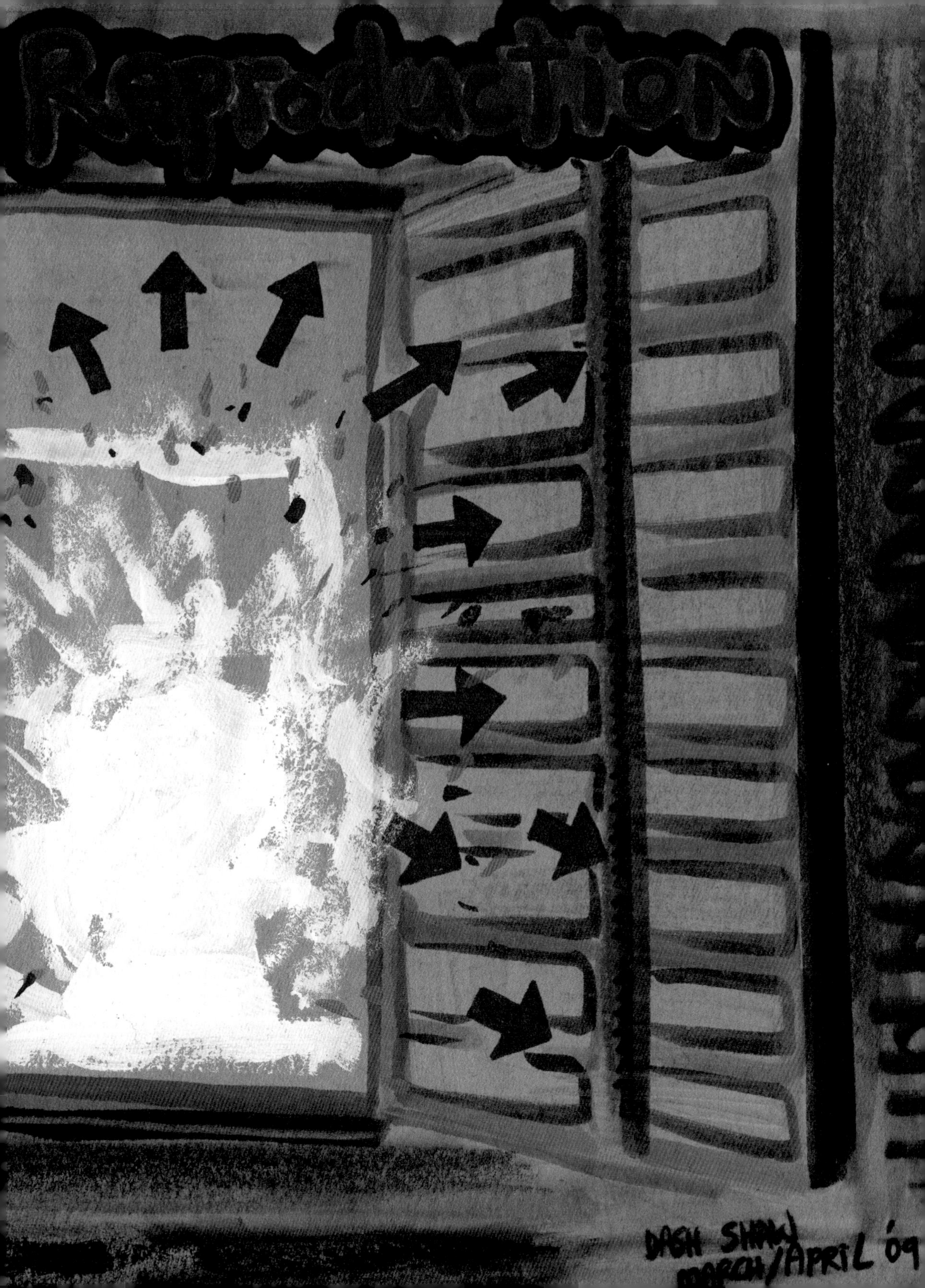
Reproduction
DASH SHAW
MARCH/APRIL 09

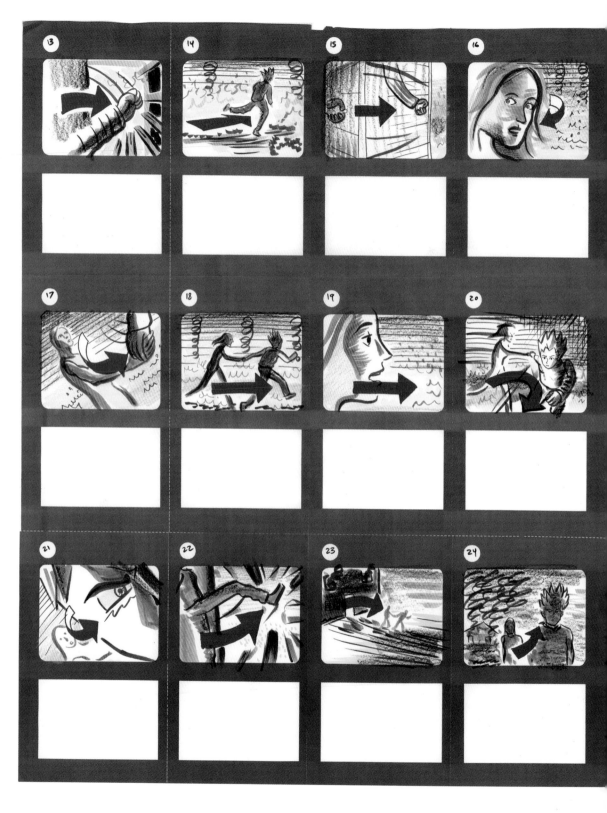

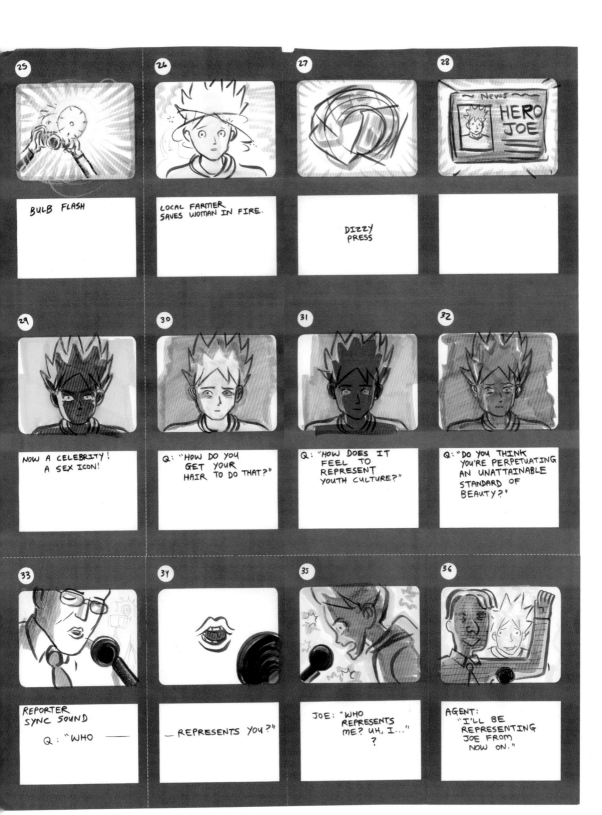

25

BULB FLASH

26

LOCAL FARMER
SAVES WOMAN IN FIRE.

27

DIZZY
PRESS

28

29

NOW A CELEBRITY!
A SEX ICON!

30

Q: "HOW DO YOU
    GET YOUR
    HAIR TO DO THAT?"

31

Q: "HOW DOES IT
    FEEL TO
    REPRESENT
    YOUTH CULTURE?"

32

Q: "DO YOU THINK
    YOU'RE PERPETUATING
    AN UNATTAINABLE
    STANDARD OF
    BEAUTY?"

33

REPORTER
SYNC SOUND

   Q: "WHO ——

34

—— REPRESENTS YOU?"

35

JOE: "WHO
     REPRESENTS
     ME? UH, I..."
       ?

36

AGENT:
   "I'LL BE
   REPRESENTING
   JOE FROM
   NOW ON."

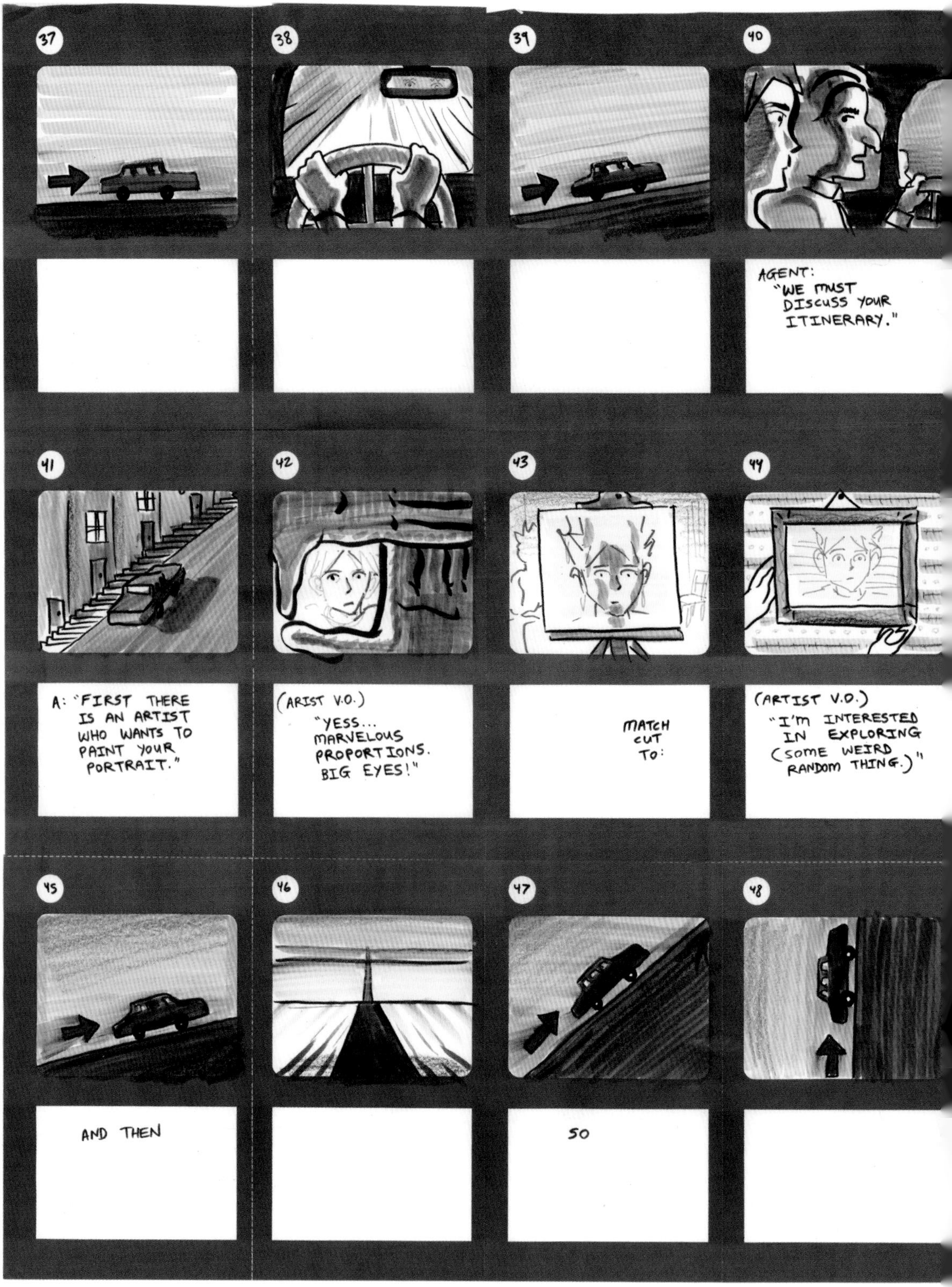
37
38
39
40
AGENT: "WE MUST DISCUSS YOUR ITINERARY."
41
42
43
44
A: "FIRST THERE IS AN ARTIST WHO WANTS TO PAINT YOUR PORTRAIT."
(ARIST V.O.) "YESS... MARVELOUS PROPORTIONS. BIG EYES!"
MATCH CUT TO:
(ARTIST V.O.) "I'M INTERESTED IN EXPLORING (SOME WEIRD RANDOM THING.)"
45
46
47
48
AND THEN
SO

49

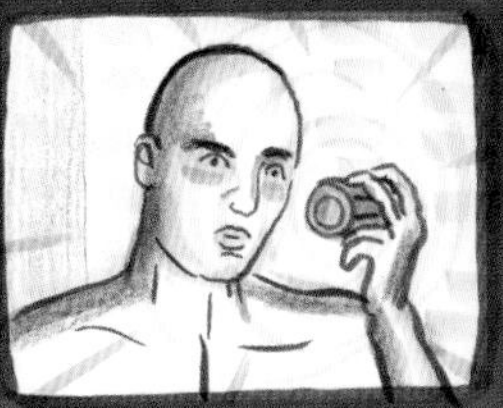

50

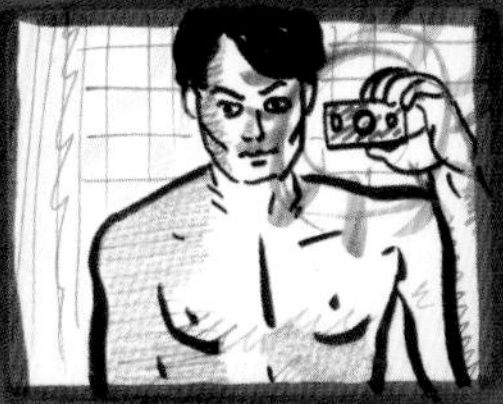

PEOPLE MAIL JOE PHOTOS OF THEMSELVES.

51

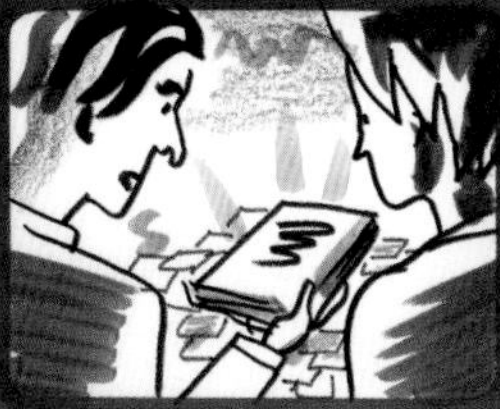

AGENT:
"YOU'RE RECEIVING SCRIPTS TOO."

52

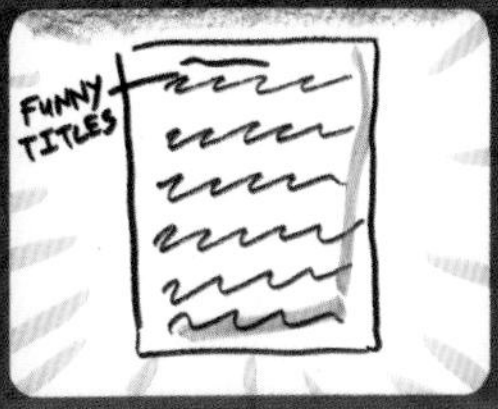
FUNNY TITLES

PLANS FOR MOVIES OR TELEVISION SHOWS PEOPLE WANT TO MAKE, STARRING JOE!

53

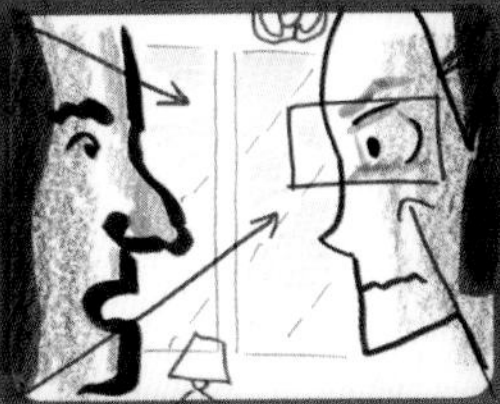

"HAVE YOU EVER CONSIDERED ACTING FOR LOTS OF MONEY?"
THEN ZOOM IN

54

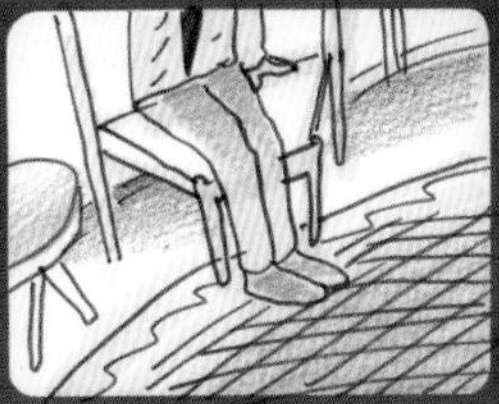

JOE'S P.O.V.

55

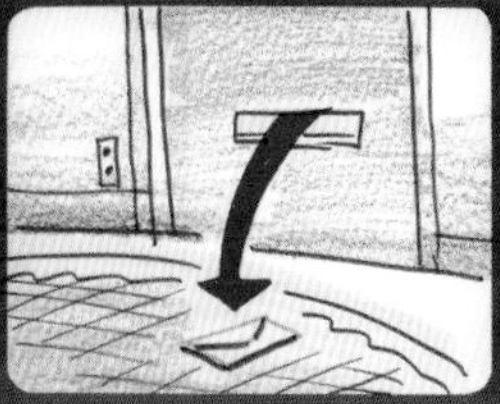

JOE'S P.O.V.

56

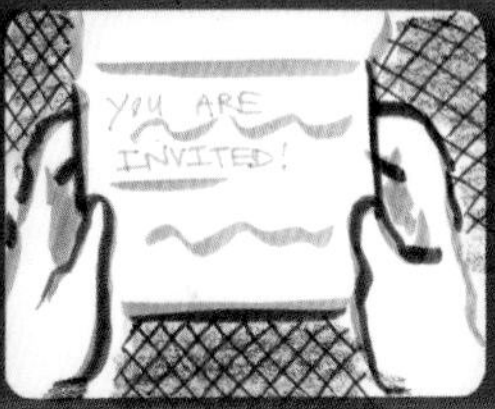
YOU ARE INVITED!

JOE'S P.O.V.
AN INVITATION TO A MASKED BALL HOSTED BY THE TOWN MAGAZINE.

57

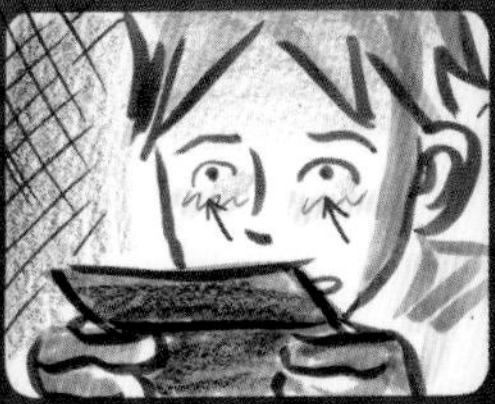

JOE: "DO YOU THINK NINON WILL BE THERE?"

58

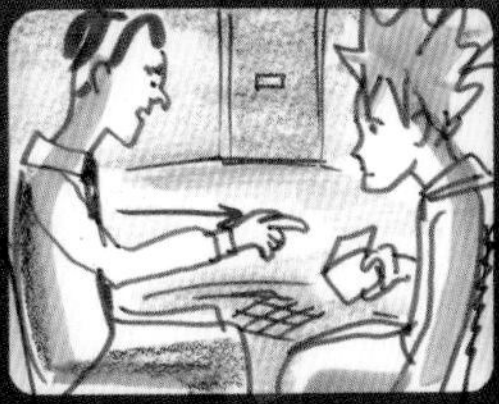

AGENT: "PROBABLY. IF YOU LIKE THAT GIRL, YOU SHOULD PRETEND TO BEFRIEND HER. IF YOU'RE TOO DIRECT NOW, YOU'LL CREATE A RESISTANCE THAT WILL NEVER WANE."

59

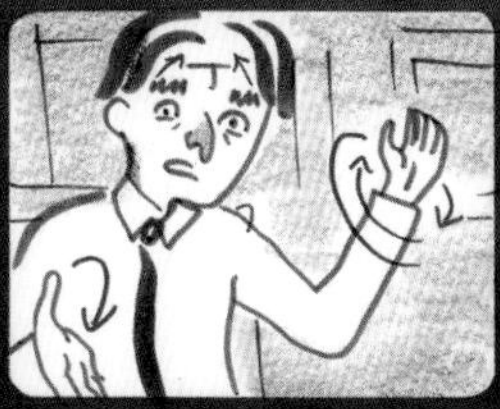

"YOU CAN'T SAVE HER AND THEN HIT ON HER. SHE'LL QUESTION YOUR MOTIVATION. CONFIDE IN HER AS A FRIEND. THEN SHE'LL TRUST YOU.
BELIEVE ME – I KNOW A LOT ABOUT THIS."

60

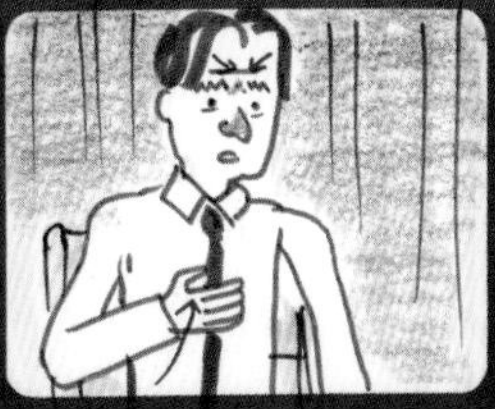

"INSTEAD OF HAVING SEX WITH ONE PERSON MANY TIMES, I HAVE SEX WITH MANY PEOPLE ONE TIME. PLUS I STUDIED PSYCHOLOGY BRIEFLY OUTSIDE OF SCHOOL."

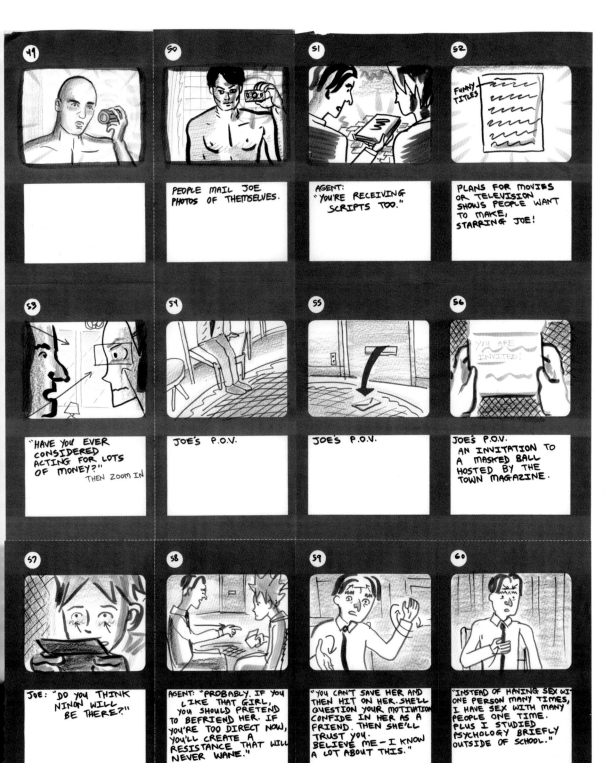

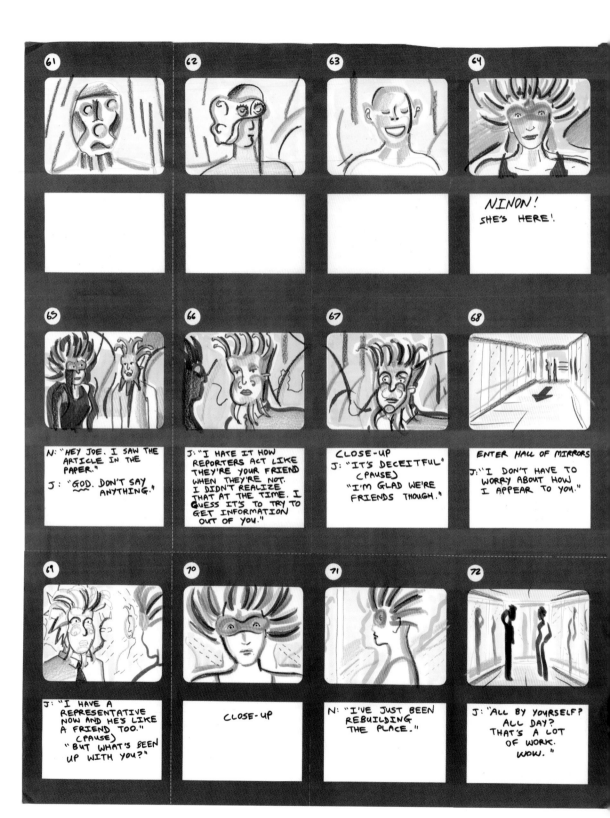

61

62

63

64 — NINON! SHE'S HERE!

65 — N: "HEY JOE. I SAW THE ARTICLE IN THE PAPER." J: "GOD. DON'T SAY ANYTHING."

66 — J: "I HATE IT HOW REPORTERS ACT LIKE THEY'RE YOUR FRIEND WHEN THEY'RE NOT. I DIDN'T REALIZE THAT AT THE TIME. I GUESS IT'S TO TRY TO GET INFORMATION OUT OF YOU."

67 — CLOSE-UP J: "IT'S DECEITFUL" (PAUSE) "I'M GLAD WE'RE FRIENDS THOUGH."

68 — ENTER HALL OF MIRRORS J: "I DON'T HAVE TO WORRY ABOUT HOW I APPEAR TO YOU."

69 — J: "I HAVE A REPRESENTATIVE NOW AND HE'S LIKE A FRIEND TOO." (PAUSE) "BUT WHAT'S BEEN UP WITH YOU?"

70 — CLOSE-UP

71 — N: "I'VE JUST BEEN REBUILDING THE PLACE."

72 — J: "ALL BY YOURSELF? ALL DAY? THAT'S A LOT OF WORK. WOW."

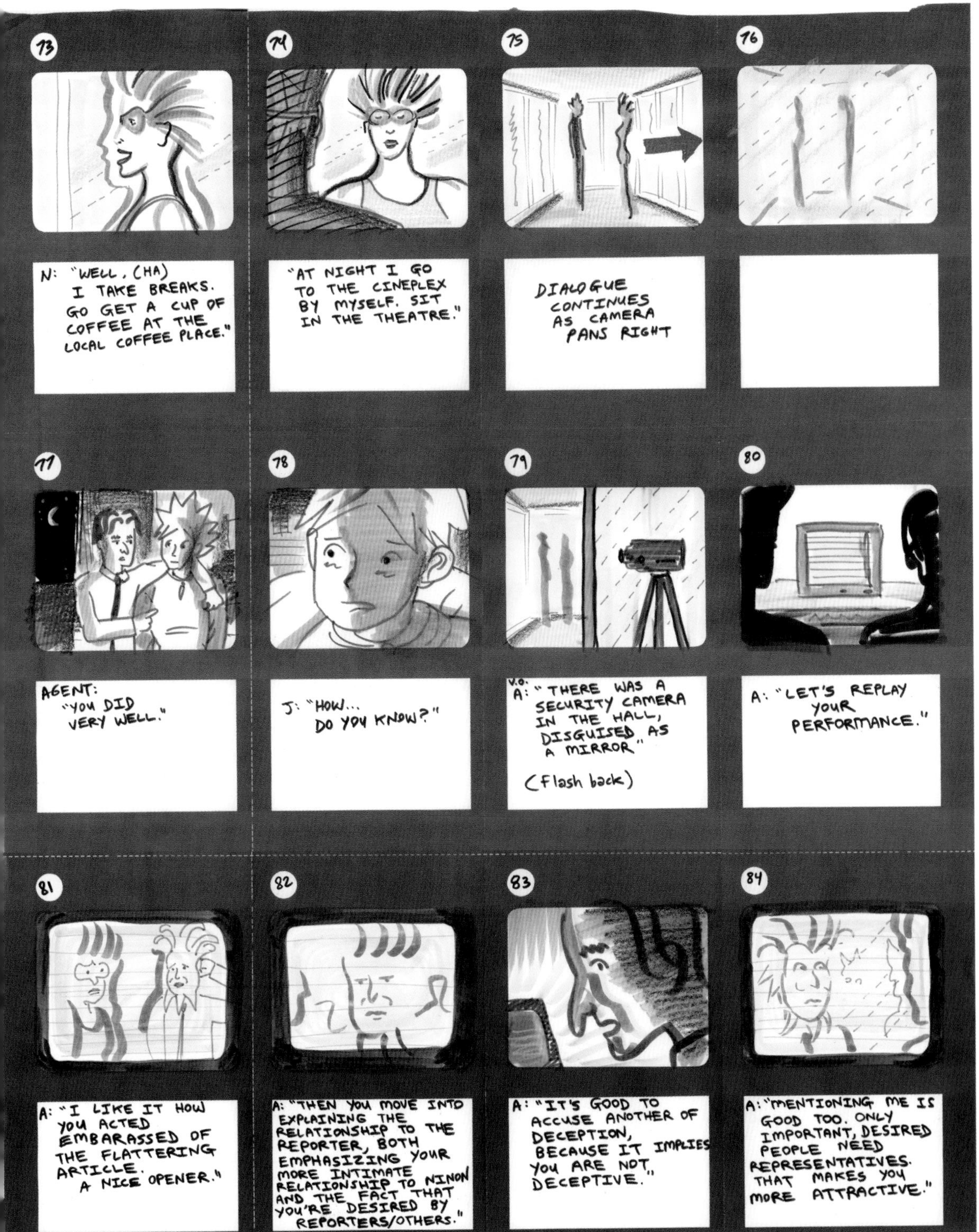
73
N: "WELL, (HA) I TAKE BREAKS. GO GET A CUP OF COFFEE AT THE LOCAL COFFEE PLACE."
74
"AT NIGHT I GO TO THE CINEPLEX BY MYSELF. SIT IN THE THEATRE."
75
DIALOGUE CONTINUES AS CAMERA PANS RIGHT
76
77
AGENT: "YOU DID VERY WELL."
78
J: "HOW... DO YOU KNOW?"
79
V.O. A: "THERE WAS A SECURITY CAMERA IN THE HALL, DISGUISED AS A MIRROR"
(Flash back)
80
A: "LET'S REPLAY YOUR PERFORMANCE."
81
A: "I LIKE IT HOW YOU ACTED EMBARASSED OF THE FLATTERING ARTICLE. A NICE OPENER."
82
A: "THEN YOU MOVE INTO EXPLAINING THE RELATIONSHIP TO THE REPORTER, BOTH EMPHASIZING YOUR MORE INTIMATE RELATIONSHIP TO NINON AND THE FACT THAT YOU'RE DESIRED BY REPORTERS/OTHERS."
83
A: "IT'S GOOD TO ACCUSE ANOTHER OF DECEPTION, BECAUSE IT IMPLIES YOU ARE NOT DECEPTIVE."
84
A: "MENTIONING ME IS GOOD TOO. ONLY IMPORTANT, DESIRED PEOPLE NEED REPRESENTATIVES. THAT MAKES YOU MORE ATTRACTIVE."

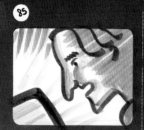

85

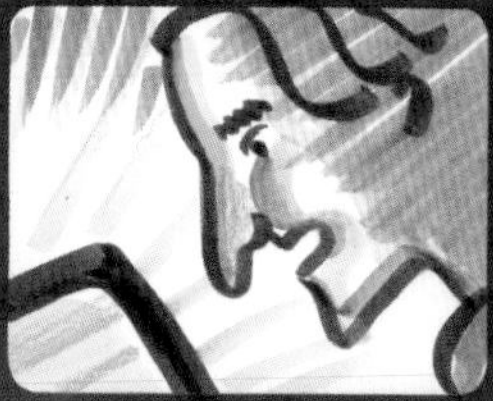

A: "THE WAY IT SEEMED INTUITIVE IN THE CONVERSATION WAS A MASTERSTROKE."

86

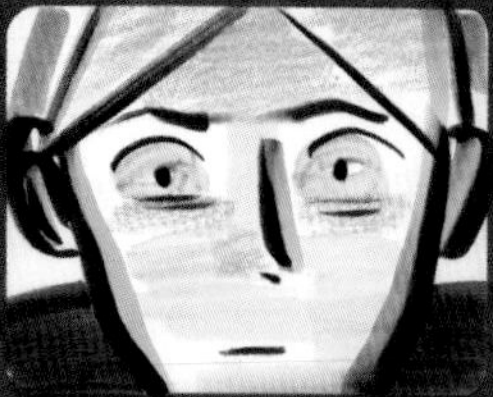

CLOSE-UP JOE

87

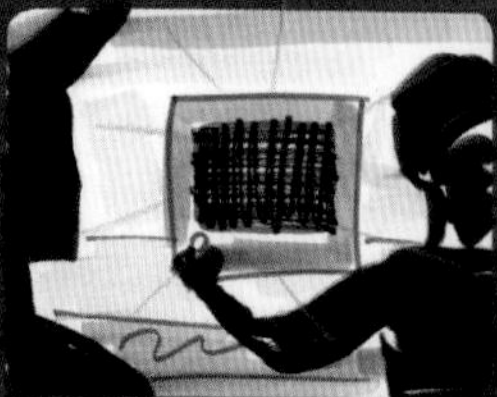

A: "IT WAS DEFINITELY THE APPEARANCE OF THE START OF SOMETHING SPECIAL."

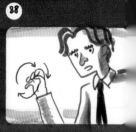

88

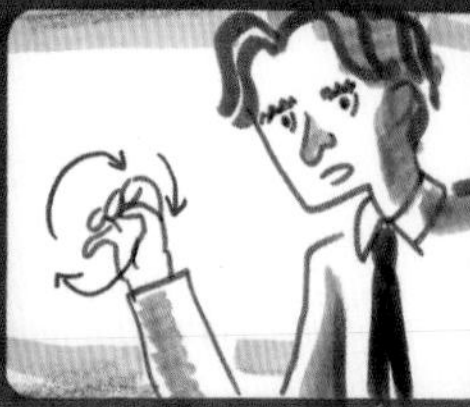

A: "THE RELATIONSHIP IS SKETCHED IN. NOW YOU NEED TO EXECUTE IT."

89

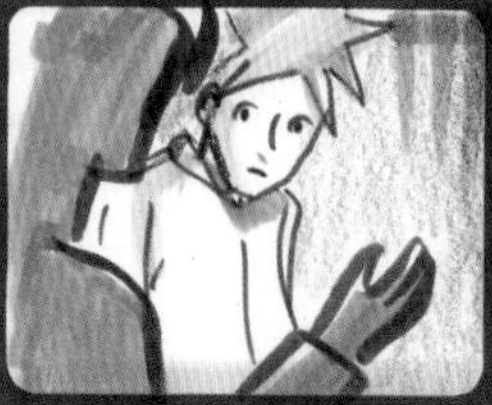

A: "SHE THINKS SHE'S YOUR FRIEND, SO YOU MUST MAKE HER REALIZE THAT YOU MEAN MORE TO HER."

90

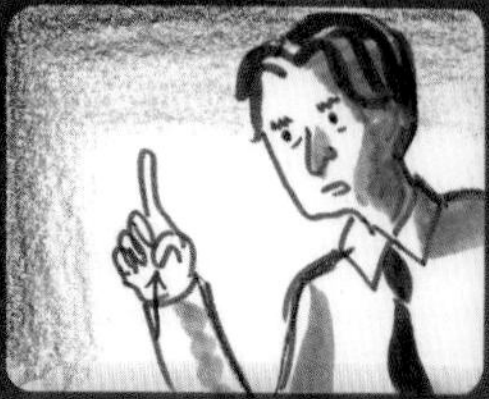

A: "THE KEY TO THAT IS JEALOUSY. PEOPLE ARE ATTRACTED TO THOSE WHO HAVE ALREADY ATTRACTED OTHERS. IF OTHERS DESIRE YOU, THERE MUST BE A REASON."

91

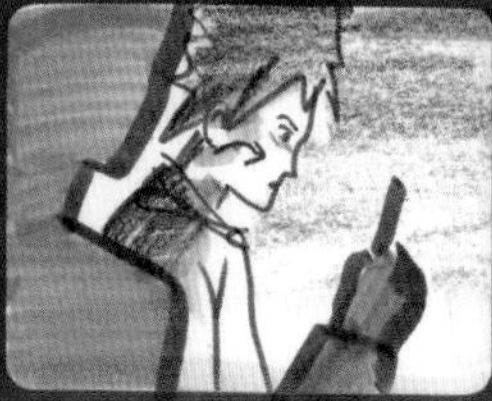

A: "SEEING YOU WITH ANOTHER WOMAN WILL MAKE HER REALIZE THIS."

92

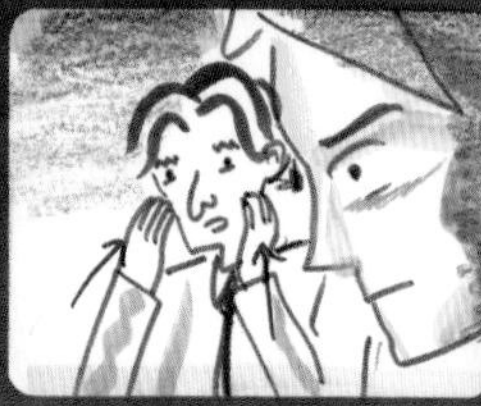

A: "IT'S IMPORTANT TO CHOOSE A WOMAN WITH A DIFFERENT APPEARANCE THAN NINON. NINON HAS DARK HAIR, SO FIND A LIGHT-HAIRED WOMAN, ETC."

93

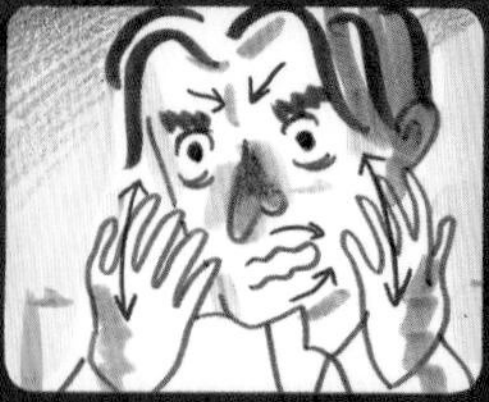

A: "THIS WILL MAKE HER FEAR SHE'S 'NOT YOUR TYPE.' THIS CREATES IN HER A FEELING OF INADEQUACY YOU HAVE THE POTENTIAL TO ABSOLVE."

94

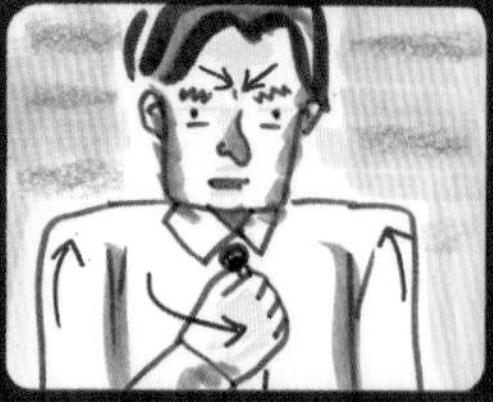

A: "IT STRENGTHENS YOUR POSITION."

95

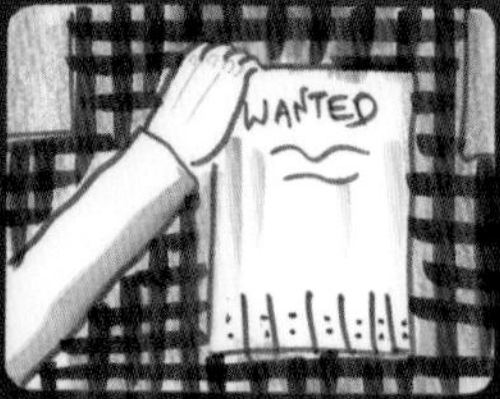
WANTED

CASTING CALL

96

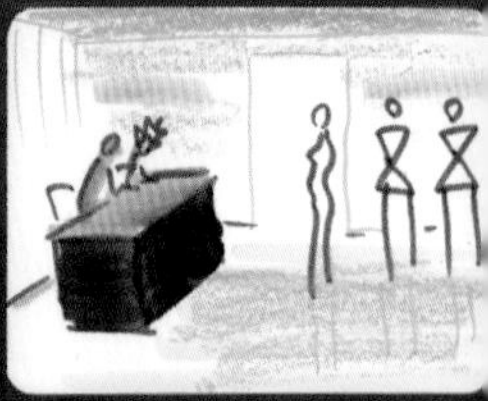

AUDITIONS

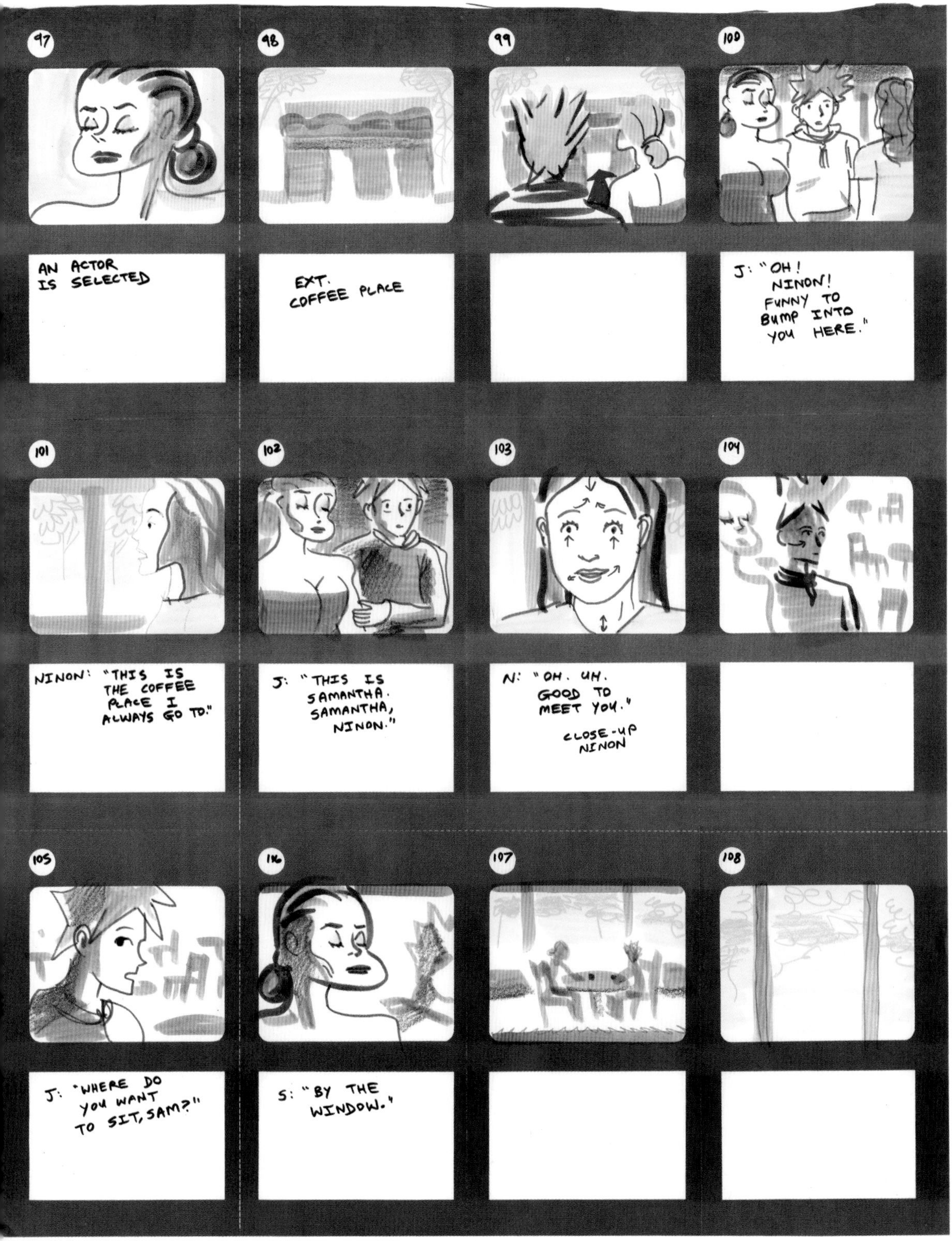
97
AN ACTOR IS SELECTED
98
EXT. COFFEE PLACE
99
100
J: "OH! NINON! FUNNY TO BUMP INTO YOU HERE."
101
NINON: "THIS IS THE COFFEE PLACE I ALWAYS GO TO."
102
J: "THIS IS SAMANTHA. SAMANTHA, NINON."
103
N: "OH. UH. GOOD TO MEET YOU."
CLOSE-UP NINON
104
105
J: "WHERE DO YOU WANT TO SIT, SAM?"
106
S: "BY THE WINDOW."
107
108

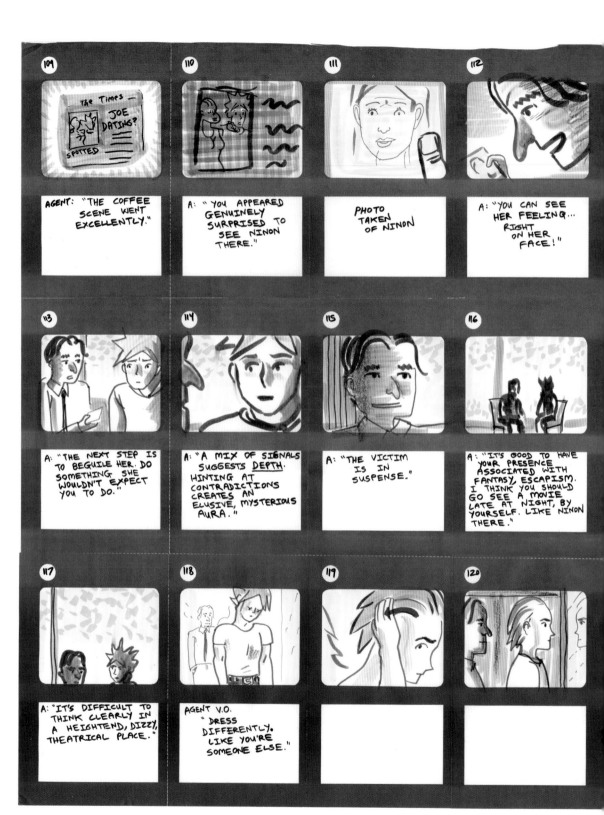

109

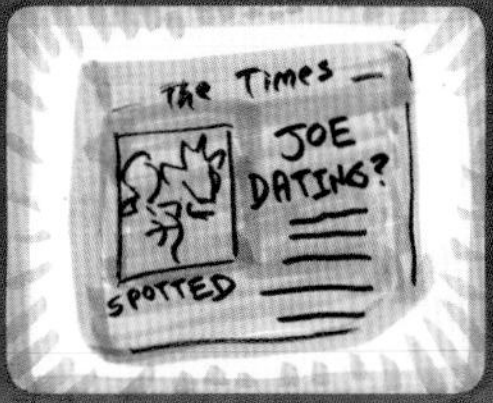
The Times
JOE DATING?
SPOTTED

AGENT: "THE COFFEE SCENE WENT EXCELLENTLY."

110

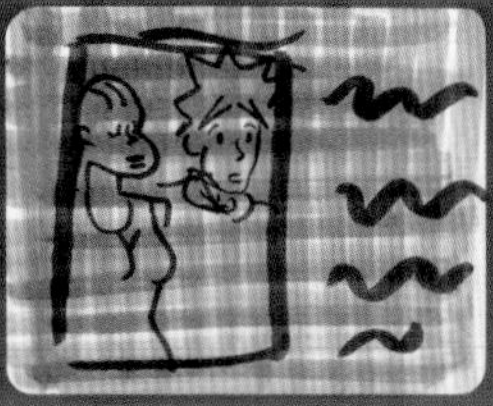

A: "YOU APPEARED GENUINELY SURPRISED TO SEE NINON THERE."

111

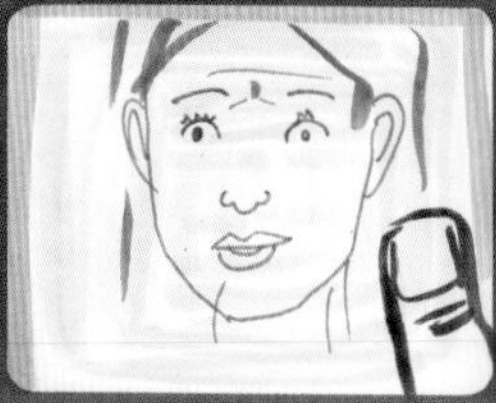

PHOTO TAKEN OF NINON

112

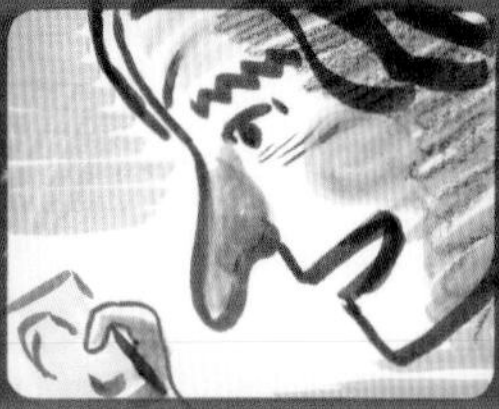

A: "YOU CAN SEE HER FEELING... RIGHT ON HER FACE!"

113

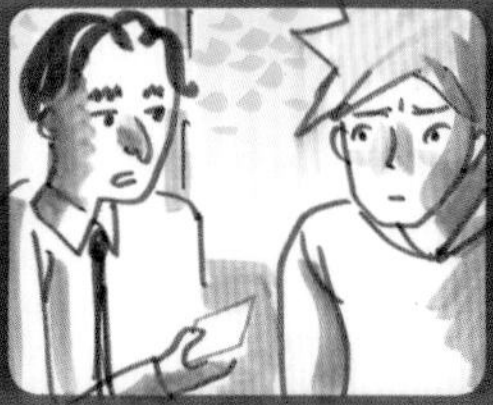

A: "THE NEXT STEP IS TO BEGUILE HER. DO SOMETHING SHE WOULDN'T EXPECT YOU TO DO."

114

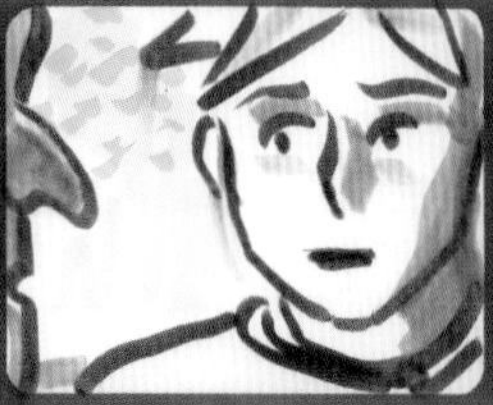

A: "A MIX OF SIGNALS SUGGESTS DEPTH. HINTING AT CONTRADICTIONS CREATES AN ELUSIVE, MYSTERIOUS AURA."

115

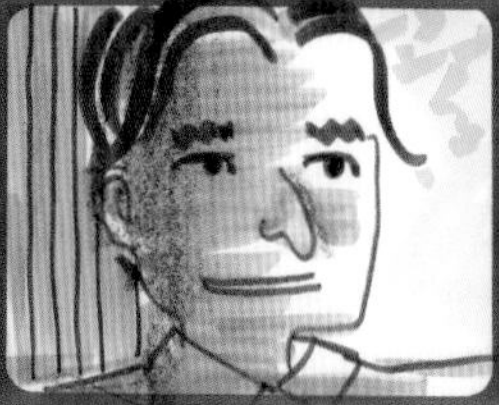

A: "THE VICTIM IS IN SUSPENSE."

116

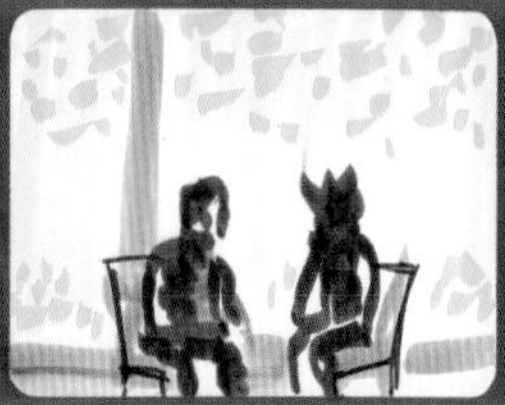

A: "IT'S GOOD TO HAVE YOUR PRESENCE ASSOCIATED WITH FANTASY, ESCAPISM. I THINK YOU SHOULD GO SEE A MOVIE LATE AT NIGHT, BY YOURSELF. LIKE NINON THERE."

117

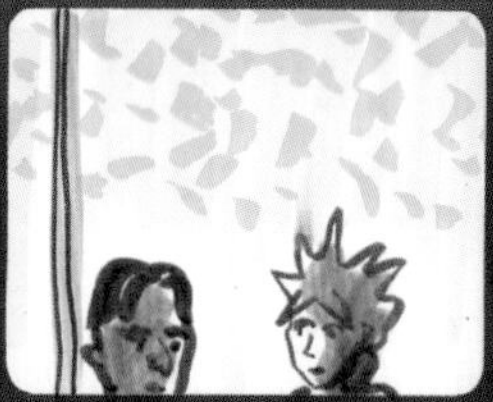

A: "IT'S DIFFICULT TO THINK CLEARLY IN A HEIGHTEND, DIZZY, THEATRICAL PLACE."

118

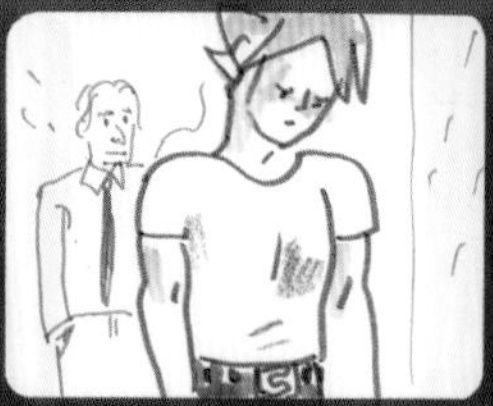

AGENT V.O.
" DRESS DIFFERENTLY. LIKE YOU'RE SOMEONE ELSE."

119

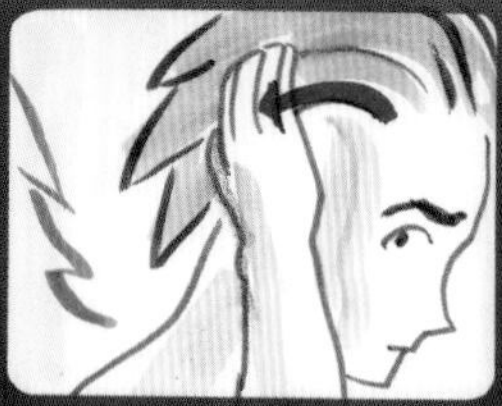

120

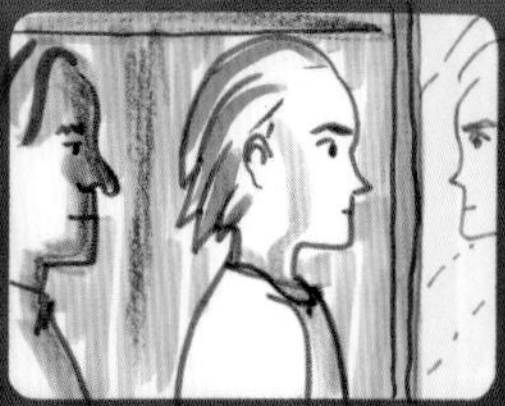

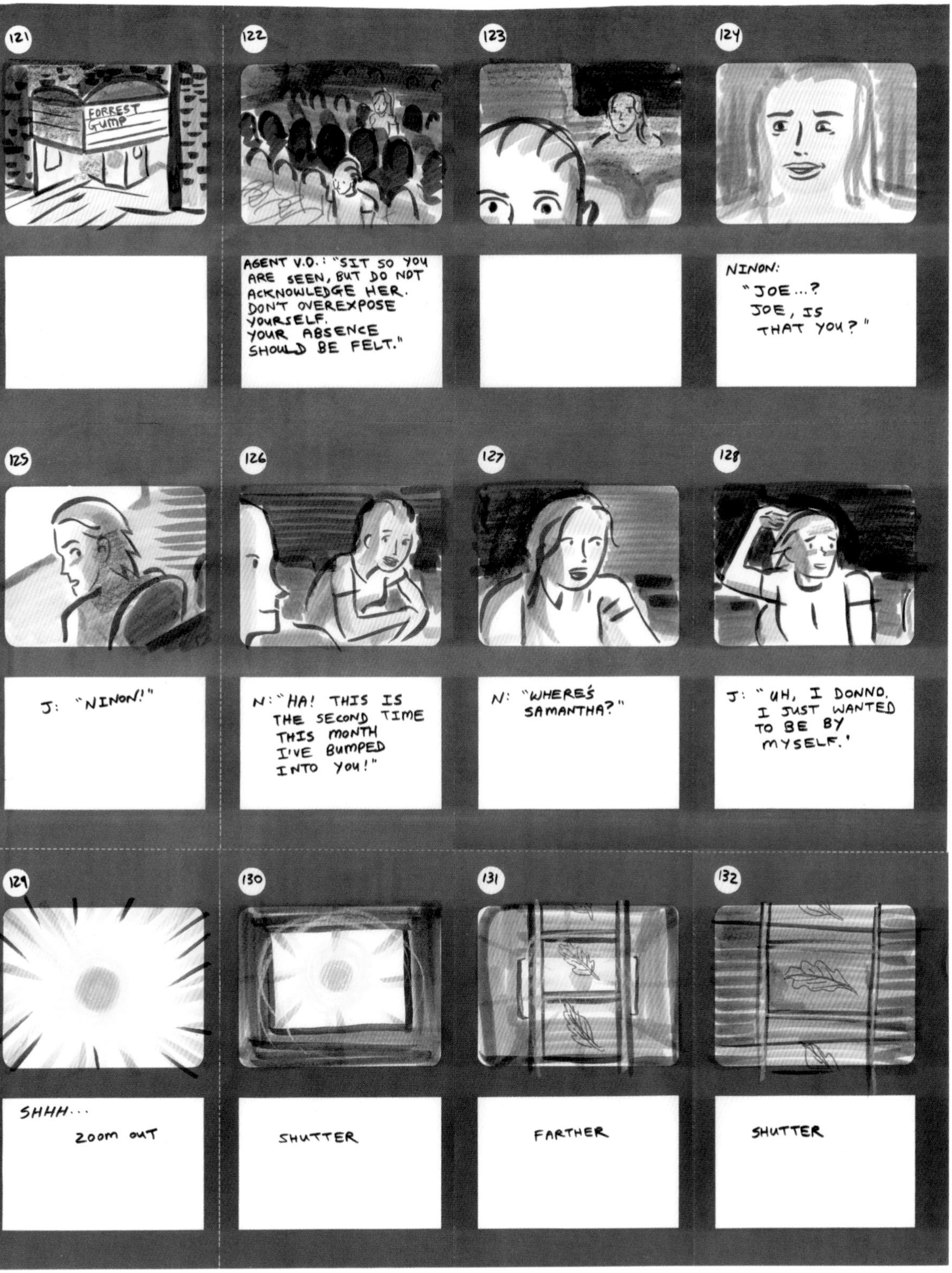
121
FORREST GUMP
122
AGENT V.O.: "SIT SO YOU ARE SEEN, BUT DO NOT ACKNOWLEDGE HER. DON'T OVEREXPOSE YOURSELF. YOUR ABSENCE SHOULD BE FELT."
123
124
NINON: "JOE...? JOE, IS THAT YOU?"
125
J: "NINON!"
126
N: "HA! THIS IS THE SECOND TIME THIS MONTH I'VE BUMPED INTO YOU!"
127
N: "WHERE'S SAMANTHA?"
128
J: "UH, I DONNO. I JUST WANTED TO BE BY MYSELF.'
129
SHHH...
ZOOM OUT
130
SHUTTER
131
FARTHER
132
SHUTTER

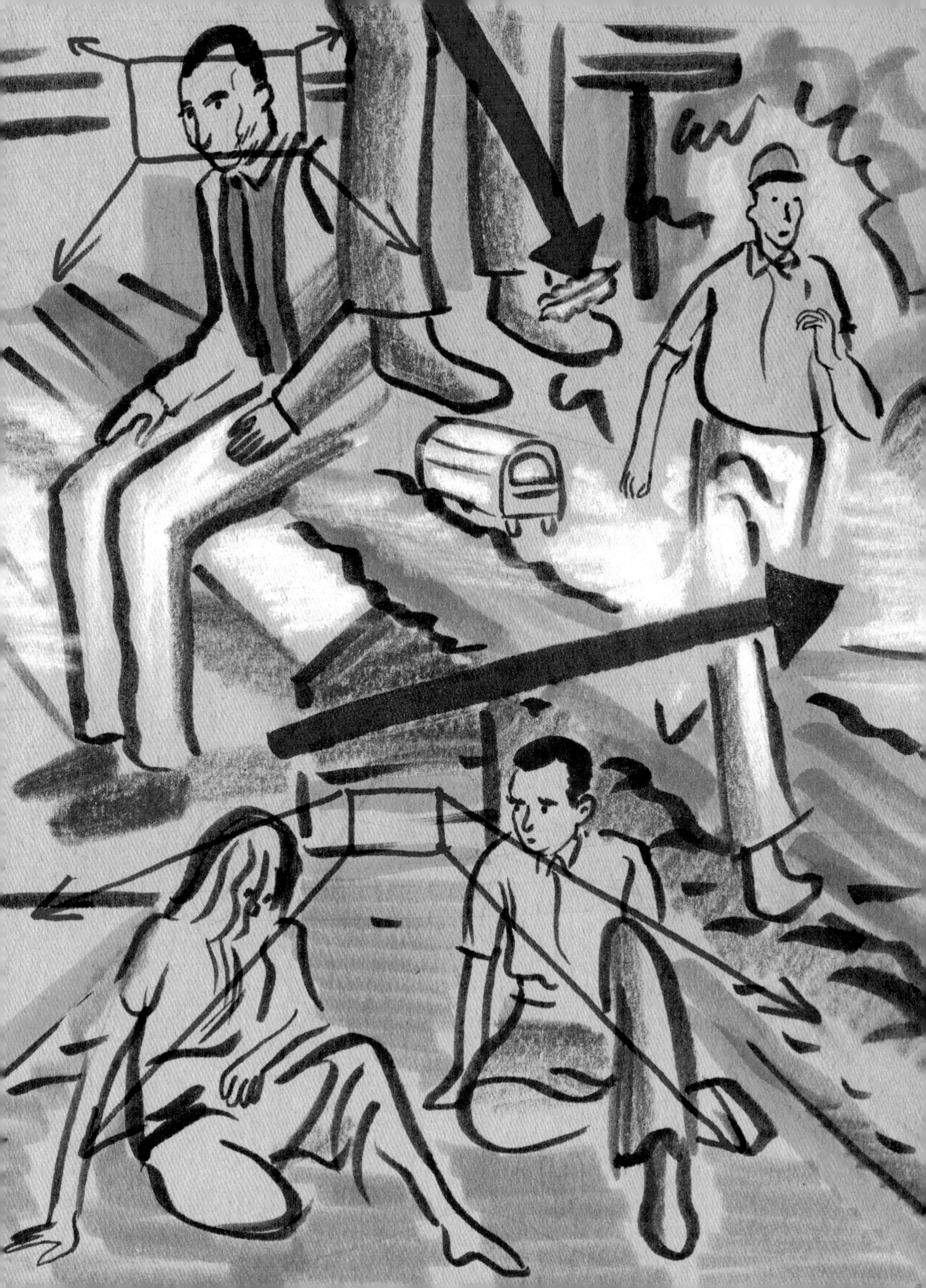

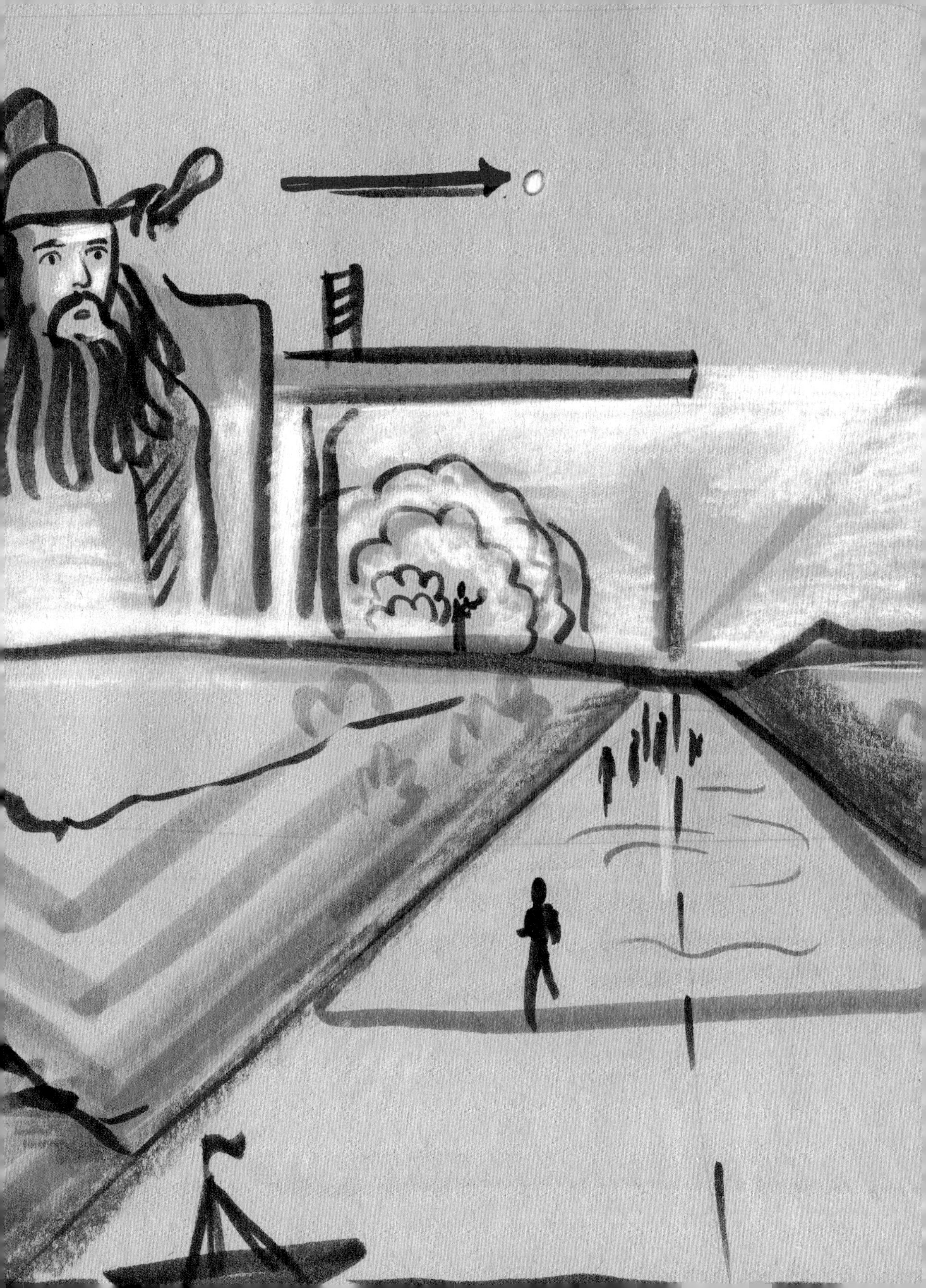

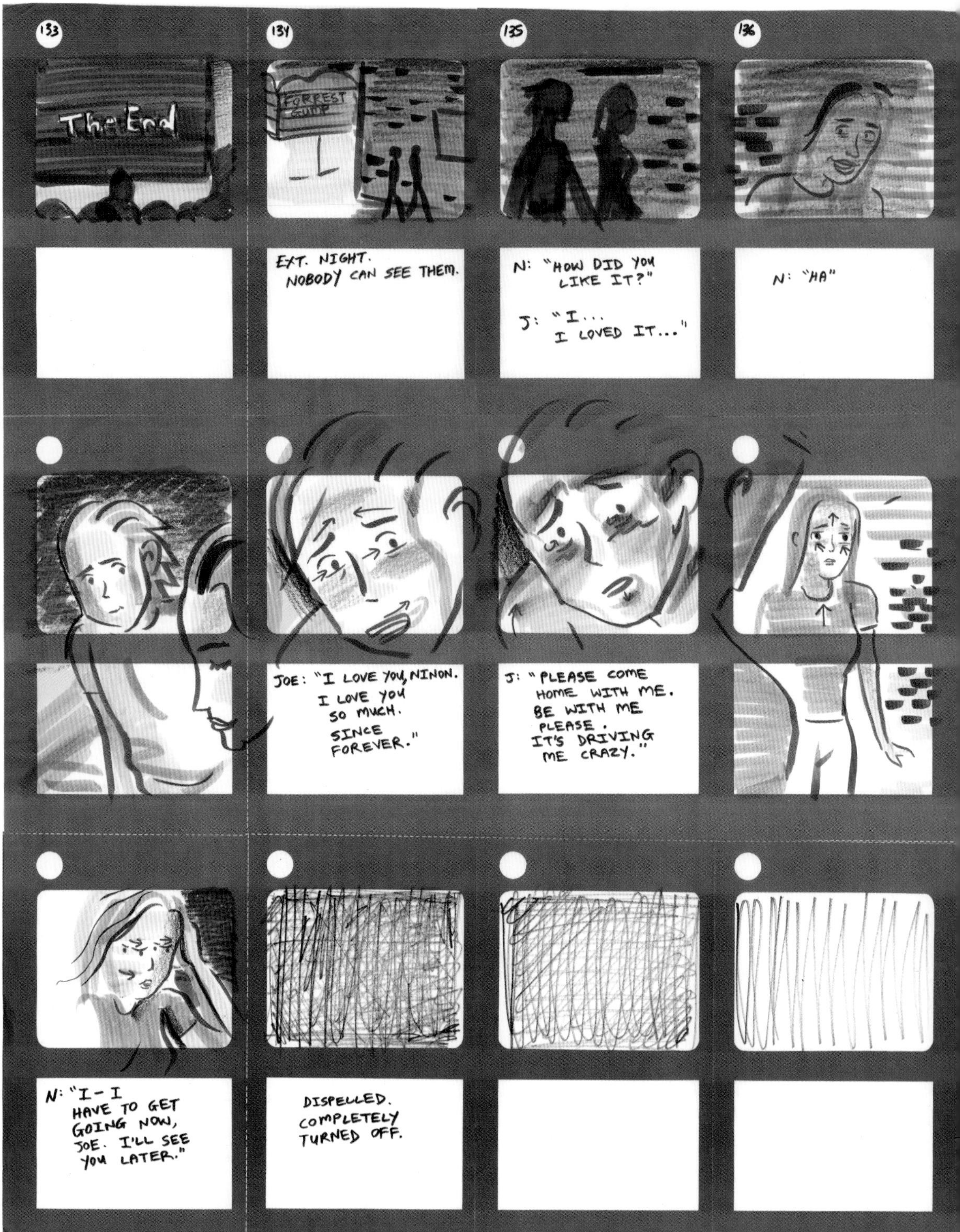
133
The End
134
FORREST GUMP
EXT. NIGHT. NOBODY CAN SEE THEM.
135
N: "HOW DID YOU LIKE IT?"
J: "I... I LOVED IT..."
136
N: "HA"
JOE: "I LOVE YOU, NINON. I LOVE YOU SO MUCH. SINCE FOREVER."
J: "PLEASE COME HOME WITH ME. BE WITH ME PLEASE. IT'S DRIVING ME CRAZY."
N: "I - I HAVE TO GET GOING NOW, JOE. I'LL SEE YOU LATER."
DISPELLED. COMPLETELY TURNED OFF.

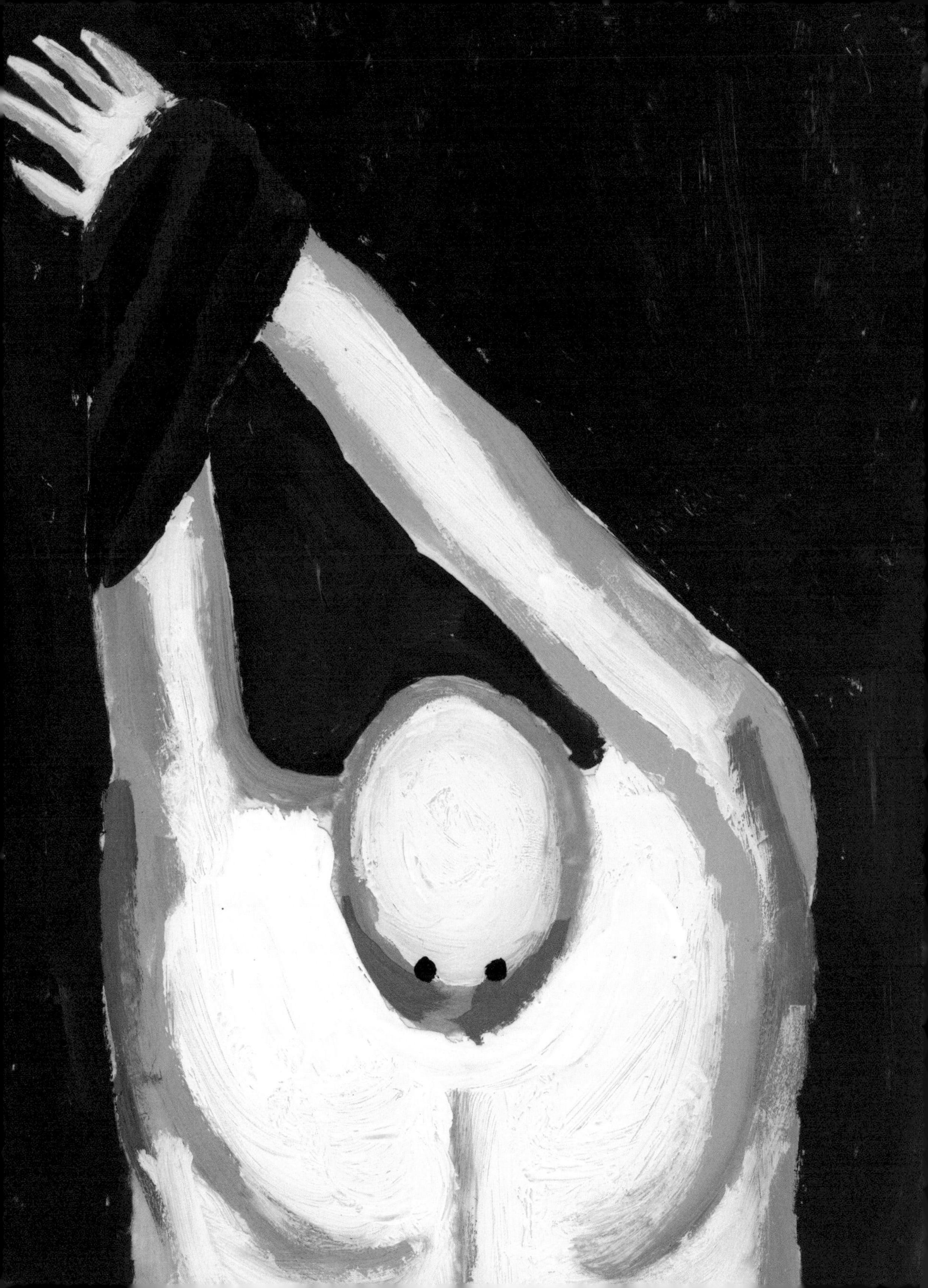